635.982 Pierce.
Pier

FITCHBURG PUBLIC LIBRARY

THIS BOOK IS THE PROPERTY OF THE
ABOVE LIBRARY.

GOOD CARE AND PROMPT RETURN IS THE
RESPONSIBILITY OF EACH BORROWER.

WITHDRAWN

FITCHBURG PUBLIC LIBRARY
WITHDRAWN

A16600 255692

D1247387

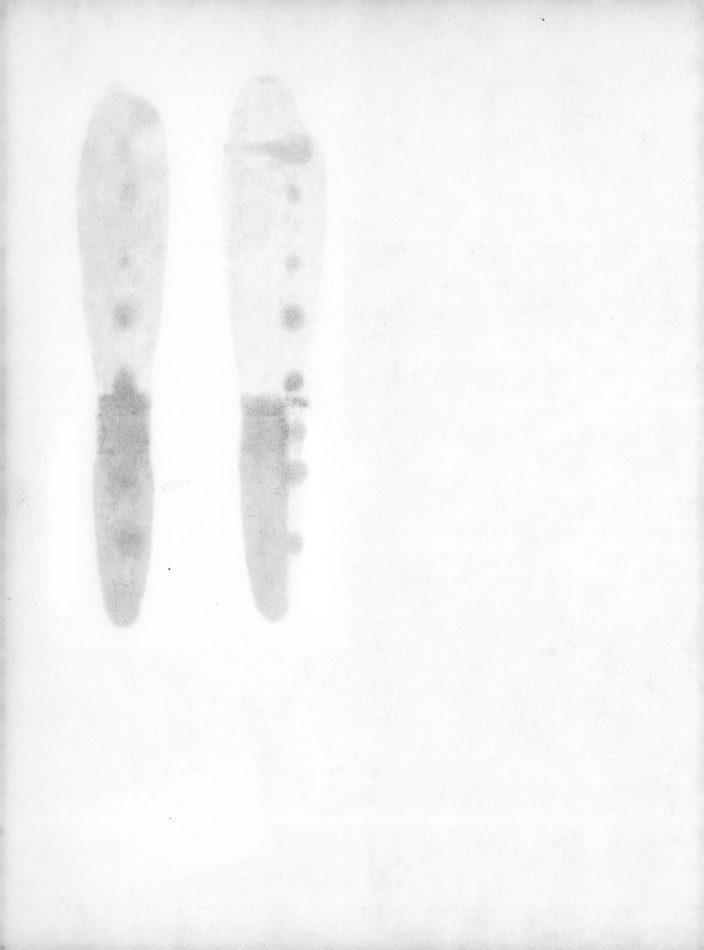

GREEN HOUSE
GROW HOW

GREEN HOUSE GROW HOW

A reference book

 JOHN H. PIERCE

Color Illustrations: Roselyn Pape
Technical Illustrations: Jon.Hersh

PLANTS ALIVE BOOKS
Seattle, Washington

While due care has been exercised to ensure the reliability of all information, the publisher makes no warranties, express or implied, as to the reliability of manufactured items.

Trade names are utilized for clarity and do not constitute an endorsement. In all cases of product usage, follow the manufacturer's directions explicitly and adhere to federal and state usage regulations.

Design: Roselyn Pape

ISBN 0-918730-01-5

No part of this book may be reproduced or utilized in any form or by any means, electronic or mechanical, including photocopying, recording, or by an information storage and retrieval system without permission in writing from the publisher. Inquiries should be addressed to: Plants Alive Books, 5509 1st Avenue South, Seattle, Washington 98108.

© 1977 by Plants, Inc.
Printed in the United States of America

R. R. DONNELLEY & SONS COMPANY, THE LAKESIDE PRESS

To my mother
Frances Hewett Pierce, who
first showed me where the
violets grew

Contents

Chapter Appendixes

No appendices for chapters 10, 13, 16, 18

Figures

Tables

Color Plates

Preface

During the past twenty-five years, I have heard questions from students in home gardening and in practical horticulture and landscaping, and have compiled answers to their questions. For as many years, I have dealt daily with the specific horticultural problems of commercial growers and propagators. At the same time, I have conducted and published research.

Worldwide, I have found that people are growing more plants both indoors and outdoors—in mini-greenhouses, such as coldframes and windowsill gardens, as well as in full-size greenhouses. Year round, a home greenhouse lets growers enjoy the beauty in color, form, and fragrance of the ornamental plants; and a greenhouse helps produce superior food plants of all kinds, including vegetables, fruits, and herbs, which taste fresher and are more nutritious than those that are mass produced.

To be successful and to have fun growing plants, however, you need information. Thus, if you are a plant grower or a student or a teacher needing access to information about greenhouses and growing, this book provides details on the methods and advantages of greenhouse growing, some basic botany, and instructions on plant care. If you have a greenhouse at home or plan to build one, you will find here structural and engineering data with schematics and step-by-step procedures, as well as many listings of sources of information and supplies, to help you construct or operate a functional, well-equipped structure.

The book is intended to be a reference that is kept at hand, and if you use it frequently, it will have been successful. Happy growing!

Plants and people live together in many houses being built

STRUCTURES

WHAT IS A GREENHOUSE?

Plants grow naturally in diverse environments around the world. A greenhouse is a specialized structure that enables us to reproduce or simulate the conditions under which plants grow in their natural habitats by controlling the amount of light, heat, air, food, and moisture for optimal growth.

Although many of us try to grow house plants on windowsills and on plant stands, the usual home does not provide sufficient light or moisture for many plants. It is impracticable, for example, to create an environment suitable for growing tomatoes in a residence during the winter. A greenhouse, on the other hand, allows us to provide the right environment for all kinds of plants at any season of the year.

WHY HAVE A GREENHOUSE?

For many people, the beauty, form, color, and design of growing plants satisfies a need to relate to nature, and a greenhouse optimizes the experience. It is fulfilling to grow plants and participate in the earth's life processes, seeing your first seed germinate, finding roots on your first cutting, and tasting your own tomatoes grown in January. In fact, in a greenhouse you can ensure the best nutritional value from your own salad greens and vegetables and have them fresh in summer and winter.

SIZE AND COSTS

Greenhouses can be any size. The smallest structures (mini-greenhouses) are called "hot caps,"

"cloches," "windowsill greenhouses," "coldframes," or "propagating cases." When the structure is walk-in size, it is called a greenhouse.

You can begin greenhouse growing with a windowsill greenhouse in a tray for less than $10.00. You also can build a simple 8-by-8-foot freestanding wood structure with scrap lumber for about $100.00 or buy a prefab 8-by-8 feet at prices ranging from $200.00 to $1,000.00, depending upon the materials and equipment involved. An 8-by-12-foot automated greenhouse may cost several thousand dollars. As with most things, the more you do yourself, the less the total cost.

LOCATING THE GREENHOUSE

How do you decide where to put the greenhouse on your property? There are at least five considerations: your own convenience, available light, air flow, and available power and water sources.

Your own convenience

On a cold winter evening or a rainy summer night you have to be a real plant enthusiast to leave slippers and a warm fireside for a trip halfway across your property to see how the new cuttings are doing. In contrast, the hobby greenhouse that is attached to the residence, or the plant room that is an integral part of the house, allows you to enjoy looking or puttering anytime—in your slippers. In short, the more accessible the greenhouse, the more you will use it.

Increasingly more people are using old sun porches as plant rooms or adding new rooms for the purpose of enjoying plants out of the weather (fig. 1). This idea is not new. It is probably as old as the existence of permanent dwelling structures. Hav-

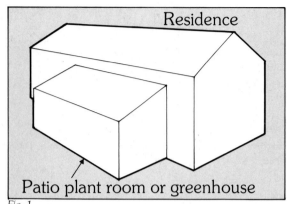

Fig. 1
Patio plant room or greenhouse

ing enjoyed plants outdoors, man brought plants into the first permanent home and created such modifications as atriums, courtyards, conservatories, covered porches, covered patios, and lanais in order to provide a suitable environment for the plants.

The atrium today is a square courtyard bounded by four walls of the residence or building *(fig. 2)*. It is

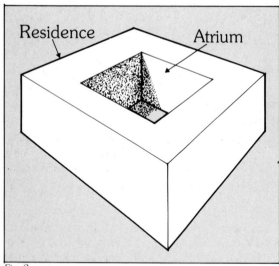

Fig. 2
House designed with an atrium

open to the sky and contains plant material and paving. In some instances, a glass or fiberglass roof converts the atrium into a plant room.

The plant room, often called a solarium, is usually part of a residence that is used by the family but also

is arranged especially for plants. It may be an extension of the kitchen, a sun porch, a bathroom, or any room in which people want maximum rapport with the color, fragrance, and beauty of plants. Such a room gives a greater feeling of living with the plants than does the less integrated lean-to structure. A plant room with southern exposure to let in warm sunshine provides an eating area reminiscent of a traditional picnic—without the ants!

If you plan to install a plant room in your home, however, it is wise to employ the services of an architect to make certain that your environmental controls and construction methods do not damage or detract from the rest of the residence. (See appendix for guidelines.)

Finally, convenience refers not only to you, the grower, but also means convenience in the sense of easy access to all the materials used. If you build a freestanding greenhouse away from the residence, make sure you can reach it easily with a wheelbarrow or hand truck to transport peat moss, soil, sand, and other materials.

Available light

Light is a prime growth factor, so locate the greenhouse to get all the light you can. A greenhouse facing south with a 45° roof angle, for example, will

Table 1
CHILL FACTOR

Temperature Fahrenheit	Wind in miles per hour				
	10	20	30	40	50
35°	21°	12°	5°	1°	0°
30°	16°	3°	−2°	−4°	−7°
25°	9°	−4°	−11°	−15°	−17°
20°	2°	−9°	−18°	−22°	−24°
10°	−9°	−24°	−33°	−36°	−38°
0°	−22°	−40°	−49°	−54°	−56°
−10°	−31°	−52°	−63°	−69°	−70°
−20°	−45°	−68°	−78°	−87°	−88°
−30°	−58°	−81°	−94°	−101°	−103°

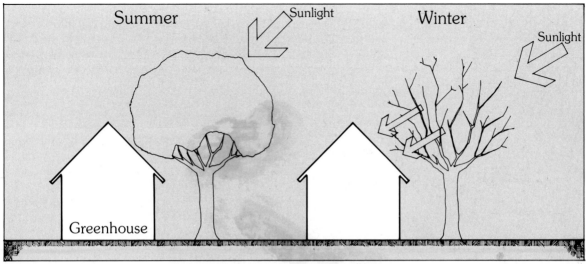

Fig. 3
Deciduous tree shades the greenhouse in the summer; winter light is maximized by siting the greenhouse parallel to the sun's movement

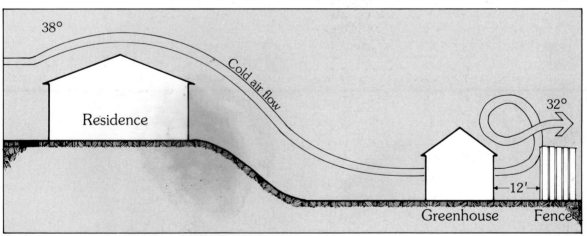

Fig. 4
Cold air runs downhill like water and can be dammed by a solid fence—keep the greenhouse at least 12 feet away from such a solid barrier

get a maximum amount of sunlight at any season of the year. In the winter the angle of the sun is lower, and the sun's rays are weaker because they have to travel farther to reach the earth *(fig. 3)*. If a southern exposure is not possible, the best solution is to supplement natural light with artificial light.

Air flow

Cold air flows downhill like water and, if confined, will collect to form a cold pocket around the greenhouse *(fig. 4)*. A solid board fence, for instance, can dam the cold air and must be modified for proper cold air drainage. Making certain that cold winter air flows over or by your greenhouse also will save on the heat bill.

In addition, when engineering the heat requirements, remember to make allowances for wind velocity and the chill factor. Cold air robs the greenhouse of heat, and when the air is traveling fast, temperature is affected as shown in *table 1*. For example, on a winter evening when your thermometer says 30°F (−1.11°C) and there is a ten-miles-per-hour wind, the actual temperature is 16°F (−8.9°C). One good way to control wind is to place a barrier of hedging where it will deflect the wind over and around the greenhouse *(fig. 5)*.

Available power and water sources

Electricity and water should be readily accessible to the greenhouse. In cold climates this means running a ditch below the frost line for the water pipe and electrical conduit. *(See appendix for installation).* Since you cannot trench through rock or a septic tank field, this type of problem must be considered in locating the greenhouse.

Experience of many hobbyists has proven that it is best to locate the greenhouse where you will spend time in it easily, even if you have to run the

12 MPH Air flow
3 MPH
12'
6' Hedge
Greenhouse

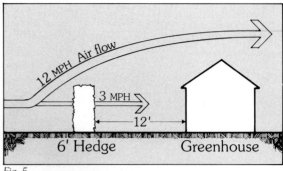

Fig. 5
Moving air strikes a barrier of hedge material and goes over the greenhouse, and air that moves through the hedge is reduced in velocity—materials for hedge should be thick evergreens such as arborvitae, Douglas fir, Scotch or black pine, sheared hemlock, or Thuja lobbi

Common types of greenhouse structures
Fig. 6

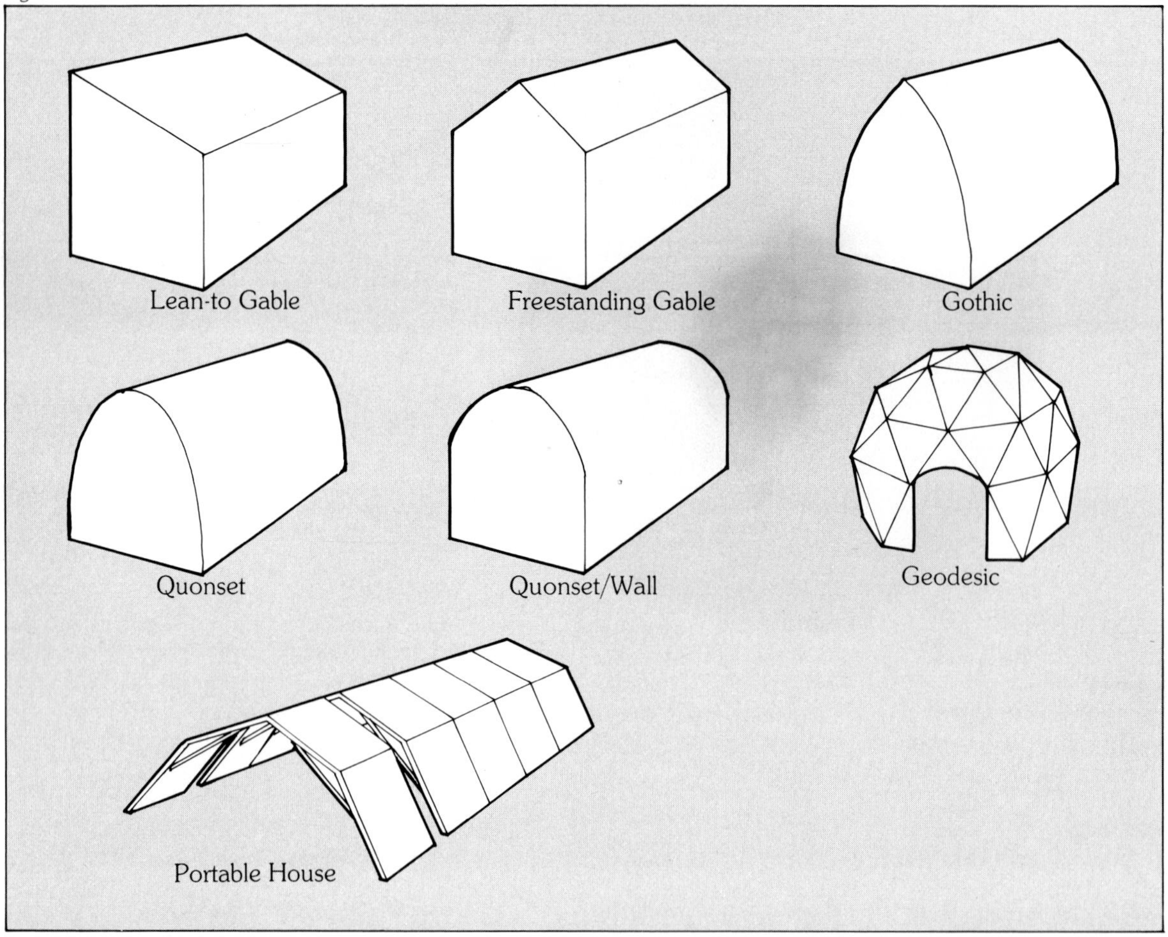

Lean-to Gable
Freestanding Gable
Gothic
Quonset
Quonset/Wall
Geodesic
Portable House

Table 2

TYPES OF GREENHOUSE STRUCTURES

Type of Structure	Size in Feet	Availability and Price	Location and Convenience	Utilities	Comments
LEAN-TO (Entry from residence only) Even span	6x8, 6x12, or 8x12 (Optional to fit residence)	Prefab or custom $200.00 and up; cost is reduced by using one wall of the residence (may involve cost of installing new door in residence)	Attach to south wall or use supplemental light—walk-in, stand-up head room; easy access in bad weather; difficult access for bulky materials such as peat and soil	Can use residence utilities; lower installation cost	Heat cost reduced about ⅓ due to one solid wall and wind protection; airborne smokes or chemicals cannot be used or residence will be contaminated; difficult to expand
(Entry from outdoors only)* Even span	Same as above	Same as above	Can be attached to barn, garage, or shed—walk-in, stand-up head room; difficult to use and service in bad weather	Utilities must be extended if attached to outbuilding	Easy access to materials; airborne smokes and chemicals may be used; difficult to expand
(Entry from residence and outdoors) Even span	Same as above	Same as above; cost of second door in the residence or greenhouse	Convenient access for people and materials when attached to house—walk-in, stand-up head room	Can use residence utilities	Airborne smokes or chemicals cannot be used or residence will be contaminated; maximum convenience
FREESTANDING Even span	All sizes (from 8x8 to 20x100)	Many prefab units from about $200.00 up; custom or homemade at about $1.00 per square foot and up	Can be connected to shed or outbuilding at gable end; maximum light available: orient on axis east and west; difficult to use and service in bad weather; walk-in, stand-up headroom	Utilities must be extended underground (see appendix)	Costs ⅓ more to heat than lean-to; no danger of airborne contamination of residence; should be screened from wind; easily expanded
PORTABLE Even span	All sizes	Custom or homemade; cost about $1.00 per square foot and up	Can be used over vegetable garden or other area for winter protection	Uitlities must be extended (may be temporary)	Useful as a temporary or seasonal structure
COLDFRAME*	Width 2, 4, or 6 by any length	Small sizes are available as prefab from about $100.00 up; custom or homemade at about $.35 to $.50 per square foot	May be freestanding anywhere or attached to sides of the greenhouse—not walk-in (bend-over); difficult to use and service in bad weather	No heat; watering by hand	Usually used as structure to get start on season, harden off plants, or overflow space for greenhouse
HOTBED*	Same as above	Same as above; additional cost for electric bottom heat	Same as above	Electric cable bottom or wall heat; utilities extended underground	An inexpensive, non-walk-in (bend-over) greenhouse; can be used for year-round crops
MINI-GREENHOUSE Cloche	1x2 or larger	Prefab $5.00 to $8.00; homemade $1.00 to $2.00	Portable	No utilities	Seasonal protection
Balcony*	To fit balcony	Prefab $100.00 and up; homemade $25.00 and up	On balcony or porch	May have electric heat	For apartment dwellers
Window sill	To fit window	Prefab $50.00 and up	As bay window or on windowsill	May have electric heat	Useful where greenhouse is not feasible
Propagation box	From approx. 1x2 to 2x3	Prefab from $5.00 to $200.00; homemade from $5.00 up; cost of electric varies	In residence (often in basement)	May have electric heat and light (basement must have electric heat and light)	To root cuttings, germinate seed, or grow small plants

*(See appendix for illustrations)

utilities some distance. If heat is a prime expense factor, the best answer is a lean-to attached to the house. Foundation procedures are in the appendix.

TYPES OF STRUCTURES

Greenhouses come in all shapes. *Table 2* (p. 5) should help you compare the types of structures and decide on the one that best suits both your needs and the climate in which you live. Popular freestanding and lean-to types, for example, are shown in *figure 6*.

In snow country

Usually the roof pitch is a ratio of 1-to-2 or 1 inch in height for every 2 inches of width (*fig. 7*). This is

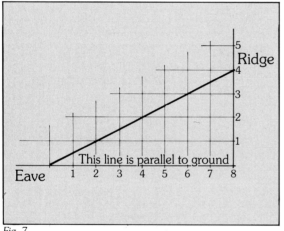

Fig. 7
The roof pitch, starting at the eave, rises 6 inches for every foot of width, a ratio of 1-to-2 or 6-to-12; in no-snow areas, less pitch can be used, but in heavy-snow areas, a ratio of 1-to-1 may be necessary

often written as 6-to-12. If the snow load is heavy, the ratio can be increased with an A-frame structure to give a pitch steep enough to shed snow. In heavy snow country, keeping the greenhouse heated will melt any snow on the roof. An unheated greenhouse, on the other hand, needs a steep A-frame or a quonset type roof, which will shed much of the snow, but requires removal of excess snow by hand after severe storms.

In hot country

Any of the structures listed on the table can be used in hot country, as long as provision is made

for maximum air movement through the structure by means such as the following:

1. A door in both gable ends that can be opened to allow full flow of air

2. Removable side or sides of the structure that are hinged and can be opened

3. Adequate shade equipment or system (*see chapter 6*)

PLANNING AHEAD

Almost everyone who builds a greenhouse soon discovers there is not enough room to keep all plant material of interest. The wise planner, therefore, ensures that it will be possible to add on and increase the space; otherwise a coldframe or hotbed adjacent to the greenhouse may be necessary. Some things to consider ahead of time include:

1. Look at as many small greenhouses as possible before buying or building your own

2. If you stay with the modular designs, you can start with an 8-by-8 foot house and add on in 4-foot sections as you need the room

3. Choose a door that is wide enough to accommodate a wheelbarrow to facilitate getting things in and out of the greenhouse

4. Check the available headroom in any prefab that you plan to buy. If you want overhead watering or hanging baskets, you may wish to have a high ridge. Often you can gain height by setting the prefab house on a low wall and adding a piece to the bottom of the door (see appendix for directions)

THE DO-IT-YOURSELF STRUCTURE

If you intend to buy the materials and build your own greenhouse, the first requisite is a good set of plans. In the appendix you will find plans for lean-to, coldframe, hotbed, and freestanding fiberglass greenhouses, as well as a window greenhouse and a balcony mini-greenhouse. A list of places to obtain other greenhouse plans is at the end of the chapter.

Table 3
GREENHOUSE WALKS

Type of Walk	Approximate Cost per Square Foot	Comments
Pea gravel	$.05-.10	Soft; walking and wheeling carts or barrows difficult
Brick (on sand)	.60	Surface grows algae and moss—gets very slippery
Wood (treated)	.40	Rots quickly—gets slippery; provides site for pathogenic organisms
Concrete (readymix)	.10-.15	Run-off—no direct drainage, may have puddles; gets slippery from algae
Porous concrete*	.10-.15	A new, stable, non-skid, quick-draining surface; directions for mixing and installing in appendix
Porous aggregate	2.00-3.00	A pea-gravel aggregate with epoxy binder; non-skid, quick draining; available in a range of colors
Stepping stones	2.00-3.00	Concrete or field stone; tendency to tilt unless full width of walk; get slippery

*See appendix for formula

Table 4
GREENHOUSE BENCHES
Coverings

Types	Air Circulation	Drainage	Costs	Comments
Metal mesh	Excellent	Excellent	$.60 per sq. ft.	Permanent if painted or coated to prevent rust; rigid; reduces site of disease
Corrugated asbestos	Poor	Fair	$.75 per sq. ft.	Permanent as is; rigid; uneven surface; reduces site of disease
Aluminum corrugated	Poor	Fair	$.75-$.80 per sq. ft.	Flexible, requires support; absorbs heat at pot level; uneven surface; reduces site of disease
Fiberglass corrugated	Poor	Fair	$.50-$.60 per sq. ft.	Flexible, requires support; uneven surface; reduces site of disease
Wood (redwood)	Good, if slats are spaced	Good	$.50-$.60 per sq. ft.	Rots unless treated—use galvanized nails; provides site for disease organisms

Supports

Types	Treatment	Cost	Comments
Pipe	Will rust unless treated (see appendix)	$.30-$.50 per foot (¾")	Fixed and rigid; no disease sites
Concrete block	No treatment required	$.50-$.75 each	Portable and rigid; some disease sites
Wood (cedar 2"x 4"x 10')	Will rot unless treated (see appendix)	$.40 per foot (2"x 4")	Requires annual treatment—use galvanized nails; many disease sites

THE PREFABRICATED STRUCTURE

Prefabricated greenhouses come in all types, the exterior stuctures costing from $200.00 up. You don't have to be a carpenter or mechanic to assemble most of the prefabricated greenhouses on the market today. Many of them bolt together and require only a few tools and a spare Saturday to have the structure up and ready for benches. Illustrations that show how such a greenhouse can be erected in one day are included in the appendix.

If you are not mechanically inclined, however, and want to have a manufactured structure delivered to your door, the section at the end of the chapter lists some of the companies who supply prefabs. If you don't find a listing near you among the resources given, the yellow pages also should be a help.

WALKS

Another consideration in building a greenhouse is the walks. You want a walking surface in the greenhouse that is easy on your feet, drains well, and doesn't get slippery. *Table 3* will help you compare different walk materials. There is a formula for porous concrete walks in the appendix.

Wood and concrete block bench
Fig. 8

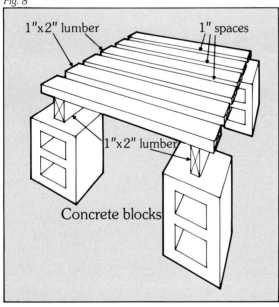

BENCHES

Over the years, growing benches have changed and improved *(fig. 8)*. Current research indicates that it does make a difference what kind of bench you use for growing plants. *Table 4*, should help you decide the type of material that best suits your needs for benches and bench frames.

SHELVES

To gain additional growing space, consider using shelves made of the same material you use for benches. Small shelves can be located in the following places to provide more space for plants *(fig. 9)*:

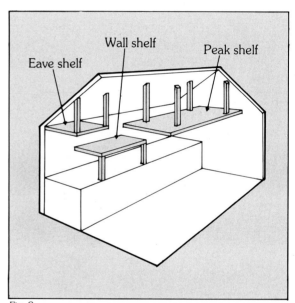

Fig. 9
Greenhouse peak shelf, eave shelf, and wall shelf

1. In the peak of the greenhouse, suspended by wire or chain

2. Along the eave wall at the back of the bench

3. Under the benches with supplemental light if necessary

4 Double-decked over existing benches and narrow enough to permit light to reach the existing bench

HOUSEKEEPING

All of us hope to spend as much time as we can with the pleasures of growing plants and as little time as possible with the structure and its attendant problems. As with any structure, however, the home greenhouse requires attention to keep it in good condition. Summer is a good time to check your greenhouse to see what maintenance is needed.

Take all the plants out of the greenhouse so they will not be damaged as you work. Summer temperatures are high enough for you to safely put all the plants outside, but they should be located in at least partial shade and be protected from wind and rain. Also keep them away from any of the outdoor garden plants that may be infested with pests or diseases. An open veranda, porch, or patio with access to a hose for easy watering may be a suitable place. Don't forget, however, to bring the plants into the greenhouse again before the chilly nights of autumn.

It is best to examine your greenhouse systematically. The following checklist should help you make certain that the greenhouse is in good shape:

☐ 1. Are there weeds under the benches?
   a. Remove by hand
   b. Spray with Paraquat at ½ to ⅔ oz. per gallon water, plus $^1/_{10}$ oz. of wetting agent such as X-77

☐ 2. Is there algae or moss on the walks?
   a. Spray with one of the following: Bromodine at 1 oz. per gallon water, Clorox or Javex at 14 oz. per gallon water, LF-10 at 4 tsp. per gallon water

☐ 3. Are there signs of rot or decay?
   a. Remove and replace rotted wood
   b. Paint with Green Cuprinol #10, a copper naphthenate ready to use out of the can; 1 gallon covers 400 sq. ft. (see appendix)
   c. Spray entire inside of greenhouse thoroughly with Clorox or LF-10 diluted as above

☐ 4. Are you disinfecting tools?
   a. Keep a can or container filled with an LF-10 or Clorox solution in which to soak small tools for thirty minutes when not in use

☐ 5. What do you do with empty pots?
   a. Soak in Clorox or LF-10 solution for one hour before storage

☐ 6. Is your spaghetti system clean?
   a. Remove and soak spaghetti tubes in LF-10 for thirty minutes
   b. Rinse in clean water thoroughly and replace

☐ 7. Does your greenhouse need repainting?
   a. Use a paint formulated for greenhouse use, with rust inhibitors and fungicide content

☐ 8. Do you have broken glass?
   a. Remove old glass and putty
   b. Replace with new glass; use putty formulated with special oils for greenhouse use

☐ 9. Is your fiberglass getting old?
   a. Check the surface—if you can feel exposed fibers, resurface as follows:
      1) Clean the surface with a strong detergent
      2) Apply liquid acrylic resin with a brush (available from greenhouse suppliers and often called fiberglass refinisher)

☐ 10. Are there holes in the fiberglass?
   a. Clean the area around the hole with detergent
   b. Apply a coating of acrylic resin to the patching piece and around the hole to be covered
   c. Apply the patch at once and press down firmly

☐ 11. Is your glass clean for winter?
   a. Spray or brush apply a strong detergent over the glass; some supply companies make a special product for this purpose
   b. Rinse thoroughly with plain water
   c. Repeat if necessary

☐ 12. Are there tears in the polyethylene covering?

a. Mend with mylar adhesive tape (available from suppliers as poly mending tape)

The purpose of this greenhouse-keeping session each year is to help grow the best of plants. Along with annual attention, you should be conscientious about cleanliness and sanitation throughout the year. It is easy to leave infected plants or dead leaves lying around under the benches when they should be removed. Such a little thing as letting the end of a watering hose lie on the ground or walkway can spread diseases. A broom clip on a wall is a good way to keep the hose nozzle or end off contaminated surfaces. You can greatly reduce your bill for chemical pesticides and fungicides with good sanitation practices.

SOURCES

General information

CANADA:
Gardening Under Glass. Jerome A. Eaton. Collier-MacMillan, 1125 B Leslie St., Don Mills, Ontario

UNITED STATES:
Build Your Own Greenhouse. Charles D. Neal. Chilton, 201 King of Prussia Rd., Radnor, PA 19089

Correspondence Aid (#34-134, contains a list of sources of information on greenhouses). U.S. Dept. of Agriculture, Washington, DC 20250

Gardening Under Glass. Jerome A. Eaton. MacMillan, 886 3rd Ave., New York, NY 10022

Greenhouse Handbook. Brooklyn Botanic Gardens, 1000 Washington Ave., Brooklyn, New York, NY 11225

WORLD:
The Complete Book of the Greenhouse. Ian G. Wall. Ward Lock, Ltd., 116 Baker St., London, England WIM 2BB

Plans
Fiberglass structures
UNITED STATES:
Environment, Box 7855, Austin, TX 78712

Greenhouse Specialties, 9849 Kimker Ln., St. Louis, MO 63127

Home Greenhouse Plans, Johns Manville Corp., 22 E. 40th St., New York, NY 10016

Liahona Greenhouses, Box 17060, Salt Lake City, UT 48117

Geodesic structures

UNITED STATES:
Dome Plan (#822-350), Quonset Plan (#822-360), and others. Extension Agricultural Engineering, Pennsylvania State University, University Park, PA 16802

The Handmade Greenhouse. Richard Nichols. 38 S. 19th St., Philadelphia, PA 19103

Plant rooms— architectural growing structures

UNITED STATES:
Your Homemade Greenhouse and How to Build It. Jack Kramer. Simon and Schuster, 630 5th Ave., New York, NY 10020

Prefabricated greenhouses

CANADA:
B. C. Greenhouse Builders, Ltd., 7425 Hedlye St., Burnaby, British Columbia

Canadian Greenhouses, Box 5000, Durham Rd., Beamsville, Ontario LOR 1BO

English Aluminum Greenhouses, 1201 Deerford Rd., Willowdale, Ontario M2J 3J3

Equipment Consultants and Sales, 2241 Dunwin Dr., Mississauga, Ontario L5L 1A3

Great Northwest Greenhouses, 71 Glencameron Rd., Thornhill, Ontario

Lord and Burnham, Dept. T, 325 Welland Ave., St. Catharines, Ontario

UNITED STATES:
Aluminum Greenhouses, Inc., 14615 Lorain Ave., Cleveland, OH 44111

American Leisure Industries, Box 63, Deep River, CT 06417

W. Attlee Burpee Co., 6055 Burpee Bldg., Warminster, PA 18974

Eden Greenhouses, Eden Aluminum Co., 5462 W. Broadway, Cedarhurst, New York, NY 11516

Enclosures, Inc., 80 Main St., Moreland, GA 30259

Environmental Dynamics, Box 996-MA, Sunnymead, CA 92388

Foray Corp., P. O. Box 1026, Kent, WA 98103

Garden of Eden, 985 E. Jericho Turnpike, Huntington Station, NY 11746

Gothic Arch Greenhouses, P. O. Box 1564, Mobile, AL 36601

Growhouse Corp., 2335 Burbank St., Dallas, TX 75235

Janco Greenhouses, Dept. PA 10, 10786 Tucker St., Beltsville, MD 20705

Pacific Coast Greenhouse Mfg. Co., 430 Burlingame Ave., Redwood City, CA 94063

Peter Reimuller, Greenhouseman, P.O. Box 2666-W1, Santa Cruz, CA 95063

Redfern Greenhouses, Mt. Harmon Rd., Scotts Valley, CA 95066

Redwood Domes, Box 666, Dept. AN, Aptos, CA 95003

Sturdi-Built Mfg. Co., 11304 S. W. Boones Ferry Rd., Portland, OR 97219

Sun-Glo Greenhouses; Fabricators, Inc., 3711 S. Hudson St., Seattle, WA 98118

Turner Greenhouses, Rt. 117 Bypass, Goldsboro, NC 27530

Wood-frame polyethylene structures

CANADA:
How to Build a Plastic Crop Shelter or Greenhouse (Catalogue #A53-1337). Information Div., Canada Dept. of Agriculture, Ottawa, Ontario K1A 0C7

UNITED STATES:
The Cornell 21 Plastic Greenhouse. Dept. of Vegetable Crops, Cornell University, Ithaca, NY 14850

Home Plastic Greenhouse (Circular #892). Virginia Polytechnic Institute, Blacksburg, VA 24060

Plastic Covered Greenhouse (Building Plan #73). Oregon State University, Corvallis, OR 97330

Slant-Leg Rigid Frame Plastic Greenhouse (Plan #139). Agricultural Engineering Dept., Rutgers University, New Brunswick, NJ 08903

Supplies
Special equipment

CANADA:
Humex, Ltd., Equipment Sales and Consultants, 2241 Dunwin Dr., Mississauga, Ontario L5L 1A3

UNITED STATES:
Kee Klamps, Inc. (for bench frames), 79 Benbro Dr., Buffalo, NY 14266

See the General Appendix, Sources of Supply, for a more complete list of materials and suppliers available if you build your own greenhouse.

Although glass is still the most common cover, other types are gaining popularity

COVERINGS

There are so many different kinds of material used to cover greenhouses that deciding which one to use can be confusing. *Table 5* (p. 15) compares the characteristics of each available material to help you select the one that best suits your needs.

Double-layer materials, such as the new Aircap, are coming on the market very rapidly. So before making a final selection, check with a supplier *(see General Appendix, Sources of Supply)* to see what's new.

GLASS COVERING

The wood- or metal-frame greenhouse glazed with glass is still the most widely used covering for the hobby greenhouse. Costs of the glass also are indicated in *Table 5,* and as you might expect, heavy, large lights cost the most.

Nails

At the present time square glazing nails are difficult to find, and glazing brads are available only from greenhouse suppliers. Glass clips, however, are readily available and easily installed *(fig. 10).* The clips cost approximately six cents each. They are made of aluminum for durability, fasten into the wood bar with one screw, and hold two panes of glass.

Glazing

Glazing with a putty knife and gum bead rolled between the fingers is an art. Since not many skilled glaziers are available today, the best idea is to purchase a caulking gun (about $10.00) and a cartridge of compound ($1.00) and do the job yourself. A step-by-step procedure is shown in the appendix.

POLYETHYLENE COVERING

Most growers are using a double-layer polyethylene covering (poly) to reduce heat loss from the greenhouse by as much as 30 percent. Many growers use a 4-mil covering underneath and a 6-mil copolymer cover on top, which usually last for two years or more. The double-poly coatings greatly reduce the annoying water condensation that is common in many greenhouses. Detailed instructions are included in the appendix regarding how to fasten and inflate the poly on your structure.

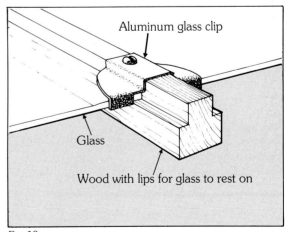

Fig. 10
Aluminum glass clips

13

FIBERGLASS COVERING

The quality of fiberglass improves each year, which is leading to increased usage *(fig. 11)*. Detailed instructions for installing fiberglass are included in the appendix.

Fig. 11
Covering a greenhouse with fiberglass

Fig. 12
One type of double-wall covering

Light transmission

When light comes through fiberglass it is diffused, or spread out, and there are no shadows cast within the greenhouse. This means less shade is required in the bright, sunny, hot months. Clear fiberglass that is used for growing transmits about 90 to 95 percent of the available light. (There are grades of fiberglass made for the construction trade with as little as 30 percent light transmission, which is not enough for healthy plant growth.)

Protective coating

Tedlar is a protective coating for fiberglass. Fiberglass coated with Tedlar is currently the best fiberglass for use on a greenhouse. The coating sheds dirt easily, protects the fiberglass surface from abrasion, and maintains good light transmission over a period of years.

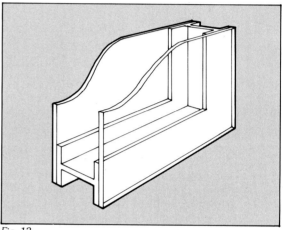
Fig. 13
Another type of double-wall covering that saves heat

RIGID DOUBLE-WALL COVERINGS

For many years we have used double-wall glass or thermopane in the residence to reduce heat loss. Now more manufacturers are using plastic and acrylic materials to make double-wall components for greenhouse use *(fig. 12)*, some of which include a baffle between the sheets of acrylic that provides an insulating dead-air layer *(fig. 13)*.

At present most double-wall rigid materials are sold as complete prefabricated greenhouses, but there are sources for individual sheets if you want to build your own structure *(see General Appendix, Sources of Supply)*. Although these panels are initially expensive, the savings in the cost of heating make them economical in the long run. As you consider new coverings for the home greenhouse that are placed on the market, however, check to make certain that light transmission is adequate: 90 percent (about 8-9,000 footcandles) or better.

Table 5
GREENHOUSE COVERINGS

Covering	Physical Data	Percentage Outdoor Light Transmitted Through Covering	Durability	Upkeep	Comments
GLASS	**Strength:** single, 1/16" double, 1/8" triple, 3/16" **Sizes for glazing:** **U.S.** 16"x 20", 18 x 24", 20"x 24", 20"x 30" **Canada** 16"x24", 20"x20", 24"x30" (or custom sizes to fit) Dutch Lites 28¾"x65"	95% Clear	Until broken, 25 to 35 years	Immerse in strong solvent or detergent, oxalic acid, fluoric acid Must be reputtied every few years Clean algae (see chapter 1)	Breaks easily Can be glazed or bedded in soft plastic or rubber You can see out of glass house 9 to 11% light loss when dirty Tempered glass is stronger **Cost:** $.25-$.35 per sq. ft.
REGULAR POLYETHYLENE (untreated plain)	**Mil* thickness:** 1, 5, 2, 4, 8, 10 3' to 40' wide 50' and 100' rolls	90% Diffused	1 year	Must be stretched tight or inflated for strength Needs frequent cleaning with mild detergent such as sodium phosphate (Tri Basic): 5-8 tsp. per gal. water, or plain water	Used in construction trades Has a tendency to split on the fold In shaded areas this material will last 2 years or more **Cost:** $.01-$.02 per sq. ft.
PLEXIGLASS	**Thickness:** .03" to 1.00" Clear acrylic resin Wear resistant **Surface sizes:** 36" to 48" to 72" to 96" (Custom sizes available)	100% Crystal clear	25 years plus	Clean with mild detergent	Does not turn yellow; resists impact **Cost:** Dupont Abcite $2.00-$3.00 per sq. ft. Other $1.50-$2.00 per sq. ft.
LEXAN	**Thickness:** .010" to .500" Glass (clear or colors) Polycarbonate resin	86% Crystal clear	Guaranteed against breakage for 3 years	Clean with mild soap and water	UV treated available Tough, break resistant, mar resistant **Cost:** $.85-$2.87 per sq. ft.
MYLAR	**Thickness:** .005" to .010" Stable polyester film Rolls 3'to 6' wide	100% Can be clear as glass or diffused	High tensile strength 5 to 8 years	Clean with mild detergent and water	Hard surface; withstands temperature to −80°F; does not yellow Chatters in wind **Cost:** $.17-$.18 per sq. ft.

*1 mil = .001 of an inch thickness

Covering	Physical Data	Percentage Outdoor Light Transmitted Through Covering	Durability	Upkeep	Comments
ULTRA-VIOLET POLYETHYLENE (UVR)	**Mil thickness:** 1, 5, 2, 4, 8, 10 3' to 40' wide 50' to 100' rolls	90% Diffused	1 to 2 years	In northern areas must be cleaned for winter light	Has been treated with inhibitors to make it resistant to ultra-violet light, which breaks down regular polyethylene Double wall reduces heat loss **Cost:** $.02-$.03 per sq. ft.
COPOLYMER POLYETHYLENE (Monsanto 602, UVR)	**Mil thickness:** 4, 6 10' to 40' wide 100' and 150' rolls —	90% Diffused	2 years	Clean as needed with mild detergent	Different resin-ethyl vinyl acetate Double the amount of ultraviolet inhibitor Tear strength twice that of regular **Cost:** $.15-$.20 per sq. ft.
WOVEN POLYETHYLENE (UVR)	**Mil thickness:** 8 Polyolefin 3-ply	90% Diffused 4% loss in 3 years	2-year guarantee	Clean as you would poly-ethylene	Polyethylene resin Usually hail-proof; not affected by low temperature; mildew proof; stands 40° below Sewn to size for larger sheets **Cost:** $.08-$.10 per sq. ft.
VINYL FILM	**Mil thickness:** 4, 8 **Widths:** 4½' 6' Clear only 7' to 40' wide 200' rolls	90-95% Clear Diffused	1 to 2 years depending on exposure	Needs frequent cleaning with mild detergent	4 mil glass-clear ESKAYLITE is available in 36" and 48" widths only Diffused-light covers wider than 6' are fabricated by electronic sealing and may be ordered in widths from 7' to 40' **Cost:** $.025-$.05 per sq. ft.
CLEAR ACRYLIC (molded or sheet)	**Mil thickness:** 8 High impact single or double wall Available pre-fab (2-year warranty)	90-95% Diffused	20 years (antici-pated by manufacturer)	Clean as needed with mild detergent	Will withstand snow load, hail, and flying objects Double wall with insulating trapped-air space reduces heat loss **Cost:** single sheet $1.00-$2.00 per sq. ft.; double sheet price unavailable

Covering	Physical Data	Percentage Outdoor Light Transmitted Through Covering	Durability	Upkeep	Comments
FIBERGLASS	Rated by weight-per-square foot **Corrugated widths:** 2', 3', 4' Up to 24' length 3' to 4' width 50' rolls (flat) UV treated	90-95% Diffused Light rated Fiberglass is special product for greenhouse use 2 oz., 4 oz., 5 oz. Loses small percent annually	10-year guarantee	Should be re-coated with clear acrylic resin as needed Low mainten-ance	Glass fibers plus at least 15% acrylic resins in better grades Depending upon location, turns yellow after several years Resistant to hail and flying objects Reduces chances of sun scorch **Cost:** $.30-$.40 per sq. ft. approximately
FIBERGLASS (Tedlar-coated)	Same sizes as above (Tedlar is florinated poly-vinyl film)	90-95% Diffused Keeps light trans-mission qualities for 20 years, with small decrease	20-year guarantee	Cleans easily Needs no refinishing	Tedlar-coated fiber-glass does not erode glass fibers **Cost:** $.50-$.75 per sq. ft.
AMER-X (UV)	**Mil thickness:** 8, 12 Vinyl 42" x 50" width	95% Diffused, milky	5-year guarantee	Clean with mild detergent	Custom sizes elec-tronically sealed **Cost:** $.10-$.15 per sq. ft.
AIRCAP (barrier-coated bubbles)	Double-layer polyethylene 4' x 300'	90% or better Diffused	Unknown	Wash with strong spray to remove dirt	Can be used the same as poly sheeting Clings to wet glass for direct application Also used as capillary mat **Cost:** $.07 per sq. ft. approxi-mately (or approximately $85.00 per roll)

SOURCES

General information

CANADA:
Cadillac Plastic & Chemical, 91 Kelfield St., Resdale, Ontario; and 156 W. 2nd St., Vancouver, British Columbia

UNITED STATES:
Cadillac Plastics & Chemical, Info-Tech Library, 15841 2nd Ave., Detroit, MI 48323

Supplies
UNITED STATES:
Continental Products Co. (putty and paint), 1150 E. 222nd St., Euclid, OH 44117

The Garland Co., 3800 E. 91st St., Cleveland, OH 44105

See the General Appendix, Sources of Supply, for a more complete list of the materials mentioned and the suppliers.

Supplemental light is added to enhance growth during the short days of winter

LIGHT AND LIGHTING

LIGHT AND GROWTH

Plants depend upon the energy of sunlight, their growth controlled by rays travelling 186,000 miles per second for 93 million miles. This energy is stored for food through the process of photosynthesis, then released for the growth of plant tissue by the process of respiration (*fig. 14*).

Photosynthesis and respiration

When light hits the surface of the leaf, it is "trapped" by the chlorophyll in the leaf cells, or the process of photosynthesis. The leaf uses the energy of the sunlight to combine carbon dioxide (CO_2) from the air with water (H_2O) from the soil. The resultant products are oxygen and sugar. The oxygen is given off into the air as a component of water vapor. The sugar (glucose) is oxidized (burned) in the plant to provide the energy for growth, or the process of respiration.

Photosynthesis

$$\text{Carbon dioxide + water} \xrightarrow[\text{energy}]{\text{light}} \text{sugar + oxygen}$$

$$6\,CO_2 + 6\,H_2O \xrightarrow{\text{light}} \underset{\text{glucose (sugar)}}{C_6H_{12}O_6 + 6O_2}$$

Respiration

$$\text{Glucose + oxygen} \xrightarrow{\text{oxidation}} \text{carbon dioxide + water + energy}$$

$$C_6H_{12}O_6 + 6O_2 \xrightarrow{\text{oxidation}} 6CO_2 + 6H_2O + 686 \text{ kilocalories of free heat energy}$$

When growing plants, you therefore need to provide the proper conditions and materials for

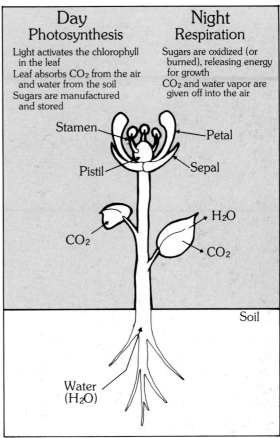

Day
Photosynthesis
Light activates the chlorophyll in the leaf
Leaf absorbs CO_2 from the air and water from the soil
Sugars are manufactured and stored

Night
Respiration
Sugars are oxidized (or burned), releasing energy for growth
CO_2 and water vapor are given off into the air

Stamen
Petal
Pistil
Sepal
H_2O
CO_2
CO_2
Soil
Water (H_2O)

Fig. 14
Plant-growth cycle

these two processes to occur. Plants need sunlight, for example, in order for photosynthesis to take place, during which the plant gives off oxygen into the air. The plant then needs darkness in order for respiration to take place, during which the plant gives off carbon dioxide into the air.

LIGHT INTENSITY

When a plant gets too much light, the tender tissues burn and the tips of the leaves turn brown. If a plant receives too little light, however, it grows tall and spindly and will not flower—a condition called etiolation. The quality of light is determined by how the wavelength affects plant growth. *Figure 15* shows plant response to light of different wavelengths.

The native habitat of any given plant has a specific range of light intensity. Since the greenhouse bench mixes plants from all over the world, it is important to study the light requirements of the natural environments and group your plants in the greenhouse according to light requirements. You can check the light conditions in your greenhouse with a light meter calibrated for footcandles of light and add or decrease the light to the proper intensity for your plants.

Measuring light intensity

You can measure the approximate light intensity with a camera that has a built-in light meter by the following process:

f/ 2.8	—	32 fc
f/ 4.0	—	64 fc
f/ 5.6	—	125 fc
f/ 8.0	—	250 fc
f/ 11.0	—	500 fc
f/ 16.0	—	1,000 fc
f/ 22.0	—	2,000 fc

For example, if the preceding procedure gives you an f/stop of 8, you have approximately 250 footcandles of light. The following illustration (*fig. 16*) should help you place the light source the proper distance above your plants for optimum growth.

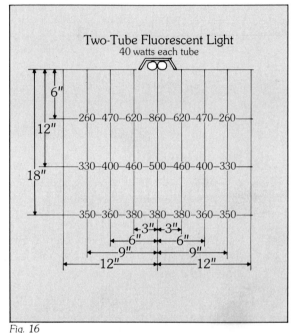

Fig. 16
Light intensity drops rapidly as plants are moved away from the light source

Light spectrum where photosynthesis occurs
Fig. 15

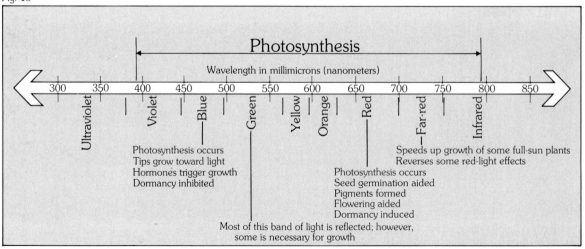

Plate 1

Cut roses grown in greenhouses are a major commercial florist crop—you can also grow beauties like this in a hobby house . . . even in mid-winter

Plate 2

Right: *You can harvest fresh produce daily from a home greenhouse. The Meyer lemon is not only ornamental, it produces fruit, too. Notice the Iron Cross begonia (B. masoniana) growing at the base of the tree*

Below: *You can grow your own plants for bedding out. Geraniums are a colorful addition to a green-house—with bright blooms even in the darkest days of winter*

Right: *One of the best fresh vegetables to grow in a cool greenhouse is lettuce, leafy types or loose-headed varieties such as a Bibb or Butter-crunch; other salad makings also do well: onions, radishes—and in a warm house, peppers and tomatoes*

Plate 3

This grape house in Oshawa, Ontario produces heavily; many grape varieties, which will not survive outside in most climates, will bear like this in a hobby greenhouse

Plate 4

Sweet 100 is a new tomato hybrid bred for heavy production over a long season. Pictures on these two pages are of the same plant; the first three showing the transition from many green fruits to . . .

Plate 5

. . . the ultimate in greenhouse gardening—succulent, red fruits you can harvest when it's freezing cold outside

Plate 6

Right: *Tropicals growing in a lean-to greenhouse attached to a residence*

Above: *This lipstick plant (Aeschynanthus) is a good representative of one of the best plant families for growing in greenhouses; the gesneriad family also includes African violets*

Right: *Many cacti and succulents deliver weird shapes, odd growth habits — and a spring dividend — an almost magical burst of bloom*

Plate 7

Most hobbyists end up raising orchids — either specializing in the many diverse kinds and colors or keeping a few in a house with other plants that want compatible temperatures

Plate 8

*Splashy combinations of color can be combined in the same pot. This planting
includes poppies, schizanthus, vinca and daisies (for later bloom), which can be started
early for instant color outside*

PHOTOPERIODISM

The response of a plant to the relative length of light and dark is known as photoperiodism. Plants may be grouped as "long-day," "short-day," and "neutral." (See *table 6*.) Photoperiodism affects flowering, and in many cases, you have to know the proper photoperiod in order to produce flowers. A short-day plant given eight hours of light and sixteen hours of dark, for instance, will flower. If there is even one minute of light from a twenty-five watt bulb at midnight, however, flowering will not take place.

This means you have to structure carefully the light environment for the plants you have in your greenhouse. You cannot get flowers on a poinsettia, for example, which should have less than ten hours of light in order to bloom, if it is sitting beside a begonia that you are lighting more than sixteen hours a day. *Table 6* also gives you the intensity and the photoperiod for a selected list of plants.

Table 6
MINIMUM LIGHT REQUIREMENTS FOR SELECTED PLANTS

Light in Footcandles*

50-500		1,000-5,000
Adiantum	Howea	Annuals (SD,N)
Aeschynanthus	Maranta	Azalea (LD)
Aglaonema	Monstera	Calceolaria (LD)
Aloe	Nephrolepis	Cattleya
Amaryllis (N)	Nephthytis	Chrysanthemum (SD)
Anthurium	Pandanus	Cineraria (LD)
Aphelandra (SD)	Peperomia	Citrus
Asparagus (N)	Philodendron	Coleus (LD)
Asplenium	Pilea	Crossandra (N)
Aspidistra	Podocarpus	Croton
Beaucarnea	Platycerium	Cyclamen
Begonia (LD)	Plectranthus	Cymbidium
Bromeliads (LD)	Pleomele	Dendrobium
Caladium	Polypodium	Epidendrum
Cereus	Polyscias	Episcia
Chamaedorea	Pseudorhipsalis	Eriobotrya
Chamaerops	Pteris	Euphorbia (SD)
Chlorophytum	Rhapis	Gardenia (SD)
Chrysalidocarpus	Rhoeo	Fuchsia (SD)
Cibotium	Sansevieria	Gloxinia (LD)
Cissus	Scindapsus	Gynura
Clusia	Selaginella	Hoya
Coccoloba	Spathiphyllum	Hydrangea
Coccothrinax	Tolmiea	Iresine
Coffea	Tradescantia	Kalanchoe
Columnea		Ligustrum
Cordyline	**500-1,000**	Lithops
Crassula		Opuntia
Cycas	Abutilon	Oncidium
Cyperus	Agave	Oxalis
Davallia	Araucaria	Pelargonium
Dieffenbachia	Ardisia	Portulacaria
Dizygotheca	Capsicum	Rosa
Dracaena	Cypripedium	Saintpaulia (LD)
Fatsia	Phalaenopsis	Saxifrage
Ficus		Stephanotis (LD)
Fittonia		Strelitzia
Hedera		Vanda
Helxine		

*N = Neutral
SD = Short day: less than 10 hours of light
LD = Long day: more than 16 hours of light

How to provide short days

The following materials are made specifically for the purpose of shading photoperiod plants (*fig. 17*) in order to provide short days:

1. Black Cloth—a tightly woven fabric (costs about $1.75 per square yard)
2. Simshade Al/blac—an opaque pvc film and an aluminized reflective film laminated on either side of a nylon mesh (price is about $.20 per square yard)

Fig. 17
Drawing shading material over Kalanchoes to reduce day length

Use of available light

There are also several ways in which you can take maximum advantage of the light available at your particular site for those plants requiring more light:

1. Orient the greenhouse toward the maximum source of light, with the long axis pointing east and west
2. Locate the greenhouse so it is free of shadow patterns from trees and buildings, especially in the winter months
3. Place the shade-loving plants in the shady part of the greenhouse and the others in full sunlight

Enhancing natural light

To get better distribution of natural light, use a reflective surface material such as aluminum foil or Roscoflex on the walls and under the benches. For maximum light during winter, reflective material

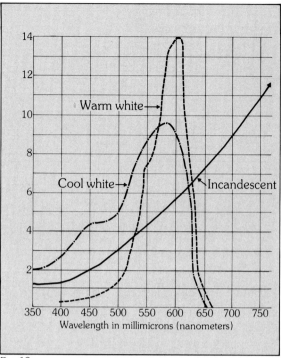

Fig. 18
Spectrum schematic of three light sources

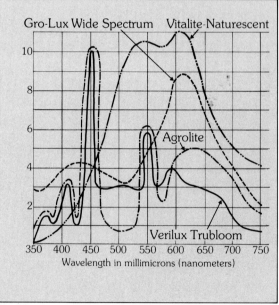

Fig. 19
Spectrum schematic of four fluorescent "grow" lamps

also can be placed on walks in areas where there is minimal traffic.

Use of supplemental light

To increase day length in winter, or to provide higher light intensity on the shady side of the green-house, you will need to use supplemental light. *Figures 18* and *19* show the spectrum of incandescent, cool white, and warm white light sources; the spectrum of four "grow" lamps; and the degree of light intensity relative to the distance from the light source. *Table 7,* which follows, should help you decide the source of light that best suits the plants you are growing. Suppliers of lamps and lighting equipment are listed at the end of the chapter.

Spot lights

If you are growing plants where it is not practicable to place the light 18 inches or less over the plants, spot lights are available that can be placed as high as 6 feet above the plants. Data on these lights also is given in the lighting table.

High intensity lamps

Lamps with higher wattage that increase the light intensity are "High Output" (HO) and "Very High Output" (VHO), or from 110 to 215 watts. "High Intensity Discharge" (HID) lamps are usually metal halide or high-pressure sodium. For home use, metal halide lamp (Nitegro) at 400 watts is now available for about $300.00 or 1,000 watts at about $400.00. Prices include an oscillating assembly that covers 50 to 90 square feet when placed 3 to 8 feet above the plants.

For the sake of safety, it is best to have the wiring of your greenhouse done by a licensed electrician. In fact, most building codes require professional installation.

A good fixture to start with is a two-tube reflector type such as shown in *figure 20.* If it is mounted with two pieces of chain that slip over hooks in the rafters, you can adjust the distance from the light source to the plant. Construction details and procedures for care of the fixtures are given in the appendix.

Lamp Guidelines:

1. Lamps decline in efficiency as they age; for good growth replace the lamp when it has functioned for 60 percent of the rated life in hours

2. Use the reflectors to increase the light intensity reaching the plants

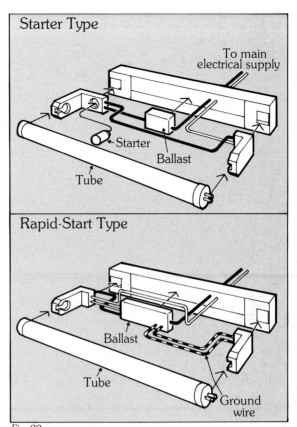

Fig. 20
Wiring diagram for starter-type fluorescent tube. Wiring diagram for rapid-start fluorescent tube*
Courtesy of "Do-It-Yourself," Reader's Digest

3. The number of lamps needed is often figured by lamp-watts-per-square-foot of growing area, as follows:

$$\frac{\text{(Growing area) x (Required lamp watts per sq. ft.)}}{\text{Individual lamp watts}}$$

A. 10 lamp watts per square foot: for germinating seed (6 to 8 inches above germinating medium)

B. 15 lamp watts per square foot: for low energy plants in the 50 to 500 foot-candle range (12 to 15 inches above plants)

C. 20 lamp watts per square foot: for high energy plants in the 500 to 2,000 foot-candle range (12 to 15 inches above plants)

Table 7
GREENHOUSE LIGHTING

Type of Lamp	Light Source	Spectrum*	Lamp Life (in hours)	Cost	Comments
Incandescent	Tungsten filament	15% B 33% Y-G 52% R	700-1,200	$.50-$3.00	Gives off heat 130V lasts longer
Fluorescent Cool white	Phosphors and mercury arc	30% B 52% Y-G 18% R	5,000	$2.00-$3.00	Change lamps every year if this is the only light source; change every 2-3 years if used as supplemental light
Warm white	Phosphors	20% B 55% Y-G 25% R	Same as above	$3.00-$5.00	Same as above
Gro-Lux	Phosphors	38% B 18% Y-G 43% R	5,000-15,000	$4.00-$5.00	
Gro-Lux Wide Spectrum	Phosphors	30% B 32% Y-G 38% R Tr FR	7,500 only	$4.00-$5.00	
Gro-Lux Plant Grower GL-1302	Phosphors	27% B 15% Y-G 39% R Tr FR	10,000	$5.00-$7.00	High intensity lamp
Agrolite	Phosphors	30% B 28% Y-G 40% R 5% FR	7,500-20,000	$4.00-$5.00	
Naturescent	Phosphors	20% B 45% Y-G 35% R Tr FR	5,000-7,500	$4.00-$5.00	
Verilux Trubloom	Phosphors	35% B 25% Y-G 40% R Tr FR	20,000-30,000	$4.00-$5.00	
Vitalite	Phosphors	32% B 46% Y-G 20% R 2% FR	13,000-33,000	$4.00-$5.00	

* B= blue
Y-G = yellow-green
R = red
FR = far red
Tr =trace

(Approximate percentages)

SOURCES

General information

CANADA:

Chatelaine's Gardening Book. Lois Wilson. McLean-Hunter, 481 University Ave., Toronto, Ontario M5W 1A7

Businesses and organizations

Civic Garden Center, 777 Lawrence Ave. E., Don Mills, Ontario M3C 1P2

ITT, Lighting Fixture Div., 1601 Ben Lomond St., Hamilton, Ontario (also other cities)

The Plant Room, 6373 Trafalgar Rd., Hornby, Ontario

UNITED STATES:

The Complete Book of House Plants Under Lights. Charles Marden Fitch. Hawthorn, 260 Madison Ave., New York, NY 10016

Florist's Review. 14 August 1975 and others. Florist's Publishing Co., 310 S. Michigan Ave., Chicago, IL 60604

Gardening Under Lights. F. H. and J. I. Kranz. Second edition. Viking, 625 Madison Ave., New York, NY 10022

The Indoor Light Gardening Book. George A. Elbert. Crown, 419 Park Ave. S., New York, NY 10016

Lighting for Plant Growth. Elwood D. Bickford and Stuart Dunn. Kent State University Press, Kent, OH 44240

Businesses and organizations

National Indoor Light Gardening Society, 128 W. 58th St., New York, NY 10019

Plants Alive, Inc., 5509 1st Ave. S., Seattle, WA 98108

Supplies

CANADA:

Equipment Consultants and Sales, 2241 Dunwin Dr., Mississauga, Ontario L5L 1A3

Ruddi Electric Wholesale, Ltd., 75 Richmond St. W., Oshawa, Ontario

Stokes Seed, Ltd., P. O. Box 10, St. Catharines, Ontario L2R 6R6

UNITED STATES:

Duro-Light Lamps, 17 Willow St., Fairlawn, NJ 07410

Famco, Inc., 300 Lake Rd., Medina, OH 44256

Floralite Co., 4124 E. Oakwood, Oak Creek, WI 53221

General Electric, Lamp Div., Nela Park, Cleveland, OH 44112

GTE Sylvania Lighting Center, Danvers, MA 01923

JD 21 Lighting Systems, 1840 130th N.E., Suite 7, Bellevue, WA 98005

Sylvania Electric Co., 60 Boston St., Salem, MA 01971

Verilux Trubloom, Dept. B, 35 Mason St., Greenwich, CT 06803

Westinghouse Electric, Lamp Div., Bloomfield, NJ 07003

Reflective material

UNITED STATES:

ROSCO Laboratories, Inc., 36 Bush Ave., Port Chester, NY 10573

Shade cloth

UNITED STATES:

Simtrac, Inc., 8243 N. Christiana Ave., Skokie, IL 60076

See the General Appendix, Sources of Supply, for a more complete list of materials and suppliers. Also consult the yellow pages of your local phone directory under lighting fixtures, nurseries, and garden centers, many of which now stock growing lights.

Most cacti prefer hot, dry conditions, as grown here in this almost circular greenhouse

HEATING

BASICS OF HEATING

Temperature control

The temperature in a plant's environment must be controlled precisely for successful gardening. A greenhouse provides the gardener with a means of not only protecting the plant year round, but of achieving optimal growth as well.

The response to temperature differs from one plant to another, but the whole plant is affected, including its ability to flower, to produce roots, to absorb nutrients, and to form tissue. Additionally, all plants have a fundamental optimal growth temperature (*fig. 21*).

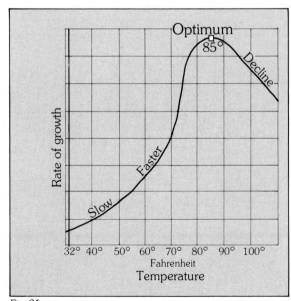

Fig. 21
Fundamental optimal growth temperatures

Native habitat temperatures

As mentioned in the previous chapters, the fundamental purpose of a greenhouse is to reproduce as closely as possible the environment in each plant's native habitat. Most of our house plants, for example, come from the tropics where they grow at 65°F-70°F (18°C-22°C). Bedding plants and perennials, which we start in the greenhouse and then put outdoors, come from temperature climates 50°F-65°F (10°C-18°C), while dwarf evergreens for bonsai and many perennials from alpine meadows grow at temperatures below 50°F (10°C). The horticultural encyclopedias listed in the appendix should help you become familiar with the native habitat of your favorite plants. *Table 8* also will give you some suggestions for plants to be grown in cool, medium, or warm greenhouses.

Figuring your heat loss

You can buy a hot water, gas, electric, or oil heating unit for your greenhouse in a variety of sizes. You need to know the BTU (British Thermal Unit) heat loss of the greenhouse, however, in order to determine the size unit you need. Your goal is to replace the BTUs lost; then using your heat loss, you can refer to *Table 9* (p. 32) to choose the heating equipment best suited to your greenhouse. To help you calculate your heat loss, first is a formula, then a diagram in *figure 22*.

Formula

A × B × C × W = Heat loss in BTUs per hour

A = The total exposed area of the greenhouse in square feet

B = The temperature differential between the coldest nights outside and the temperature you wish to maintain inside the greenhouse right through the winter

C = The construction factor:

Single-layer poly	1.20
Double-layer poly	.80
Old glass glazing	1.80
New glass glazing	1.50
Fiberglass or rigid plastic	1.20
Lean-to attached	.80

W = The wind factor:

15 mph	1.00
20 mph	1.20
30 mph	1.25
40 mph	1.30

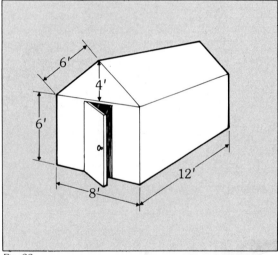

Fig. 22
Example showing how to figure heat loss of greenhouse

Table 8
GREENHOUSE TEMPERATURES

Cool	Medium	Warm
Night: 50.0°F Day: 60.0°F	Night: 60.0°F Day: 70.0°F	Night: 65.0°F Day: 75.0°F
10.0°C 15.6°C	15.6°C 21.0°C	18.3°C 24.0°C
Achimenes	Acalphya	African violet
Aloe	Aglaonema	Anthurium
Ardisia	Aphelandra	Caladium
Asparagus	Aralia	Cattleya seedlings
Azalea (to force bloom)	Azalea (to initiate buds)	Dendrobium
Baby tears	Begonia	Gloxinia
Beaucarnia	Cattleya (except seedlings)	Maranta
Boston fern		Nephthytis
Cactus	Chrysanthemum	Oncidium
Calceolaria	Coffea	Palms
Chlorophytum	Cordyline	Phalaenopsis
Cissus	Croton	Pleomele
Citrus	Cryptanthus	Sansevieria
Crown of thorns	Dieffenbachia	Scindapsus
Cymbidium	Dracaena	Spathiphylum
Cyclamen	Epidendrum	Stephanotis
English ivy	Episcia	Vanda
Jade plant	Ficus	
Odontoglossum	Fittonia	
Paphiopedilum	Fuchsia	
Philodendron	Gardenia	
Plectranthus	Geranium	
Rhapis	Gynura	
Wandering jew	Hemigraphis	
Zamia	Hoya	
	Hypoestes	
	Jacobinia	
	Kalanchoe	
	Miltonia	
	Monstera	
	Paphiopedilum, mottled leaf	
	Pellionia	
	Peperomia	
	Pilea	

Conserving heat

Every year there are developments that make it easier to have a comfortable greenhouse all winter. Currently, some commercial houses are using two layers of polyethylene over their greenhouses, the layers separated by forced air from a small squirrel-cage blower. This method is also effective on home greenhouses and requires much less work than trying to put one layer inside and one layer outside as with the old double-covering method. The blower style works well over both fiberglass or glass. Procedures for installing double polyethylene are given in the appendix of chapter 2.

Heating costs

The following data on the heating value of fuels should help you to figure the cost of heating the greenhouse in your area:

Propane	91,000 BTU per gal.
Natural gas	1,000 BTU per cu. ft.
Coal	13,000 BTU per lb.
Fuel oil	138,000 BTU per gal.
Gasoline	122,300 BTU per gal.
Electricity	3,413 BTU per kw. hr.
Wood (birch)	4,300 BTU per lb.
Nord and Presto logs	65,000 BTU per lb.

Stand-by generators

If you have a choice collection of plants, it is advisable to have stand-by power in order to avoid disaster in case of power failure. (Become familiar with the use of the stand-by generator before you have an emergency.)

Gas-driven, air cooled generator:
1,500-4,000 watts, 5,119-13,651 BTU;
from $200.00 up

Minimizing freeze damage

Most freeze damage is caused by rapid thawing that tears the plant's leaf and stem tissue. If you are not able to provide enough heat in an emergency, there are materials available to minimize freeze damage to plants. If a freeze at night is followed by bright sun and a temperature rise the next morning, for example, there would be extensive damage. Spray plants thoroughly that night with a liquid polyethylene such as Wilt-pruf, Vapor Guard, or Foliar Gard, which will not prevent the tissue from freezing, but will slow down thawing and reduce the damage.

Locating the heat source

The upper surfaces of most leaves are transparent in order to trap light energy, but thick and wax-coated to resist excessive radiation. By contrast, the lower leaf surface is thin, exposed, and covered with openings (stomata) that permit the exchange of gases. Since the upper-leaf surface is so much better protected, the greenhouse's heat source should be above the plants.

Sun heat, for example, comes through the glass as radiant short waves. It is absorbed by the plants, the soil, and interior greenhouse structure. Excess heat is radiated back to the air as longer waves that do not readily pass through the glass, therefore maintaining warmth in the greenhouse. Heating from above offers the additional benefits of allowing the soil to remain cooler than the surrounding air, thus promoting healthy root growth, and of retarding moisture evaporation, so less water is needed.

TEMPERATURE INSTRUMENTS

Thermometers

In order to keep track of the temperature in the air and in the soil, you need good thermometers. For air temperature, use a large-figure, white-mer-

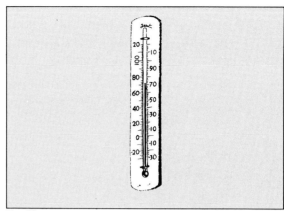
Fig. 23
Easy-to-read thermometer

cury thermometer (fig. 23). For soil temperature, use a bimetallic probe thermometer.

You should take your initial air temperature readings when you first install the heating system; it is worthwhile to check the heat distribution throughout the greenhouse. Record the temperature in the four corners and in the center of the structure. (See appendix for detailed instructions.) If there is wide variation in temperature, the heating system should be adjusted to provide uniform heat all through the greenhouse.

In addition, a maximum-minimum thermometer (fig. 24) can tell you how low the temperature has

Maximum-minimum thermometer
Fig. 24

gone overnight and how high it goes on a bright sunny day. Measuring these extremes in temperature lets you further adjust the heating system so heat is uniform throughout the day and night. An indoor-outdoor thermometer *(fig. 25)* is recommended for adjusting the heating system to provide for these outdoor temperatures since it has one sensing device inside the greenhouse and one outside.

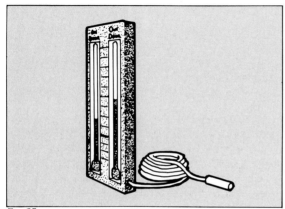
Fig. 25
Indoor-outdoor thermometer

When taking the soil temperature, place the probe thermometer in a pot, on a bench, or in the ground. You should also keep a soil thermometer in a pot on the bench at all times to make certain that your heating system is providing a minimum 60°F (15.6°C) soil temperature.

Cultural directions that say "grow at 65°F (18.3°C)," for example, mean that not only the air, but also the soil in the pot should be at the specified temperature. Often the soil temperature will fall below the air temperature, so this monitoring is important.

Should you wish to keep a precise record of the relationship between temperatures and growth, you also will need a recording thermometer. This thermometer will give you a continuous record of temperature fluctuations over a seven-day period.

Thermostats

A thermostat *(fig. 26)* is an instrument that automatically maintains a constant set temperature. If the temperature deviates from the setting, an electrical current is activated that turns the heater on or off to correct the temperature.

Fig. 26
Thermostat

For many greenhouses, a single-stage thermostat that will operate one piece of equipment and can be connected to either fan or heater is adequate. If more power is needed, however, a thermostat can operate several fans, two-speed fans, or more than one heater.

Temperature alarm

One of the best ways to protect against a power failure in your greenhouse in the middle of the night is to set up a battery-operated temperature alarm *(fig. 27)*. The alarm can be connected to the bedroom and attached to a bell so you will be alerted to a power failure as soon as it happens.

It is not difficult to hook up such a device, and it can mean the difference between losing and saving all the plants in your greenhouse. Temperature alarms are available from greenhouse suppliers and

Fig. 27
A warning alarm

cost from about $20.00 to $25.00. Alarms also have an upper-limit contact that will ring a bell if the greenhouse gets too hot so you can attend to a ventilation problem (*see appendix, chapter 15 for detailed instructions*).

HEATED BENCH

Growing plants in the winter depends upon heat conservation. With the current energy shortage, plan to do your growing with a minimum use of heat energy!

One way to conserve energy is to heat a bench for growing, rather than heating the entire greenhouse. Even with a double layer of poly on the greenhouse, you are heating a lot of space that is relatively non-productive. By using the same double layer of poly on a heated bench, you can have two-zone heat in one greenhouse.

In addition, more and more people are thinking about the merits of growing their own food, especially salad greens. In fact, many have done this during the spring and summer in vegetable gardens or in outdoor coldframes and hotbeds. But it makes good sense—as well as good eating—to continue the garden right through the winter. This can be accomplished with a heated bench in your home greenhouse where you can tend your vegetables in relative comfort. If by chance you already have a propagation bench, you are one step ahead; it can be converted easily to a heated winter-garden bench. See detailed instructions for constructing a heated bench in the appendix.

Environmental control

Maintaining a productive growing environment on a heated bench requires control of the light, water, heat, and ventilation. In many areas, for example, it is necessary to provide supplemental light for good growth, the use of which is detailed in chapter 3. Additionally, water practices are critical, but the method depends upon the crop being grown. Chapters 7 and 15 contain detailed discussions of watering practices. The maintenance of warmth and ventilation are discussed in the following paragraphs.

Heat

If you have trouble maintaining the desired temperature for your heated bench, a small electric heater can be installed at one end. For about $20.00 you can purchase a 1,320 watt heater that puts out 4,500 BTUs. This data and *Table 9* should help you select the electric heater you need:

ELECTRIC HEATER	BTU/HR.
650 watts	2,218
1,320 watts	4,500
2,000 watts	6,825
3,000 watts	10,238
4,000 watts	13,650
5,000 watts	17,064
1 BTU/hr. = .293 watts	$\frac{watts}{.293}$ = BTU/hr.

Ventilation

One of the primary problems with the heated bench is providing sufficient ventilation and air circulation to prevent disease. For a cubic area 3-by-10-by-2 feet, for example, a 2-inch exhaust fan rated at 250 cfm (cubic feet per minute) mounted in one end of the heated bench would be ample (priced at about $10.00). The fan should be controlled by a humidistat so it will be activated by excessive humidity to exhaust the moist air (see appendix for detailed installation procedures).

Potato vine (Solanum jasminoides) blooms vigorously all summer

Table 9
GREENHOUSE HEATERS

Type of Heater	Size of Greenhouse	BTU* Output	Cost	Fuel	Installation	Comments
MAIN HEAT SUPPLY Oil-fired Fan-driven	8'x8' 8'x12'	5,000 20,000	$ 100 200	Stove oil Diesel oil Kerosene	Available with self-contained tank or separate tank	Vent necessary unless burner has afterburner that provides complete combustion; larger units should be professionally installed
Gas Fan-driven	8'x8' 8'x12'	20,000 50,000	$ 200	Natural or propane	Small portable models or fixed	May be used with poly tube vent system to distribute heated air
	12'x30' and up	50,000 500,000	$ 300 1,000	Same	Fixed models	
Gas Catalytic	8'x8' 8'x12'	3,000 20,000	$ 50 300	Propane	Fuel from a disposable bottle or refillable tank	Does not produce flame or carbon monoxide; no vent necessary
Electric Fan-driven	8'x8' 8'x12'	1,000 5,000	$ 25 150	Both 110V and 220V	Portable plug-in or fixed models	Should have totally enclosed motor to withstand humidity
	12'x 20' and up	17,000 85.000	$ 200 600	Usually 220V	Permanently fixed	Should be professionally installed
Hot water	For a small greenhouse, a professional heating expert can extend the residence hot water heating system into the greenhouse. The hot water tank system shown in the appendix is another alternative. Larger greenhouses requiring a boiler and hot water pipe distribution system should be engineered and installed professionally.					
STAND-BY-HEAT SUPPLY Salamander or hard hat	8'x8' 8'x12'	Up to 150,000	$ 300 and up	Kerosene Diesel	Portable No installation	Most have afterburner for near complete combustion; one filling lasts 10 to 20 hours
Others	In an emergency, camping stoves using white gas, alcohol, or kerosene may be used.					

*1 BTU/hour = 0.293 Watts

SOURCES

General information
CANADA:
Ball Red Book. Twelfth edition. Ball-Superior, Ltd., 1155 Birchview Dr., Mississauga, Ontario L5H 3E1

UNITED STATES:
Ball Red Book. Twelfth edition. Geo. J. Ball, Inc., P.O. Box 335, West Chicago, IL 60185

Greenhouse Climate Control Handbook. Acme Engineering and Mfg. Corp., P.O. Box 978, Muskogee, OK 74401

Greenhouse Handbook for the Amateur. Vol. 19, No. 2. Brooklyn Botanic Gardens, 1000 Washington Ave., Brooklyn, New York, NY 11225

WORLD:
The Complete Book of the Greenhouse. Ian Walls. Ward Lock, Ltd., 116 Baker St., London, England WLM 2BB

Supplies
See the General Appendix, Sources of Supply, for a list of materials and suppliers.

Solar energy provides heat for Provident House, an experimental home in King City, Ontario

Provident house, King City, Ontario, is a solar house of the future—solar and wind energy are used extensively

SOLAR HEAT

HISTORICAL BACKGROUND

Since very early times, man has been using simple structures to trap the heat energy of the sun for himself as well as for plants. The Navajo in southwestern America and early man in Europe, for example, learned to orient both living and growing areas in order to get the maximum radiation from the sun. Later, through most of the Middle Ages, plants were grown in sun pits throughout Europe and the Mediterranean countries. Modern sun pits, descended from the medieval archetype, are discussed later in this chapter.

Interest in solar heat did not reappear until there was a flurry of activity in the early 1900's when thousands of solar hot water heaters were sold in Florida and California. The interest was short lived, however. In the more recent past, countries including Japan, Australia, and Israel have used solar heating to some extent, but the low cost of fuels in those countries discouraged interest in solar energy.

Now that the other forms of energy have become expensive and limited, there is renewed world-wide interest in solar energy, and research is underway to develop solar heat and power. Consequently, the next few years may well see the use of solar cells, photovoltaic cells, eutectic salt storage, and high-efficiency optical collectors to trap the energy of the sun in order to heat greenhouses and other structures.

SUN-HEATED PIT

Particularly for cold locations, the sun-heated pit is still an economical way of growing plants out of season. The pit is basically a trench four feet deep

that serves as the walk, with benches at ground level on either side. Above this is an A-frame structure of any of the common greenhouse covering materials. The heat source is primarily the sun, although supplemental heat is sometimes used. Details of construction are in the appendix.

SOLAR-HEATED GREENHOUSE

A glass greenouse is a natural heat trap. The shortwave radiation energy from the sun, in the form of light, easily goes through the glass of the greenhouse, and once inside, the energy is converted to heat in the form of long waves that will not pass back through the glass as readily as the light (fig. 28).

There are some simple methods of trapping

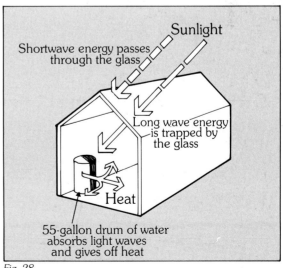

Sunlight

Shortwave energy passes through the glass

Long wave energy is trapped by the glass

Heat

55-gallon drum of water absorbs light waves and gives off heat

Fig. 28
Greenhouse as a heat collector

solar energy to heat your own greenhouse. If you use a 55-gallon drum full of water or stones to support a bench in your greenhouse, for example, and let the sun shine all day on the black side (*fig. 29*), it will act as a collector. When the sun goes down at night, the drum releases heat to the air of the greenhouse. This simple structure is a solar heater that collects, stores, and releases the energy of the sun.

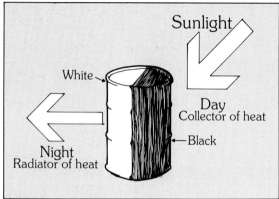

Fig. 29
Fifty-five gallon drum filled with water is simple heat collector

Collecting solar energy

Placing the collector of sun energy under the bench is obviously not the best location for optimum exposure to the sun. Most of the current research is directed toward collectors on top of the greenhouse, with transfer to a storage device and release from storage into the greenhouse through a distribution system.

The Bradenton Agricultural Research Center in Florida, for instance, is experimenting with a collector made of black hollow metal plates (*fig. 30*) through which water flows. Cool water enters the collector and comes out heated to temperatures as high as 200°F (93°C). This collector shows an efficiency of 55 percent—which will doubtlessly be improved with further research. Bradenton research further indicates that a collector should be one-tenth the square-foot area of the greenhouse. Thus an 8-by-12-foot greenhouse would have a collector that measures 10 square feet.

For trial purposes, you might try a grid of black painted aluminum pipe as a collector. You can also heat air by pumping or forcing it through such a collector and into a rock storage "battery."

Fig. 30
Bradenton solar research house has solar collectors on the roof

Fig. 31
The heated water goes to an insulated storage tank

Storage as heated water

The heated water goes from the collector to a water-storage tank (*fig. 31*). The storage capacity should be 10 gallons per square foot of collector area. For an 8-by-12-foot greenhouse, for example, this would mean a 100-gallon tank. At Bradenton the storage tank is insulated with 5 inches of urethane foam, enough insulation so there is almost no heat loss directly from the storage tank over a two-month period.

For a small greenhouse you might use a 100-gallon domestic water heater wired so the electricity will cut in to heat the water whenever the solar heat is not functioning. At present, the best use of solar energy is probably to supplement electrical energy.

Storage as heated air

Heated air from the collector is usually stored in rocks or stones (see appendix) that are called a solar battery in much of the current literature. Solar-Aire, one of the solar furnaces for a residence, for example, requires 225 cubic feet or about 25,000 lbs. of 1.5 inch stone for the storage area. This is too large a battery for the small greenhouse, although if properly engineered, it might be possible to use a stone battery under the benches. There is additional solar data in the appendix.

SOURCES

General information
UNITED STATES:

Energy for Survival. Wilson Clark. Anchor Books, Doubleday, 277 Park Ave., New York, NY 10017

Introduction to the Use of Solar Energy. George G. Laf. McGraw-Hill, 1221 Ave. of the Americas, New York, NY 10020

Practical Applications of Solar Energy (Leaflet #83). University of Florida, Gainesville, FL 32611

Businesses
Bradenton Agricultural Research Center, Dr. R. F. Lucas or Dr. C. D. Baird, 5007 60th St. E., Bradenton, FL 33505

Solar Energy Research Corp. ($2.00 information kit), 10075 E. County Line Rd., Longmont, CO 80501

Zomeworks Corp., P.O. Box 72, Albuquerque, NM 87103

Supplies
UNITED STATES:

C & C Solarthermics, Inc., P.O. Box 144, Smithsburg, MD 21783

Enclosures, Inc., 80 Main St., Moreland, CA 30259

Solar-Aire, 1565 9th St., White Bear Lake, MN 55110

Solar Comfort, Inc., 1031 S. Meeting St., Statesville, NC 28677

Solar Dynamics, Inc., 4155 E. Jewell St., Denver, CO 80206

Solar Mfg., 40 Coneaut Lake Rd., Greenville, PA 46125

Solar Power, Inc., 201 Airport Blvd., Doylestown, PA 18901

Solarstor, Parker, SD 57053

Solar-Thermics Enterprises, Ltd., P.O. Box 248, Creston, IA 50801

Sunglow, Inc., 12500 W. Cedar Dr., Lakewood, CO 80228

One common way of cooling a greenhouse is with roller shades

COOLING AND SHADING

GROWTH AND TEMPERATURE

Nature has evolved an intricate system for regulating the climate to support plant and animal life, two important aspects of which are the length of daylight and the intensity of the sun's rays. In this chapter we are concerned with the sun's intense radiation in the summer and its effect on plants.

During the summer the earth revolves at its highest angle, so the sun's heat energy is concentrated. The longer days give more chance for surface materials to accumulate heat; the shorter nights allow less time for the excess heat energy to dissipate. It therefore is necessary to provide both shading and cooling in our greenhouses during the summer to prevent the plants from becoming dehydrated or burned as we try to simulate nature's best growing conditions.

Fig. 32
A large exhaust fan for extracting large volumes of hot air

Temperature range

Plants show a wide diversity in temperatures needed for optimum growth. Most plants, however, show a rapid decline in growth as well as sunburn and wilting in temperatures above 85°F (29.4°C). Exceptions are the desert xerophytes (cacti and succulents), which survive high temperatures with very little water.

As the hot season approaches, check the thermometers in your greenhouse. If they go to 80°F (26.7°C), you need cooling. If you live in a subtropical or tropical climate, cooling year-round may be necessary.

COOLING METHODS

Circulating cool air

If your climate provides outside air ten to fifteen degrees cooler than inside air, you can simply open the doors and let the air blow through. You will probably need an exhaust fan to move hot air out and draw cool air in (*fig. 32*), as hot air must be moved rapidly for cooling to take place. *Table 10* (p. 40) should help you select the proper fan to cool your greenhouse. It gives data for air exchange once every minute, which is the optimum for cooling, as well as fan and pad requirements, and information about a wet pad cooler that is complete and ready to install. Construction, installation, and operation details are in the appendix.

SHADE

As mentioned, the sun climbs higher in the sky in the summer, giving excess light and heat. Many growers protect their plants with about 50 percent shade, but it is worthwhile to determine the specific shade needs for your location. As in other growing practices, with experience you eventually will be able to tell the shade requirements of individual plants.

First, look up the light conditions in the native habitat of the plants you are growing. Most cacti grow in the desert in full sun (about 10,000 footcandles), for example, while the majority of ferns grow in moist, shady woods with as little as fifty footcandles.

Second, use a footcandle meter and adjust your shade to the recommended light levels. (Chapter 3 has a list of the light requirements of a number of plants that can serve as a guide.)

Third, watch the plants for signs of tip burn or scalding. As a final check, measure the growth rate

to see if it is declining. Many kinds of materials are used for shading greenhouses. *Table 11* (p. 42) shows the characteristics of several that are readily available. A discussion of each shade type follows the table.

Interior shade systems
Roller shade

A system that lets you adjust the amount of shade to suit conditions is by far the best. Roller shades work well in a small greenhouse—up to 8-by-12 feet *(fig. 33)*—in which inexpensive cloth window shades are mounted along the ceiling ridge and pulled to the eaves as needed. If your greenhouse has many hanging baskets, however, this system may be inconvenient.

The shades should be white to reflect as much

Table 10
GREENHOUSE COOLING

Size of Greenhouse	Air Exchange (in cfm° per sq. ft.)			Required Exhaust (cfm°)	Fan Sizes and Ratings	Air Exhange	Cost
8'x 8'	x	12	=	768	12" — 650 cfm 16" — 870 cfm	1 — min. 1 — min.	$ 45.00 60.00
8'x 12'	x	12	=	1,152	16" — 870 cfm 18" — 1,625 cfm	1 — min. 1 — min.	60.00 80.00
12'x 20'	x	12	=	2,880	20" — 2,600 cfm 22" — 3,500 cfm	1 — min. 1 — min.	135.00 140.00
20'x 50'	x	9	=	9,000	24" — 4,500 cfm 30" — 8,500 cfm 36" — 10,300 cfm	1 — min. (use 2 fans) 1 — min. 1 — min.	250.00 300.00 350.00

°cfm = cubic feet per minute

PAD AND FAN DATA

Use 1 square foot of pad for every 150 cfm of fan velocity

To determine how much pad you need: $\frac{\text{Fan velocity}}{150}$ = square feet of pad required

For example: 8'x 12' house has 18" fan: $\frac{1,625 \text{ cfm}}{150}$ = 10.8 square feet of pad required

Water: Use ⅓ gallon per minute, per lineal foot of pad, without regard to height

WET PAD COOLER

Air capacity from 2,000 cfm @ $275.00 to 5,500 cfm @ $475.00 ready to hook up to water and electricity. The unit contains cabinet, fan, cooling pads, re-circulating water pump, float valve, and louvres. Larger models available up to 15,000 cfm

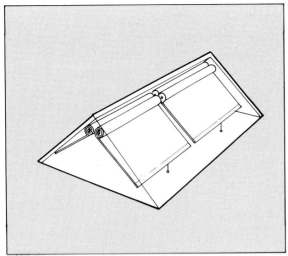

Fig. 33
Roller shades inside greenhouse

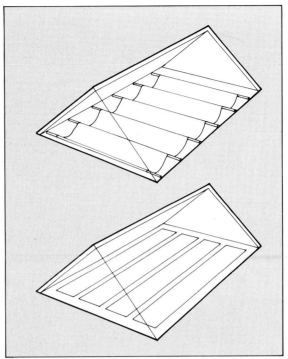

Fig. 34
Draped cheesecloth
Stretched cheesecloth

light as possible, but not made of plastic since plastic window shades do not stand up well under conditions of intense heat. After installing the shades, you need excellent ventilation and cooling to keep the temperature down to a reasonable level. A good fan system can circulate the air between the roller shade and the glass so the heated air eventually is moved out of the green-house by the exhaust fan.

Drape-cloth shade

You can also use a good grade of cheesecloth or Windsor Aster cloth draped or stretched as needed to provide shade inside the greenhouse (*fig. 34*). Fine burlap, old sheets, muslin, or almost any white fabric will work well for temporary interior shade.

Venetian-blind system

The Humex Sunvisor shown in *figure 35* is an example of an inside aluminum venetian-blind system for use in the summer. In the winter, the individual slats can be removed readily to allow maximum light entry. This type of shade can be adjusted to suit almost all conditions.

Poly on glass

It is possible to apply poly sheeting directly to wet glass on the inside—some colored poly is available for this purpose. These shades are not adjustable, however, which is a disadvantage.

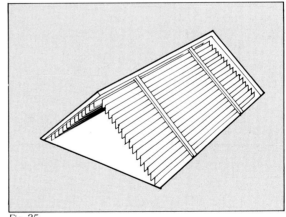

Fig. 35
Venetian-blind system

Snap-in shade

White fiberglass panels that fit between the rafters on the roof and the studs on the side wall are currently manufactured. These panels pop in and are easily removed. They provide approximately 50 percent shading.

Table 11
GREENHOUSE SHADE COVERINGS

Covering	Physical Data	Shade	Durability	Comments[*]
Polypropylene	1% shrinkage Tough plastic Black only	25%-100%	10-20 years	Available flame-proof or regular; sewn to custom sizes and fitted with taped edges and grommets—install tightly **Cost:** $.15-$.20 per sq. ft.
Saran	3% shrinkage Polyvinylidene Chloride Green, black, and natural	6%-94%	10-12 years	Not as tough or strong as polypropylene, lasting qualities vary with exposure—install loosely **Cost:** $.12-$.20 per sq. ft.
Polyshade	Polypropylene Black	47%-73%	Unknown	Sewn to custom sizes—new fabric, first available in 1975 **Cost:** $.20 per sq. ft.
Simshade K-65	Knit construction, 100% polyester yarn Light color	65%	4-5 years	New material, 1975; fire resistant, custom fabricated to size **Cost:** $.20 per sq. ft.
Windsor Aster Cloth	Cotton yarn Natural fiber color 8x10 mesh (threads to the inch) 200" widths	30%	3-5 years, depending on exposure	Sewn to specification; available with mildew inhibitor **Cost:** $.35-$.40 per sq. yd.
Propagating Cloth	White muslin 8x12 mesh	10%-20%	1-2 years	Light shade over seed and seedlings **Cost:** $.40-$.50 per sq. yd.
Natural Windsor Shade Cloth	Cotton yarn 16x16 mesh	70%	1-2 years, depending on exposure	Sewn to specifications in multiples of 40" **Cost:** $.40-$.50 per sq. yd.
Venetian Blinds	Aluminum or plastic	Adjustable	20 years plus	Can be controlled with light sensor for automatic shade control

[*]Costs are approximate

Exterior shade systems

Exterior shade systems are more popular with growers since they do not clutter up the inside of the greenhouse. Because they are subject to more abuse from the weather, however, they must be more durable.

Roller shade

A roller shade of bamboo, wood slat, or fabric (fig. 36) can be fastened at the ridge and installed with pulleys. On cloudy days it can be rolled up easily; a pull of the string will release the roller to provide cover on a hot sunny day.

Awning shade

We have used awnings on residences for many years, and the same principle adapts to greenhouses (fig. 37). Cooling is improved because the

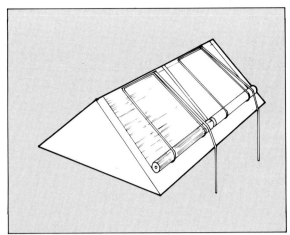

Fig. 36
Bamboo roller shades

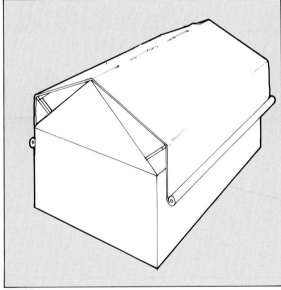

Fig. 37
Awning shade

Lath-house system

There are localities where the heat is so intense that it is worthwhile to build a lath house over the greenhouse (*fig. 38*). A lath house can provide as much shade as necessary and could be fabric covered for additional shade. Usually, a lath house is a wood structure consisting of posts and rafters that are covered with lath. The lath can be spaced to provide a given amount of shade, but once nailed down, it is not adjustable.

Spray shade

Commercial greenhouses use a soluble powder or liquid shade applied directly to the glass. Some

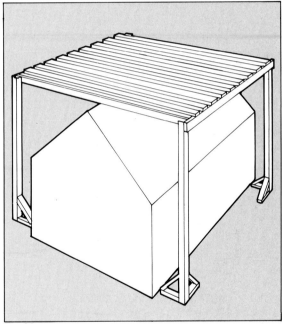

Fig. 38
Lath shade

air flows between the shade material and the surface of the greenhouse.

Venetian-blind system

A greenhouse at the University of Vienna has vertical venetian blinds that are controlled automatically by a photoelectric cell. The blinds are well suited to a hot climate region and can be adapted for use on a small greenhouse.

ranges of 20 acres or more use a helicopter to spray on the shade compound. The compound is formulated to dissolve and wash off by the time the fall rains begin—but frequently must be scrubbed off, and if the shade is stubborn, the growers often end up trying to scrape it off with a razor blade. It is difficult to remove spray shade from fiberglass or polyethylene using any method. For the small greenhouse, any other system is more efficient and convenient.

SOURCES

General information

CANADA:

Ball Red Book. Twelfth edition. Ball-Superior, Ltd., 1155 Birchview Dr., Mississauga, Ontario L5H 3E1

UNITED STATES:

Ball Red Book. Twelfth edition. Geo. J. Ball, Inc., P. O. Box 335, West Chicago, IL 60185.

Greenhouse Climate Control Handbook (#7).

Acme Engineering and Mfg. Corp., Box 978, Muskogee, OK 74401

Greenhouse Handbook for the Amateur. Vol. 19, No. 2. Brooklyn Botanic Gardens, 1000 Washington Ave., Brooklyn, New York, NY 11225

WORLD:

The Complete Book of the Greenhouse. Ian G. Wall. Ward Lock, Ltd., 116 Baker St., London, England W1M 2BB

Supplies

See the General Appendix, Sources of Supply, for a list of materials and suppliers.

Display greenhouse at a flower show illustrates the use of roller shades on exterior for heat and light control

Water is still the vital resource for plant growth—watering methods have expanded dramatically in the last few years

WATER AND WATERING

THE ROLE OF WATER IN PLANT GROWTH

Water is one of the basic constituents of plant tissue, making up as much as 85 percent of the bulk of the living plant. It is water, for example, that maintains the form and position of the leaves by turgor pressure. If water is lacking, the cells of the leaf collapse and we say the plant "wilts."

In addition, water is necessary for the manufacture of food. Nearly all fertilizer compounds in the soil are carried into the root system by water, and the movement of chemical materials in the plant tissues takes place in the water.

Transpiration

Large amounts of water are taken into the plant through the root system and eventually are transpired into the air through the leaves in the form of water vapor. On a bright sunny day, for instance, a single silver maple tree 50 feet high would transpire about 60 gallons of water per hour. If there is a strong air movement over the surface of the leaves, then water also is lost due to evaporation. Additionally, as the temperature rises, water loss from both transpiration and evaporation increases.

Water balance

Physiologically there should be a balance between the amount of water available in the soil and the amount being transpired. Hence, plants in bright, warm sun or under strong lights, and plants that are growing rapidly must be watered more often to maintain the water balance. If there is too little water, the plant droops and wilts. If there is too much water, the roots are unable to get oxygen and the plant literally drowns. Knowing when to water or when not to water is one of the secrets of growing healthy plants.

IDENTIFYING WATER NEED

Overwatering symptoms

To determine if you are overwatering, look for these symptoms:

1. Light green or yellow leaves

2. Leaves with brown edges or tips

3. If you have the first two symptoms, tap the plant out of the pot and look for root symptoms such as a sparse root system that is weak and has few root hairs, or

4. The larger roots are soft, mushy, or rotten

If the first two symptoms occur with the third and fourth symptoms, the reason is almost always overwatering. If you have the first and second symptoms but the root system is good, check for other causes of the leaf condition (*see chapter 10*).

Spaghetti tubes for hanging baskets

Underwatering symptoms

To determine if you are underwatering, look for the following symptoms:

1. Water shortage often will show first in the soft young leaves as a droop at the tip

2. Rub the soil from the pot between your fingers; if it is powder-dry and dusty, watering is indicated

3. Tap the plant out of the pot and see if the root system is dry—most plants are damaged if the entire root system dries out thoroughly because the small feeder roots and root hairs have been destroyed

Sensing devices

Moisture meters such as those shown in *figure 39* are inserted in the pot and read for the relative moisture content of the soil (see appendix for details on the moisture meter). Tensiometers *(see chapter 15)* often are used as sensing devices with automatic watering systems. The tensiometer makes

Fig. 39
One of many kinds of moisture meters

or breaks an electrical current according to the moisture reading. If the soil moisture is insufficient, for example, the tensiometer completes the circuit and turns the watering system on.

There are other devices for controlling watering based on the evaporation rate, such as the Mist-A-Matic shown in *figure 40*. Complete climate control systems use tensiometers, thermometers, and humidistats in combination to provide nearly perfect water balance. No sensing device is a complete

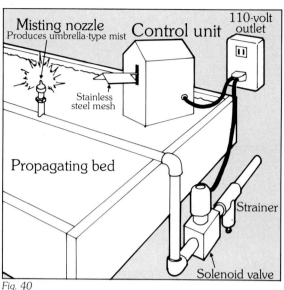

Fig. 40
Misting controlled by evaporation: when the small screen is saturated, it moves down, and the mist shuts off; when the screen dries, it rises again, activating the mist

substitute for the judgment of the experienced grower, however.

WATERING PRACTICES

The following procedures will help you arrive at sound watering practices for pots with drainage holes as well as those without:

1. Water thoroughly and let the water drain out of the pot

2. Water again when the top inch of soil mix becomes dry

Pots without drainage:
1. Insert a tube and a dipstick (a piece of wood) into the pot

2. Water until the end of the dipstick is wet

3. Water again when the top inch of soil is dry

VARIABLES AFFECTING THE NEED FOR WATER

Growth stage

Both germinating seeds and growing plants have

a special need for water. Seeds, for example, must absorb water before the process of germination can begin. A freshly germinated seed is trying to establish a shoot and root system, and the availability of water at this stage is critical. It should be kept moist all the time—even a short period without water will collapse a seedling, and it will die. When a mature plant begins to grow rapidly, there also is an extra demand for water to accomplish growth of new leaves, flowers, and roots.

Seasonal variation

Remember that spring is usually the time when the most active growth is taking place; many plants flower and set buds for the next season, and the water requirements are high. Then as summer comes along, new growth stops and the plant begins to harden tissue, and less water is required. Finally, in fall and winter you should water more sparingly because light is reduced and temperatures are down, making even less need for water.

Pot size

If you use an automatic system for watering, pot size becomes a factor—large pots require more water than small pots. Many growers maintain even watering by segregating the plants according to pot size. Hand watering allows individual adjustments for each pot, so the segregation is not necessary.

Water retention of planting mixes

The need for water is also affected by the type of ingredients used in preparing a planting mix. The ideal mix drains rapidly enough to prevent drowning the roots, yet retains enough moisture for good growth.

Wetting agents

When preparing soil mixes, a class of products known as wetting agents, also as surfactants or adjuvants, can be a help to the home greenhouse owner. A bale of peat moss, for example, is often difficult to get wet because of the surface tension at the interface where the water meets the peat moss. When you add a wetting agent, the surface tension is lowered, and the peat picks up water more easily. There are many wetting agents with such names as Water-mate, Aqua-gro, Water-in, and X-77, all of which are available at most garden centers and nurseries.

The following water retention list should help you relate water retention to the planting mix ingredients (*see chapter 9 for additional data*):

WATER RETENTION		
High	Medium	Low
Sphagnum moss	Fine sand	Coarse sand
Viterra	Perlite	
Calcined clay	Vermiculite	
	Baled peat	
	Sawdust	
	Bark	
	Compost	

WATER QUALITY

Before you do much watering in the home greenhouse, it is worthwhile to have your water tested by a local laboratory. (See yellow pages of the telephone book under laboratories or testing laboratories.) Many growers have spent time and money trying to diagnose plant problems only to discover that the water supply is at fault. Costs vary, but are in the $50.00 and up range, depending on how detailed an analysis you request.

Fluorides

There are reports that fluorides in the water may cause browning of the leaves of some tropical foliage plants, particularly the lily, maranta, and aralia families (for example, draceana or spider plants), although usually the concentrations are too low to be toxic. If you suspect this as a source of trouble, however, experiment with distilled water. When using distilled water, make sure you add a full complement of minor trace elements, which are absent (*see chapter 11*).

Soluble salts

If salts are in your water supply naturally, perhaps a clean source of water—either distilled or clean rainwater—will be necessary. *(See chapter 11 for a discussion of salt damage, including symptoms and treatment.)*

Water temperature

Many of us water out of the tap without testing the water temperature, not realizing that a plant's soil solution normally is 60°F (15.6°C) or higher, and that the water we apply should be about the same. Most house plants are tropical and cannot tolerate a cold water temperature any more than they can a cold air temperature, especially in the winter. When watered with cold water, the plant undergoes shock, many small root hairs are destroyed, and the growth process stops while the plant adjusts to the temperature change.

To remedy this, if your greenhouse has piped water, you can run the water pipe close enough to the heat source to warm the water, or you could wrap heat cable around the supply pipe before it gets to the plants (*see appendix*). If you are watering with a sprinkling can, simply mix hot and cold tap water until it feels warm to the touch before putting it on the plants.

WATERING TECHNIQUES

Hand watering

In a small greenhouse, the traditional method of watering has been the watering can. Unless you have a great many plants, that is the best way to water, since it allows you to apply varying amounts of water to a wide assortment of plants. If you have a larger greenhouse, however, a hose or automated system usually is necessary in order to keep an adequate moisture balance.

Watering cans are available in plastic from $2.00 to $3.00, or in copper such as the Schneider can (*fig. 41*), which runs from $20.00 to $40.00 depending upon the size. A variety of nozzles is available for fine to coarse watering.

Hose watering

A garden hose and nozzle permit more rapid watering. You must be careful, however, not to splash too much water on pots and benches, which would spread fungus and bacterial spores.

A real convenience with hose watering is the self-closing shut-off. These water breakers are designed to put out a lot of water in a soft stream that will not damage plant material (*fig. 42*). They often are used with an extension handle that makes it easier to reach the back of a bench or a hanging basket (*fig. 43*). The rose nozzles have low output with a very fine stream for delicate plants such as seedlings (*fig. 44*), and even finer is the Fog-It nozzle that actually makes a cloud of fog (*fig. 45*). There are four orifice sizes to suit your needs; use the superfine for freshly planted seed where you don't want to disturb the surface.

Fig. 41
A watering can is especially useful for gentle watering of new seedlings

Fig. 42
Water breaker

You must also be sure not to leave a hose on the walk or the ground when finished watering, since this too is one of the quickest ways of spreading fungus spores and bacteria. A simple solution is to put a peg in a convenient spot on which to hang the hose.

When purchasing a hose, as with many other things, it pays to buy good quality. (If a 50-foot hose costing $10.00 lasts five years, for example, it costs $2.00 per year; if a 50-foot hose costing $5.00 lasts one year, that is $5.00 per year.) The better garden hoses are made of virgin formulated materials, often a vinyl-rubber combination reinforced with nylon cord. This gives you a hose with high bursting strength, flexibility, and light weight. The heavy duty milled couplings of solid brass on the better hoses also will last longer, and you will avoid the common problem of having the fitting flattened out so you cannot connect it to a faucet.

Pipe and valve distribution watering systems

Running a water supply into the greenhouse and piping it along the benches allows you to turn on one or two valves *(fig. 46)* and water the entire greenhouse at once. It also permits a fully automatic system using electric valves that will take care of the watering even when you are away on vacation.

Fig. 43
Water breaker with extension handle

Fig. 46
Greenhouse piped for automatic watering—note solenoid valve

Fig. 44
Rose nozzle

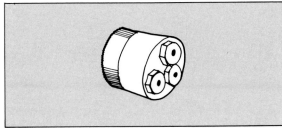

Fig. 45
Fogg-It nozzle

There are two kinds of pipe commonly used for such systems. The first type is made of polyethylene, is very flexible, and comes in rolls of 100 to 300 feet. To plumb the polyethylene, you need only a sharp knife and stainless steel clamps for each fitting *(fig. 47)*. The second type is made of polyvinyl chloride (PVC), a more rigid pipe that comes in 20-foot lengths. It cuts with a handsaw or hacksaw. The fittings are easily installed with PVC cement and do not require clamps. Both kinds of pipe are sold according to wall thickness, and for most purposes, Class 200 PVC is thick enough to withstand pressures of up to 200 pounds per square inch (psi).

The most efficient manual valve for a small greenhouse is the gate valve, which is threaded to fit metal pipe. A very versatile valve, however, is the

Fig. 47
Steel clamp for poly pipe

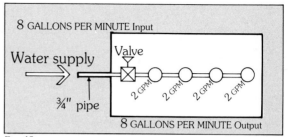

Fig. 49
Water output: match output at each delivery point (tubes, nozzles, sprinklers) or the supply will become unbalanced

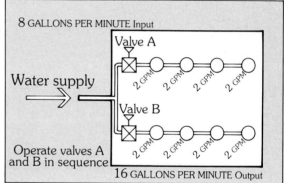

Fig. 50
Shut off one valve or the other when watering to assure adequate supply

Fig. 48
One-quarter turn valve

one-quarter turn valve, which is made to fit pipe or garden hose *(fig. 48)*.

Control systems for pipe and valve distribution are discussed in chapter 15. See the appendix for schematics of one- and two-valve systems.

Flow rates of pipe

There is a direct relationship between the size of pipe and the amount of water carried as shown in *figure 49*. If you have ¾-inch pipe coming into the greenhouse, it gives you approximately 8 gallons per minute (gpm) to distribute through nozzles, tubes, or sprinklers. Each of the nozzles is rated for the gpm needed to get good coverage. The distribution system should be balanced so that you are not trying to distribute more total water than the available supply. If more output is needed, a two-valve system may be required *(fig. 50)*.

Capillary watering systems

For many years, European growers have been watering with the capillary mat, a fiberglass or matted-fiber mat that permits a pot to "wick-up" water by capillary action through the bottom of the pot. Until recently, however, the mat had not been available in North America. Now the system is creating a whole new era in watering since it is inexpensive, easy to install, and promises better plants with much less labor. (See appendix for installation procedures.) What can a capillary mat do for you? Here are some advantages:

1. You can go away for a week or two and be certain that all your plants will get sufficient water

2. Commercial growing experience indicates that you will get a better plant, with more lush green foliage and larger, brighter blossoms

3. You can combine automatic watering with

Plate 9

Left: *Impatiens and coleus
are two warm season plants that
develop quickly*

Below: *Many kinds of plants can be
grown in the same greenhouse. Here
euonymus is being propagated for
use as a ground cover outside; ivy
geraniums are ready to be planted in
hanging baskets, and begonias are
close to a colorful summer outside*

Plate 10

Right: *Camellia bushes can be grown in cool hobby greenhouses throughout temperate climates; attractive in form and foliage throughout the year, the bloom in late winter and early spring is gorgeous*

Below: *Succulents in strange shapes take on the character of bonsai. This plant is Euphorbia lactea cristata, a relative of the poinsettia*
Far right: *Some of the more unusual things you could grow include such settings as this miniature tropical rain forest where tiny humidity-loving plants perch on a moist rock*

Plate 11

*Chilean guava (Myrtus ugni) is a superb candidate for indoor bonsai. A hobby greenhouse
expands the range of possibilities in all areas of plant growth—it lets you experiment with a
whole set of new plant materials in any growing technique*

Plate 12

Spring comes early by forcing tulips, daffodils, and other spring bulbs, such as hyacinths and crocus

Plate 13

Above, left: *These anemones were grown from seed germinated in a hobby greenhouse*
Above: *Tuberous begonias started in a greenhouse are one of the more colorful plants for bedding out*

Left: *A street flower stand in Salzburg, Austria. European use of flowers and plants is more widespread than here*

Plate 14

Hobby greenhouses are not a new idea. This one, built in Vienna for Emperor Franz Josef of Austria, is now used as a restaurant. Greenhouses as restaurants and as hotel lobbies are now being incorporated into modern building design

Plate 15

Left: Another hobby greenhouse —this one was built as a plaything for Empress Maria Theresa of Austria

The public conservatory in the Tadjik Botanical Garden, Tadjik, Russia. This is the part of the world where some of our temperate tree fruits, such as apples, may have originated

Another view of Emperor Franz Josef's hobby greenhouse—larger than many of today's commerical greenhouses

Plate 16

Right: *Interior view of Empress Maria Theresa's hobby greenhouse . . . reminiscent of the long ago time when greenhouses were available only to the wealthy*

Below: *Automatic roller shade on a European greenhouse. When the light intensity reaches the pre-set intensity, a photoelectric cell triggers un-rolling of the shade*

Right: *Today's hobby greenhouses are modestly priced. Many are offered in kit form for do-it-yourself hobbyists or can be built from plans shown in this book or from sources listed here*

automatic feeding by using timed-release fertilizers

4. Each plant on the bench gets the proper amount of water: a big 10-inch pot will take up what it needs alongside a few 2-inch pots.

5. This is nature's way—supplying the water so the plant takes what it needs and no more; large-leaved plants take up more than small-leaved plants. You avoid the most common mistake of the hobby grower—overwatering!

6. You improve the humidity and create a more favorable climate in the greenhouse, especially for the subtropical and tropical foliage plants (with increased humidity, however, remember you need adequate air circulation)

7. No electric valves, hydraulic valves, time clocks, or tensiometers are necessary, and the cost is only about 15 to 20 cents per square foot

Start the action

Once you have the mat down, you must consider what water-supply system to use. There are several types of tubes on the market for carrying water to the mat. Perhaps the easiest system for the home grower, however, is running a length of ¾-inch poly-ethylene pipe down the center of the bench using enough spaghetti tubes to place one on each square foot of mat *(fig. 51)*. The pipe can be supplied with water from a hose or pipe, cracking the gate valve or quick-turn valve just enough to trickle all the time, keeping the mat moist. If your watering is not over-done, you will not need sides on the bench.

Every few days it is good to check the rate of the water supply in order to be sure to provide enough water on the sunny days when both evaporation from the mat and transpiration from the leaves create a need for more water. Conversely, in dark cloudy weather, you will need to reduce the water supply. The objective is to keep the mat constantly moist, but not dripping wet, so the plants on it do not develop water stress. This means never letting the mat dry out either, which would break the capillary flow from mat to plant.

The first time you water after placing your plants on the capillary mat, you will want to water from the top down through the pots with a hose or a watering can to ensure starting the capillary action. It is also a good idea to add a wetting agent, such as Aqua Gro or X-77, to the water for the first top application to aid the mat in absorbing the water. Thereafter, as long as the mat remains moist, there is no need for top watering.

Pots and soils

You can use any pot with multiple drainage holes in the bottom with a capillary mat; single-drainage hole pots do not work well. Some of the plastic pots that have side drainage also do well on the mats *(fig. 52)*; even plastic flats or cell-packs with good drainage holes will work well.

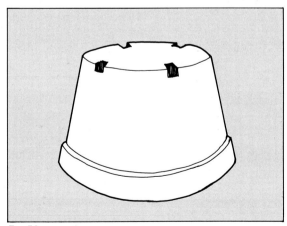

Fig. 52
Capillary action works if pots have drain holes cut where the bottom meets the side—these are commonly available, and are called "side-drain" pots

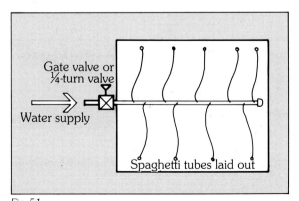

Fig. 51
Spaghetti tubes are laid on the mat—the water is turned on long enough to saturate the mat

Additionally, you need careful attention to the soil mix when using capillary watering. Experience thus far suggests that a mix of about 50 percent peat and 50 percent perlite, bark, or vermiculite is good. If you plan to use garden soil, compost, or loam, then try not more than one part loam or soil to three parts peat and one part perlite or vermiculite.

Bench or ground poly-tube watering systems

If you are growing winter vegetables or flowers in ground beds, a good distribution system is the perforated polyethylene tube. This differs from pipe in that it is thin-walled, usually 4-, 8- or 12-mil thickness, and can be rolled up on a spool. One type is a single tube with pores throughout that permit the water to ooze out all along the tube. A second type is a double tube with holes punched at engineered intervals in both tubes to equalize the pressure so you get the same water output at both ends of a long tube. The same type of tube also is made with a stitched edge through which the water oozes. For a schematic diagram see the appendix, which shows typical installation used on a bench or on the ground.

Perimeter watering systems

The perimeter system consists of polyethylene pipe mounted on the perimeter of the raised ground bench or raised bed with little nozzles inserted in the pipe, as shown in *figure 53* if your bench is 42 inches wide or less, or in *figure 54* if your bench is wider than 42 inches. The nozzles are only a few cents apiece and easily installed: simply punch or drill a hole in the pipe the same size as the nozzle and thread the nozzle in by hand. Be careful, however, not to turn the nozzle too far and strip the threads; poly pipe is soft, and once the hole is loose it will leak.

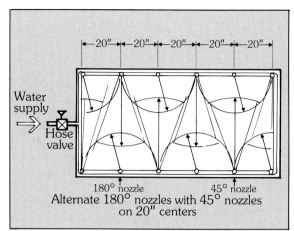

Fig. 54
Layout for perimeter watering system on benches over 42 inches

Spaghetti watering systems

The spaghetti system *(fig. 55)* consists of small plastic tubes with weights on the end that are inserted into a supply pipe *(fig. 56)*. Each weight holds a tube in a pot and helps spread the water evenly over the surface. Different length tubes are available.

Fig. 55
Spaghetti watering system installed and tube inserted in each pot

Some tubes also have a manual shut-off weight on the end—as plants are removed from the bed, a quick push on the end of the weights shuts off the individual tubes, a feature that saves both water and

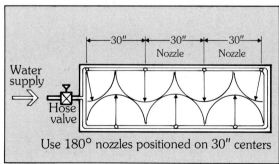

Fig. 53
Perimeter watering system for benches up to 42 inches

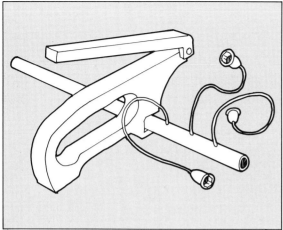

Fig. 56
Tubes are easily punched into polyethylene supply pipe

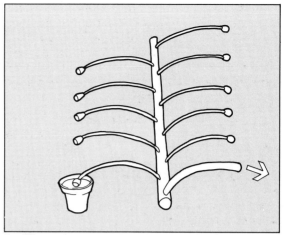

Fig. 58
Long-header watering system

fertilizer. The on-off tube is also ideal for hanging baskets since it prevents the water from running from the overhead tubes without plants. Up to 400 containers can be watered at a time from the average ¾-inch water supply.

You also can attain flexibility in watering various quantities of pot plants with Add-A-Headers *(fig. 57)*, or a long-header system *(fig. 58)*. Another option, the water loop, is a very efficient means of getting the water spread out evenly over the soil surface of the large potted plants. To install spaghetti tube components, see appendix.

Fig. 59
Spray-stake watering system in operation

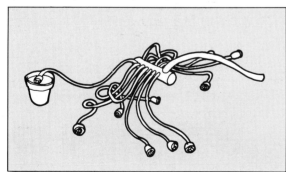

Fig. 57
Add-A-Header watering system

Sprinkler nozzle watering systems

Leader tube types are nozzles that are fed by a supply tube, which is inserted by hand into the pipe. The first type, the stake system, *(fig. 59)* is set in the ground and is most adaptable to vegetables grown in ground benches. The second, the hanger system, is more suitable for mounting over the bench for pots or bench-grown crops. See appendix for installation details.

Mini-spray watering systems

The mini-spray nozzle *(fig. 60)* is inserted by hand into poly or PVC pipe. It is a versatile nozzle, and has the capacity to water at pressures below 25 pounds psi, or to mist at pressures of from 40 pounds psi up.

Plumbed-in sprinkler watering systems

There are many sprinklers that plumb into pipe with standard fittings to give broader coverage watering. The Roberts spinner *(fig. 61)*, for example,

Fig. 60
Mini-spray nozzle

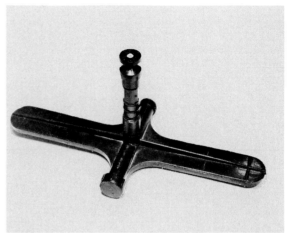

Fig. 62
Toro head

Fig. 61
Roberts spinner

Fig. 63
Line strainer

adjusts by turning the nozzles at either end of the spinning arm. The Toro head *(fig. 62)* adjusts by raising or lowering the screw in the center of the head. Either of these will water efficiently up to 25 feet in diameter. See appendix for details.

Attachments for watering systems

Line strainers

In any watering system, the flow of water carries tiny bits of debris that can plug up nozzles and tubes. To avoid this, you should plumb in a line strainer *(fig. 63)*.

Sand separator

If your water source has a lot of sand, and the line strainer fills too rapidly, you should use a sand separator *(fig. 64)*. The separator is a two-stage

Fig. 64
Sand separator

centrifugal device that collects sand or heavy silt in an outer jacket while fine sand and silt are spun through a series of tangent openings in the inner shell and collected in the bottom. The bottom can be vented by hand or automated with a solenoid valve and time clock. If you are pumping water from a pond or river, this device will keep both nozzles and sprinklers clean and functional.

SOURCES

General information

UNITED STATES:
Control of Wilting in Potted Plants (Bulletin #532). February, 1974. Ohio Florist's Assoc., 2001 Fyffe Ct., Columbus, OH 43210

Gardening Under Glass. Jerome A. Eaton. Mac-Millan, 866 3rd Ave., New York, NY 10022

House Plants Indoors/Outdoors. Ortho Books. Chevron Chemical Co., 200 Bush St., San Francisco, CA 94104

Water—Its Role in Greenhouse Crop Production (bulletin). April, 1961. Minnesota State Florists, University of Minnesota, St. Paul, MN 55108

Supplies

Companies specializing in watering equipment

CANADA:
Humex Equipment, Ltd., 2241 Dunwin Dr., Erinmills, Mississauga, Ontario

The Toro Co., Robert G. Eckel, Box Brooklin, Ontario

Chris Walter Sales, Ltd. (Solarmist System), RR4 Salmon Arms, British Columbia

UNITED STATES:
Chapin Watermatics, Inc., 368 N. Colorado Ave., Watertown, New York, NY 13601

The Dramm Co., P.O. Box 528, Manitowoc, WI 54220

Equipment Consultants and Sales, 9705 Shawnee Run Rd., Cincinnati, OH 45243

Fischer Greenhouse, Dept. 4, Oak Ave., Linwood, NJ 08221

Roberts Irrigation Products, 700 Rancheros Dr., San Marcos, CA 92069

Skinner Irrigation Co., 2530 Spring Grove Ave., Cincinnati, OH 45214

Spraying Systems Co., 3201 Randolph St., Bellwood, IL 60104

The Toro Co., Irrigation Div., 5825 Jasmine St., Riverside, CA 92502

WORLD:
Wright Rain, Ltd. (Solarmist System), Ringwood, Hampshire, England BH24 1PA X

A light, buoyant atmosphere contributes to success in growing

AIR

COMPOSITION OF AIR

Air, a major component of the plant's environment, is made up of the following major and minor elements:

Major: nitrogen, hydrogen, carbon, oxygen
Minor: argon, xenon, helium, krypton

The major elements supply the raw materials for the manufacture of plant tissue and for the process of photosynthesis. The minor elements exist in very

The Atmosphere
78.3% Nitrogen, 21% Oxygen,
.03% Carbon Dioxide, .93% Argon, .0018% Neon,
and traces of Xenon, Helium, Krypton,
and Hydrogen (as water vapor)

Respiration   Photosynthesis

Carbon Dioxide   Oxygen   Oxygen   Nitrogen   Carbon Dioxide   Carbon Dioxide   Oxygen

Soil

Carbon Dioxide

Nitrogen   Oxygen

Bacterial symbionts fix nitrogen
(legumes, alder, ceanothus)

Roots

Fig. 65
The atmosphere

small quantities and research to date does not indicate that they are involved in plant growth *(fig. 65)*. Any other elements or compounds found in the air are considered pollutants.

OXYGEN AND ROOTS

Oxygen is just as necessary for respiration in the root system as it is in the leaf; in order for the roots to grow, there must be energy provided by the oxidation of sugars. Since the oxygen is not transported inside the plant, it must be accessible down through the soil. Good soil aeration ensures that the oxygen will be available *(see chapter 9)*.

Other beneficial organisms in the soil break down organic matter and release nitrogen for the plant. These organisms also must have a good supply of oxygen in order to function *(see chapter 9)*.

POLLUTION

Symptoms and sources

Some air pollutants are injurious to plants. The most common of these are listed in the following pollution table. In addition to those listed, there are other gases that occur less frequently, such as chlorine, which may also cause plant damage or restrict growth.

A new field in plant study called allelopathy explores chemicals introduced into the environment by plants and the effects these chemicals have on other plants and man. Terpenes, for example, are hydrocarbons volatilized by certain plants, such as forest vegetation, that may have some adverse effect on greenhouse plants. These terpenes are the cause of the blue haze in the air that probably is respon-

Table 12
POLLUTION

Gas	Symptoms	Level at which Damage Occurs	Source	Comments
Ozone	Tiny tan and white spots; progresses to soft, mushy areas between the veins	.10 ppm[†] for 8 hrs.	Auto by-products (e.g., nitrogen oxide, hydrocarbons, terpenes)	Old leaves yellow and fall off or droop
Sulphur dioxide	Thin, papery; bleached tan to white areas between the veins	48 ppm for 4 hrs. .28 ppm for 24 hrs.	Soft coal, electrical generators, sulphur ores	Synergistic effect with ozone at levels of .03 ppm of SO_2 increases damage
Ethylene	Petioles depress, lower leaves turn yellow and drop; plant stunts, thick stem Delays flower on short-day plants	.1 ppm for 8 hrs. 1-2 ppm	Plastics manufacture, auto exhaust, greenhouse heaters	Grow tomato as a sensitive indicator of the presence of ethylene
Fluorides	Tip and edge bur brown to black	.1 ppb[†] for 5 weeks[*]	Aluminum reducing factories	Check the amount in your own water supply—call the water department
PAN (smog)	Lower leaf surface glazed or shiny silver; tissue collapse at tip of upper leaves or base of lower leaves	20-30 ppb	Manufactured in polluted air: nitrogen dioxide and volatile petroleum by-products	High light intensity increases susceptibility

[†]ppm = parts per million
 ppb = parts per billion
[*]Marlin N. Rogers, Univ. of Missouri

sible for the name of the Blue Ridge Mountains and the Blue Mountains of Washington and Oregon.

Particulate matter

In addition to the chemical pollutants, we find air currents carrying particulate matter that is harmful to plants, such as blown sand, dust, soot, fly ash, bacteria and fungus spores, and pollen. Although there are air filters available (for example, the Dorex), their high cost makes them impractical for a small greenhouse. A simpler solution is to plant deciduous trees in a position that allows the air first to move through them and then into the greenhouse, thus achieving some air scrubbing.

Rainwater

When rain falls through polluted air, it accumulates the chemicals and particulate matter present, so the rainwater also can cause problems with plant growth. The pH of rainwater, for instance, depends upon the pollution content and is often quite acidic (pH 3 to 4). If you water with rainwater, protect your plants by making certain it is pollution free. One good method is to allow the water to settle in an open container for twenty-four hours.

CARBON DIOXIDE

Effect on growth

Since about 50 percent of a plant is carbon, if the amount of carbon dioxide (CO_2) available to the plant is reduced, growth is restricted; and conversely, increasing the amount of CO_2 in the air increases growth. When outside air is normal, the CO_2 is about 300 parts per million (ppm) or .03 of 1 percent. For optimum growth, from 1,000 ppm up to 3,000 ppm is considered desirable. Whenever the CO_2 is increased, however, the other factors that limit growth — such as water, nutrients, light, and temperature — must be increased proportionally.

The CO_2 content of a greenhouse may increase during the night when plants respire. As soon as daylight arrives, photosynthesis begins, and the plants use up the CO_2 that accumulated during the night. The level can drop to less than 100 ppm, and as long as the greenhouse is closed, the level of CO_2 will not be increased until nightfall. In northern areas, or in any location if the greenhouse is tight, there is likely to be a shortage of CO_2. Some growers solve this problem by structuring their greenhouses to permit air to enter through cracks, thereby maintaining close to 300 ppm of CO_2 at most times.

Adding carbon dioxide to the air

The easiest way to add CO_2 to the home greenhouse is to open the ventilators and let outside air come in. This will raise the CO_2 content to about 300 ppm. It is difficult to do this in the winter, however, without damaging soft tropicals. The best answer, therefore, is to install equipment made to add CO_2 to the air in the greenhouse.

Sources of carbon dioxide

Whatever you burn as a source of CO_2, it must be free of sulphur dioxide and ethylene, both of which damage plants. There are several manufacturers of CO_2-generating equipment. The generators normally burn propane or natural gas. One unit will maintain 2,000 to 3,000 ppm in a greenhouse up to 20-by-40 feet and is adjustable for lesser output. For a smaller greenhouse, the CO_2 generator should be operated intermittently, based on the information from the manufacturer as to hourly output of CO_2. Prices for these units range from $100.00 to $200.00, depending upon the accessory equipment involved.

For a small greenhouse, try burning ethyl or methyl alcohol in a kerosene lamp. If the greenhouse is 8-by-12 feet, for example, 3 ounces will give you about 2,000 ppm over one twenty-four hour period.

Another source of CO_2 is dry ice, which is simply CO_2 in solid form; it turns into a gas when heated. Place a two-pound block in the greenhouse and let it vaporize. The block will maintain about 2,000 ppm for one day.

If you are growing in ground beds where you are using manure or other organic matter, you have a ready source of CO_2 as decomposition takes place. The supply of CO_2 is undependable since it varies with the rate of decomposition. You must also continue replenishing the supply of organic matter.

Carbon dioxide detectors

No inexpensive CO_2 detectors are available. The Kitigawa, for instance, is $100.00 or more. If you are producing crops for sale, this expense is warranted. For the home greenhouse, however, simply following the directions of the generator manufacturer should be adequate.

Quantity of carbon dioxide

Research currently is under way that will eventually give us specified amounts of CO_2 for particular varieties of plants. At present, the best we can do is to say that CO_2 has proved effective in improving growth of roses, chrysanthemums, irises, geraniums, some orchids, and foliage crops. As with many other phases of growing plants, the best procedure is to experiment, using CO_2 to see what it does for the particular plants you are growing.

HUMIDITY

Relative humidity

The term most often used to designate the invisible water vapor in the air is "relative humidity." This is the amount of moisture in the air expressed as a percentage of the maximum that the air could hold at a given temperature and pressure. Warm air holds more water vapor than cool air; a rule of thumb is that the holding capacity of the air doubles with every 20°F (11.1°C) increase in temperature.

Air can become so saturated with water that the excess (fig. 66) is condensed into droplets. The temperature at which this happens is called the "dew point," or 100 percent relative humidity. When air at 80°F (26.7°C) and 100 percent relative humidity is cooled down to 60°F (15.6°C), for example, it loses half its water content by condensation, and the relative humidity becomes 50 percent.

Fig. 66
Misting is an artificial way of saturating air with moisture

Amount of humidity

How do you know the optimum relative humidity for the plants you are growing? The best way to learn is to check an encyclopedia of horticulture to find out where the plant is native, then reproduce the native growing conditions in your own greenhouse as nearly as possible.

Humidity data for most kinds of plant material is not readily available, but by experimenting with the native habitat conditions in mind, you can arrive at your own data. African violets from Tanzania, for example, grow in a relative humidity of 75 percent or higher. For many tropicals, in fact, 75 percent relative humidity is probably a minimum. At the other end of the scale, however, are the cacti *(fig. 67)* that grow in desert areas where the relative humidity is less than 30 percent. If you are growing

Fig. 67
Use plastic curtains to partition plants preferring low humidity from those that need a moist atmosphere

a variety of plants that require different humidities, you should partition the greenhouse with plastic to create separate climate zones.

To germinate seeds, you normally would use a covered flat or tray in which the relative humidity approaches 100 percent. A glass cover *(fig. 68)* works well since you can see the condensation and

Fig. 68
Glass covers maintain high humidity around germinating seeds

raise the glass at intervals to provide ventilation. When the seedlings are up, the glass cover should be removed and the relative humidity kept at close to 75 percent until the seedlings are well along *(for additional information, see chapter 17).*

If you are rooting cuttings on propagation benches, on the other hand, you need a relative humidity of about 75 percent. An intermittent mist system will provide the humidity if you mist often enough. The nozzle-mist system, for example, gives time for evaporation from the foliage, allows good air circulation and still maintains adequate relative humidity.

Measuring humidity

To measure relative humidity you use an instrument known as the wet-bulb psychrometer. You can make your own with two thermometers as indicated in *figure 69.*

1. Cover the bulb of thermometer B with muslin to act as a wick; leave thermometer A uncovered for a dry-bulb reading

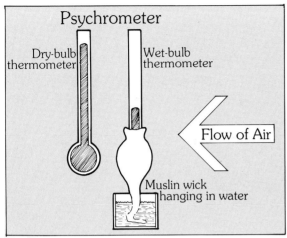

Fig. 69
Measuring relative humidity

from plant surfaces, and can only be removed by proper ventilation. In dry parts of the world, it is easy to control relative humidity by exhausting air with high moisture content and bringing in air with low moisture content. Even in the more humid areas you can control humidity by air exchange. In some older greenhouses, for example, there are enough cracks so the colder, drier air from the outside infiltrates on its own, and the warmer, more humid air escapes. In the new tight houses, however, humidity control is accomplished best with exhaust fans to keep the proper moisture balance.

In general, humidity should be high during the day when photosynthesis is occurring and low at night when respiration is taking place. You can put water vapor into the air with a mist-nozzle system or with a humidifier *(fig. 70).* The humidifier works well

2. Place the wick in a small bottle of water to make a wet-bulb thermometer

3. Place both thermometers in the air stream of a small fan—the water evaporating from the wick will lower the temperature of the wet-bulb thermometer

4. You can determine the relative humidity using the following formula:

Formula:

$A = 100 - [300 (D-W)]$ D

(A = approximate relative humidity
D = dry-bulb temperature
W = wet-bulb temperature)

Example:
If the dry bulb reading is 80°F (26.7°C) and the wet bulb reading is 70°F (21.1°C) we would have:

$A = [100 - 300 \frac{(80-70)}{80}]$ or 62.5 relative humidity

Another instrument that measures relative humidity is the hygrometer. It uses the expansion and contraction of human hair to move a pointer on a dial that indicates the percentage of humidity.

Controlling humidity

Eventually, all the water brought into the greenhouse must somehow leave. It usually becomes water vapor through transpiration, or evaporation,

Fig. 70
One kind of humidifier

for the small greenhouse because it atomizes the water into very small droplets that do not collect on surfaces.

First, water goes into the base of the humidifier and surrounds a cone. When the cone revolves, the water travels up the cone and strikes the vanes —which break it up into very fine droplets to force a fog through the outlets and into the greenhouse. Humidifiers of all sizes are available to suit your needs.

In addition, humidistats have been developed that turn humidifers on and off automatically. A humidistat is made like a hygrometer, except the expansion and contraction of the human hair element makes or breaks an electrical circuit that turns the humidifier on and off. The humidistat usually is wired to an electric solenoid valve so the humidifer vaporizes water into the air until the desired humidity is reached; at that point, the humidistat breaks the circuit and shuts off the humidifier *(fig. 71)*. The upper limit of the humidistat also can be wired to operate

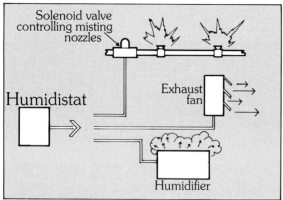

Fig. 71
You can use a humidistat to control a humidifier, exhaust fans, or to operate mist lines

exhaust fans that will expel excessive humidity from the greenhouse and bring in cooler outside air to lower the relative humidity. For details on humidity control, see the appendix.

AIR CIRCULATION

While some plants achieve optimal growth with high humidity, this same condition also is ideal for pathogenic bacteria and fungi growth. For this reason, proper air circulation is imperative.

Testing for air circulation
Perhaps the best way to determine the air circulation in your own greenhouse is to place a piece of smoldering wood in a tin can, set it on a bench, and watch the movement of smoke. If the smoke just hangs in clouds, you have stagnant air. If the smoke moves slowly and gently, you may have adequate air circulation. You do not need a draft that you can feel unless you are exhausting heated air in the summer.

Winter air circulation
Air circulation in the winter is a problem—you want to maintain a constant, gentle movement of air that is not too cold for the tropicals that you very

likely are growing. This means that when you introduce cold air from outside, there should be a mixing-box system *(fig. 72)* to blend the cold outside air with the warm inside air before it moves over the plants.

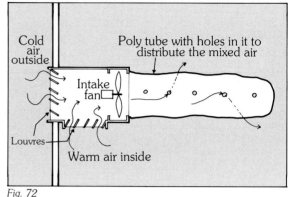

Fig. 72
How an air-mixing and distribution system works

This type of aerodynamic equipment is available; Acme Engineering, for example, manufactures a unit called a "Fan-Jet." After the unit is installed, you open a louvre in the greenhouse end wall, and the air is drawn into a mixing box by the fan, where it meets warm air from inside. When there is a thorough mixing, the fan drives the air down a polyethylene tube *(fig. 73)* and out through some openings. This gives a very uniform distribution of air throughout the entire greenhouse and allows you to introduce fresh, cold air without damaging drafts.

Fig. 73
An air-mixing and distribution system

While the Acme system using a "Fan-Jet" is excellent for ventilation in the winter, it cannot be counted upon to provide the additional cooling you need in summer. Unless you have a properly engineered system that includes both ventilation and cooling equipment, you probably will create excessive air circulation. As air moves over the pots, it speeds up the evaporation of water, and excessive air movement means you have to adjust your watering schedule.

The more you work with a small greenhouse, the more expert you become at maintaining the delicate balance of temperature, light, water, and food that it takes to grow healthy plants. Developing this expertise is one of the pleasures of greenhouse growing!

Turbulators

In some commercial greenhouses you also will find a fan called a "turbulator" that is used for gentle, low velocity air circulation. The turbulator fan develops about 200 rpm so the velocity is low, even though it discharges about 4,000 cfm. It sells in the $65.00 to $85.00 range. When you are working in a greenhouse where a turbulator is providing the air circulation, you are not conscious of a draft or breeze; it is probably as close as you can get to the zephyrs of the natural habitat.

If you cannot find a turbulator, shop for a low-rpm, low-velocity fan that will stir the air gently rather than blow a breeze. You may have to hunt, because most fans are made to cool humans who feel cooler if there is a breeze blowing across their faces. Have the store plug the fan in so you can feel how it circulates the air. Fans ranging from 500 to 800 rpm commonly are stocked.

SOURCES

General information

   CANADA:
Ball Red Book. Twelfth edition. Ball-Superior, Ltd., 1155 Birchview Dr., Mississauga, Ontario L5H 3E1

   UNITED STATES:
Air Pollution Injury to Vegetation (Publication #AP-71). National Air Pollution Control Administration, Superintendent of Documents, Washington, DC 20402

Ball Red Book. Twelfth edition. Geo. J. Ball, Inc., P. O. Box 335, West Chicago, IL 60185

Greenhouse Climate Control Handbook (Publication #C7A). Acme Engineering and Mfg. Corp., Muskogee, OK 74401

Greenhouse Handbook for the Amateur. Vol. 19, No. 2. Brooklyn Botanic Gardens, 1000 Washington Ave., Brooklyn, New York, NY 11225

"Is Air Pollution Choking Your Profits?" John K. Springer. *American Vegetable Grower.* March, 1972. Meister Publishing, Willoughby, OH 44094

Plants, People and Environmental Quality (Stock #2405-0479). Superintendent of Documents, U. S. Government Printing Office, Washington, DC 20402

Supplies

See the General Appendix, Sources of Supply, for a list of suppliers and equipment needed for air circulation and carbon-dioxide generation.

Hydroponic growing often uses gravel as the medium — the gravel supplies no nutrients

SOILS AND MEDIA

Growing plants need a medium that will provide anchor and support; one in which water, nutrients, and oxygen can be stored and transferred; and one that permits the grower to move, handle, and display the plant in a pot. A good soil mix has been every gardener's delight! For the past few years, however, there has been a trend away from using soil alone, and instead using soilless or partly soil growing media.

SOIL

If we consider the native habitat of plants, we find a tremendous variation in the types of soil that will support growth. Following are the five constituents common to all:

1. Weathered particles of rock make up the mineral fraction of most soils

2. The decomposed remains of plants, animals, and microorganisms form the organic portion of the soils

3. Oxygen and carbon dioxide largely make up the soil atmosphere

4. Water is the soil moisture, with whatever soluble materials are at hand

5. Essential nutrients are present in the organic, the mineral, and the water solution components

Root zone

There is a complex relationship between the five common soil components and the numerous microorganisms that co-exist in the root zone (fig. 74). Fertilizer applied to the surface, for example, goes into solution in the soil water, where it is acted

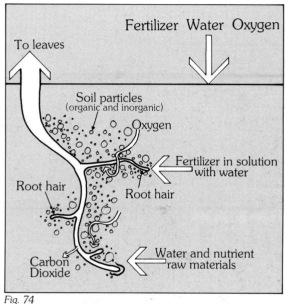

Fig. 74
Activity in root zone

upon by microorganisms before being taken into the root hairs and on through the plant to be used as raw material for the growth process. Water poured onto the surface also seeps down through the soil, and carrying nutrient raw materials, it goes into the root hairs, then completely throughout the plant. Additionally, oxygen filters through the air spaces between soil particles, and thus is available for growth process of the roots themselves.

Availability

Not everything you put on the surface of the soil gets into the plant, however, thus the term "availability," or "available to the plant." There are chemical, physical, and electrical attractions for molecules of water and fertilizer that "tie up" these soil components so they cannot go into the root hairs and on into the plant. Consequently, there may be 1 pound of potassium in 1 square foot of ground, but only a fraction of an ounce available to the plant. Methods of identifying and correcting these conditions are discussed in chapter 11.

GROWING MIXES

As mentioned, growers are using mixes that include other components as well as soil. When making your own soil mix, you will want to keep the best properties of soil, being certain that the pathogenic microorganisms and weed seed commonly found in soil are eliminated, and also to take advantage of the positive characteristics of some nonsoil media components by adding fine sand, perlite, or vermiculite to the fraction of inorganic materials, and peat moss, ground bark, sawdust, or compost to the portion of organic components. *Tables 13* and *14* should help you select basic ingredients. For detailed information on specialized media components and ready-to-use mixes, see the appendix.

FERTILIZERS

Nutrients are carried by water and then absorbed with the water by the plant's root system. Nutrients not available naturally in the plant's soil must be supplied through the application of water-soluble fertilizers. Soilless mixes contain no nutrients, thus fertilizers are the plant's only source of nutrition and must be applied regularly. Long-lasting, or slow-release, fertilizers work well for this purpose. For a detailed discussion of plant nutrients, see chapter 11.

RELATIVE ACIDITY pH

The concentration of hydrogen ions in a solution, or the pH factor, makes the solution either acidic or alkaline *(fig. 75)*. Pure water has a pH of 7, which is neutral, and as the hydrogen-ion concentration is decreased, the solution becomes more acidic. In North America, soils range from 9.5 when alkaline to 3.5 for some peat, or acidic, material.

Most plants will tolerate a range of pH values, but

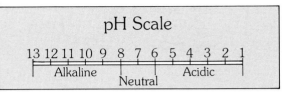
Fig. 75
pH scale

there is an optimum pH for many plants. Some of the nutrients in the soil may be "tied up," for example, and unavailable to the plant if the pH is not correct. For the general run of plants in the home greenhouse, however, a range of 4.5 to 7.0 is good. A list of suggested pH values as well as instructions for testing your soil are in *table 15* (p. 72).

Testing for pH

For home greenhouse use, the simplest device for measuring the pH value is test paper such as the Hydrion Vivid-09, which comes in a double-tape roll like Scotch tape *(fig. 76)*. One tape covers pH from 0 to 9.0 and the other from 9.0 to 13.0.'

Fig. 76
One method of determining pH is with tape

First, mix one part of soil to two parts of tap water. Stir thoroughly, and allow the solution to settle. Dip the paper for thirty seconds. Match colors on the dispenser to get a pH reading, being careful to handle the tape with forceps or tweezers so you do not get skin oils on the paper. (If you handle the tape with your fingers, you may be reading the pH of your skin rather than that of the soil mix.)

The pH tape costs about $2.00 per roll. For repeated pH tests, there are more accurate devices such as the Kelway meter, which costs about $50.00, and the new Beckman pHistol, at about $175.00.

Table 13
PLANTING MEDIA

Medium	Water Retention	Available in Uniform Material	Costs	Comments
Calcined clay	High	Yes (as Turface, Terra-Green, etc.)	$4.00-$5.00 for 50 lbs.	Improves air-water relationship
Fine sand	Medium	Yes	$5.00-$6.00 per yd.	If you collect your own fresh-water sand, take the top 12″ to get micro-organisms
Coarse sand	Low	Yes	$5.00-$6.00 per yd.	Some builders' sand may originally be from salt water sources
Perlite	Medium	Yes (also as Sponge Rock)	$4.00-$5.00 for 4 cu. ft.	Holds 3-4 times its own weight in water; silica derivative; may contain fluorides (see chapter 6)
Vermiculite	Medium	Yes	$4.00-$5.00 for 4 cu. ft.	Expanded mica; avoid compressing, or aeration qualities are lost
Sphagnum moss	High	Yes (coarse or milled)	Milled: $2.00 for 5 qts. Coarse: $7.50 for 20 lb. bale	Holds up to 15 times its own weight in water; collected green from the top of the bog
Sphagnum— baled peat (coarse)	Medium	Yes	$5.00-$6.00 for 4 cu. ft.	Holds 5-6 times its own weight in water; often from below the surface of the bog
Sawdust	Medium	No	Widely variable, depending on location	Not uniform, from different kinds of wood; requires nitrogen to decompose
Bark	Medium	No	Widely variable, depending on location	Different kinds—such as white fir and pine for orchids; available composted
Compost	Medium	No	Homemade	Varies with materials used; introduces beneficial microorganisms
Viterra	High	Yes	$35.00-$40.00 for 15 lbs.	Use ½ lb. to 1 cu. ft. of mix; holds up to 20 times its own weight in water
Charcoal	Medium	Yes·	$12.00-$15.00 for 50 lbs.	Purifies soil mix; reduces chances of excess salt accumulation
Osmunda fiber	Medium	Yes	$5.00-$6.00 for 3 lbs.	A growing medium for orchids

Table 14
TESTED SOIL MIXES

Soil Mix and Medium Data

General purpose mix	⅓ soil, ⅓ peat, ⅓ perlite or sand
African violets	½ peat, ½ vermiculite
Azaleas	All peat
Begonias	½ soil, ½ peat
Foliage plants	½ peat, ¼ vermiculite, ¼ perlite
Gardenias	½ soil, ½ acid (peat pH 4.5-5.0)
Cattleyas	½ perlite; ½ fir bark, osmunda or redwood, fiber or peat
Cymbidiums	⅓ fir bark, ⅓ osmunda or redwood fiber, ⅓ perlite

Bedding plants	⅓ soil, ⅓ peat, ⅓ perlite
Seed germination	½ fine sand, ½ peat
Bonsai	⅓ soil, ⅓ sand, ⅓ peat

Five Basic Univ. of California Soil Mixes

1. Root cuttings (primarily)	All fine sand
2. Bedding plants and potting-on	¾ fine sand, ¼ peat moss
3. Pot plants and cuttings	½ fine sand, ½ peat moss
4. Transplanting, seed germination	¾ peat moss, ¼ fine sand
5. Azaleas and some other acid-loving plants	All peat moss

Fertilizers
To each of the mixes, add small quantities of the following specified fertilizers:[*]

Soil Mix	Blood Meal or Hoof and Horn	Potassium Nitrate	Potassium Sulphate	Single Super-Phosphate	Dolomite Lime	Lime Calcium Carbonate	pH	Gypsum
1	2.5 lbs.	8 oz.	4 oz.	2.5 lbs.	1.5 lbs.	—	7.0	2.5 lbs.
2	2.5 lbs.	6 oz.	4 oz.	2.5 lbs.	4.5 lbs.	1.25 lbs.	6.8	1.25 lbs.
3	2.5 lbs.	4 oz.	4 oz.	2.5 lbs.	7.5 lbs.	2.5 lbs.	6.5	—
4	2.5 lbs.	4 oz.	4 oz.	2.0 lbs.	5.0 lbs.	4.0 lbs.	6.0	—
5	2.5 lbs.	6 oz.	—	1.0 lb.	2.5 lbs.	5.0 lbs.	5.7	—

[*] Amount per cubic yard (1 cubic yard = 21.7 bushels = 27 cubic feet = a box 3'x 3'x 3')

John Innes Horticultural Institute Mixes

SEED COMPOST (by volume)

7.0 parts composted loam[*]
3.5 parts peat moss
3.5 parts coarse sand
To this add the following fertilizer:[**]
2 lbs. superphosphate (18%)
1 lb. calcium carbonate (chalk) for acid-loving plants
(substitute 1 lb. flowers of sulphur to get pH 5.0-6.0)

POTTING COMPOST (by volume)

7 parts composted loam
3 parts peat moss
2 parts coarse sand
To this add the following fertilizer:[**]
2 lbs. hoof and horn meal (13% N)
2 lbs. superphosphate (18%)
1 lb. sulphate of potash (48% K)
1 lb. calcium carbonate (chalk)

[*](If you are making your own well balanced compost, use it in place of the seven parts composted loam)
[**]Amount per cubic yard

Cornell Mixes

The Cornell Tropical Mixes* (peat lite) are formulated for growing tropical plants. The Foliage Plant Mix** and the Epiphytic Mix** formulas are adapted specifically for their respective plant types. They are modifications of the original peat-lite mix.

Cornell has used Osmocote 14-14-14 and Peters 14-7-7 fertilizers with the tropical plant mixes with good results. Other nutrient fertilizers are omitted with the exception of dolomitic limestone and 20 percent superphosphate, which are added to adjust the pH and to maintain adequate phosphorus levels. Peter's Fritted Trace Element Mix is added to assure a balance of minor elements.

*"Cornell Tropical Plant Mixes" by Russell C. Mott
**L. H. Bailey Hortorium, Cornell University, Ithaca, New York

CORNELL PEAT-LITE MIX

½ peat (sphagnum)
½ perlite or vermiculite

To this add the following fertilizer:*

10 lbs. dolomitic limestone
4 lbs. ammonium nitrate
2½ lbs. superphosphate
½ lb. potassium chloride (omit if you use vermiculite)

*Amount per cubic yard

CORNELL FOLIAGE PLANT MIX

Material	1 Cubic Yard	1 Bushel
Sphagnum peat moss (screened ½" mesh)	½ cu. yd.	½ bu.
Horticultural vermiculite (No. 2)	¼ cu. yd.	¼ bu.
Perlite (medium grade)	¼ cu. yd.	¼ bu.
Ground dolomitic limestone	8¼ lbs.	8 Tbs.*
Superphosphate 20% (powdered)	2 lbs.	2 Tbs.
Fertilizer (10-10-10)	2¾ lbs.	3 Tbs.
Iron sulfate	¾ lbs.	3 Tbs.
Potassium nitrate (14-0-44)	1 lb.	1 Tbs.
Fritted trace element mix (e.g., Peter's FTE)	2 oz.	omit
Granular wetting agent (e.g., Aqua-Gro)	1½ lbs.	3 Tbs.

*Level tablespoon

The Cornell Foliage Plant Mix was developed for those plants that need a growing medium with high moisture-retention characteristics. Plants having a fine root system or possessing many fine root hairs are included in this group.

CORNELL EPIPHYTIC MIX

Material	1 Cubic Yard	1 Bushel
Sphagnum peat moss (screened ½" mesh)	⅓ cu. yd.	⅓ bu.
Douglas, red, or white fir bark** (⅛"-¼" size)	⅓ cu. yd.	⅓ bu.
Perlite (medium grade)	⅓ cu. yd.	⅓ bu.
Ground dolomitic limestone	7 lbs.	8 Tbs.*
Superphosphate 20% (powdered)	4½ lbs.	6 Tbs.
Fertilizer (10-10-10)	2½ lbs.	3 Tbs.
Iron sulphate	½ lbs.	1 Tbs.
Potassium nitrate (14-0-44)	1 lb.	1 Tbs.
Fritted trace element mix (e.g., Peter's FTE)	2 oz.	omit
Granular wetting agent (e.g., Aqua-Gro)	1½ lbs.	3 Tbs.

* Level tablespoon
** Fir bark comes from Douglas fir, white or red fir, or redwood, ground and screened to a definite size. Finely ground bark (⅛"-¼") has a dry weight of 11.5 pounds per cubic foot. Fresh bark has a pH of about 5.0. Upon weathering, it becomes slightly more alkaline. The bark contains some nutrients, but these will not meet the requirements of growing plants.

The Cornell Epiphytic Mix was developed for plants that require good drainage, aeration, and have the ability to withstand drying between waterings. Plants having coarse, tuberous, or rhyzomatous roots are in this category.

Table 15
SUGGESTED pH VALUES
FOR MANY HOUSE PLANT SOIL MIXES*

pH 4.5-5.5

House Plants:
Achimines
Adiantum
African violet
Aloe
Amaryllis
Aphelandra
Aurucaria
    (Norfolk pine)
Azalea
Begonia
Caladium
Calathea
Crossandra
Cyclamen
Dieffenbachia
Epiphyllum
Gardenia
Hydrangea
Impatiens
Maranta
Pellaea (ferns)
Peperomia
Pilea
Polypodium
Primula
Rechsteineria
Saxifraga
Scindapsus
Streptocarpus
Syngonium
Zygocactus

Vegetables/fruit:
Radish
Raspberry
Sweet potato

pH 5.5-6.5

House Plants:
Anthurium
Bromeliad
Bulb
Cattleya
Columnea
Cymbidium
Cypripedium
Daffodil
Gladiolus
Hyacinth
Iris
Narcissus
Phalaenopsis

Platycerium
Rhipsalidopsis
Tulip
Vanda

Vegetables/fruit:
Endive
Grape
Parsley
Pepper
Rhubarb
Soybean
Strawberry
Tomato

pH 7+

House Plants:
Abutilon
Agave
Asparagus
Aspidistra
Asplenium
Beleperone
Bouganvillea
Cactus
Campanula
Ceropegia
Chlorophytum
Chrysanthemum
Cineraria
Cissus
Citrus
Clivia
Coleus
Cordyline
Crassula
Croton
Cypress
Diplademia
Dizygotheca
Dracaena
Echeveria
Euphorbia (poinsettia)
Fatshedera
Fatsia
Ficus
Fittonia
Fuchsia
Geranium

Gynura
Hedera
Hibiscus
Hoya
Iresine
Kalanchoe
Lily
Monstera
Nephrolepis
Nerium
Palm
Pandanus
Passiflora
Peperomia
Philodendron
Phoeo
Pittosporum
Pteris
Rhoicissus
Rochea
Sansevieria
Schefflera
Stephanotis
Tradescantia

Vegetables:
Asparagus
Beet
Broccoli
Brussels sprouts
Cabbage
Carrot
Celery
Cucumber
Leek
Lettuce
Onion
Spinach
Swiss chard

* Many tropicals are pH tolerant and will do well in mixes with a pH value from 5.5 to 7.0

Do-it-yourself soil analysis

There are soil-test kits available *(fig. 77)* that test not only the pH, but also the fertilizer element content of the soil mix. These kits permit you to use color matching to determine the approximate amounts of nitrogen, phosphate, potash, and other elements in your mix, as well as the pH value. The kits come with complete directions and cost $25.00 and up.

Fig. 77
Many kinds of soil-testing kits are available

Professional soil analysis

If you wish to have a professional soil analysis, consult the lists at the end of the chapter for agencies that provide this service. Following are some guidelines for submitting soil samples:

1. Send about ½ pound that truly represents the composition of all the soil you will be using

2. Put the soil in a rigid, clean container; mark on the outside the plants you are growing, comments on the condition of the plants previously grown in the soil, and your name and address

3. If you are sending new soil or a mix that never has been used, state the source of the material on the outside of the container

4. When you get the soil test results back, the following chart should help you interpret the results:

INGREDIENT	LOW	NORMAL	HIGH
	In parts per million (ppm)		
Nitrogen	0-5	6-15	15 up
Phosphorus	0-6	7-16	16 up
Potassium	0-30	30-59	60-79
Calcium	0-125	125-200	200 up
Magnesium	0-4	4-5	5 up
Sulfate	0-100	100-200	300 up
pH		6-7	
Total salts	0-29	30-79	80 up

SOIL STERILIZATION

The untreated soil from your yard or from your own compost pile may contain a variety of weed seed, disease fungi and bacteria, nematodes, and soil insects; therefore, unless you treat your soil mix, you may be introducing these causes of disease and damage into your greenhouse. The soil treatment should kill the undesirable organisms, but not destroy the decomposition bacteria that break down raw materials for use by the plant. Following are several methods of achieving partial sterilization, or pasteurization.

Heat treatment

Temperatures up to 180°F (82°C) will kill pathogenic organisms and most weed seeds, but will not harm the useful bacteria. Simple heat sterilization procedures are detailed in the appendix.

For larger batches of soil mix, there are electric soil pasteurizers on the market such as the Dillon and the Famco (fig. 78). These devices automatically heat to the proper temperature and then shut

The Famco sterilizer will sterilize ⅛ cubic yard in three hours
Fig. 78

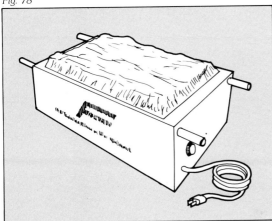

off. They plug into a 110- to 120-volt outlet and treat the soil for a cost of about seven cents per yard—the capacity is ⅛ yard per batch. Purchase cost is from $350.00 to $500.00; operating cost is comparable to a home clothes dryer.

Chemical treatment

One of the safest and most readily available chemicals for soil treatment is 40-percent formaldehyde. The formaldehyde should not be used inside the greenhouse, however, because the fumes will kill most plants. The procedures for chemical treatment are listed in the appendix.

Storage

There is little use in treating the soil mix if it is then placed in untreated flats or pots where it will be contaminated immediately. Pots, tools, benches, and shelves should all be disinfected as follows before using with sterilized soil:

1. Use 10 percent Clorox or Javex at the rate of 1 part Clorox to 9 parts water to disinfect surfaces—soak tools and pots for thirty minutes in straight 10 percent Clorox, then allow to air overnight before using

2. As an alternative, use LF-10 diluted to 4 teaspoons per gallon of water to scrub surfaces—soak tools for thirty minutes and pots for one hour

Pre-packaged pasteurized mixes

There are many brands of packaged, pasteurized soil mixes available at most garden centers and nurseries. These can be purchased in small bags for about $1.00, or in large bags and bales up to 10 cubic feet that cost from $10.00 to $20.00.

With the prepared mix there is the ultimate convenience of just opening the bag and using the material as it comes from the package. Pots or flats still should be treated before use, however, or the prepared mix also will become contaminated quickly.

HYDROPONICS

Hydroponics is the practice of growing plants in water or in an inert soilless medium, such as plain sand, with the nutrients supplied through water. Growing plants by this method requires specialized equipment and precise control of the growing process in order to avoid problems of disease.

The laboratory permits optimum conditions of sanitation and precise mixing and application of nutrient solution. Solution cultures in aerated water and an inert medium have been used for years under laboratory conditions for plant physiology research. It is difficult to handle formulas that require fractions of ounces or grams of dry nutrient ingredients in the home. Thus it is probably better to purchase prepared nutrient formulas for home use.

Hydroponic pot

A good way to begin growing in a soilless medium is with a single hydroponic pot. The growing medium can be sand, cinders, small gravel, vermiculite, perlite, or scoria. The medium usually should have a variety of particle size, about 80 percent (by weight) approximately ⅛ inch in diameter and the remainder less, to permit good aeration.

Potting procedure

1. Place large stones or broken pieces of crockery in the bottom of the pot *(fig. 79)*

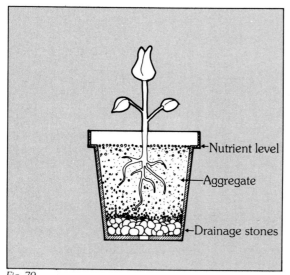

Fig. 79
Single pots can be used for hydroponic growing

2. Fill the pot with hydroponic aggregate and water thoroughly (your tap water should be tested to make certain it is correct for hydroponic use—improper salt content or other components can be damaging to the plants when applied directly to the roots rather than filtered through soil)

3. Seed or plant in the pot same as in soil

4. Add nutrients *(see chapter 11 for feeding nutrient solutions)*

Hydroponic bench

For more growing area, make a vinyl- or poly-lined growing box; set it up as shown in the appendix. If the installation is to be permanent, the box might be galvanized sheet metal. Installation directions for a permanent bench also are in the appendix. For installation of a complete hydroponic greenhouse, consult the references at the end of the chapter.

NATURAL RECYCLING

The earth's ecosystem has evolved a complex and intricately balanced system for recycling both organic and inorganic materials. In the organic, living-to-living cycle, leaves containing carbon, in the form of cellulose, fall to the ground. Decomposition releases the carbon from the leaf, and it rises in the air as carbon dioxide. The same carbon atoms return to a growing leaf during photosynthesis to be used over again as energy for growth. This process is natural composting *(fig. 80)*. Less than 1 percent of the carbon near the surface of the earth

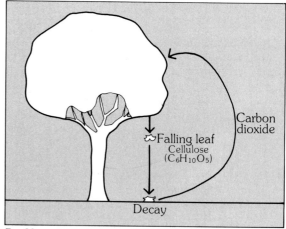

Fig. 80
Living-to-living cycle

is in this rapid living-to-living cycle, however; most of the elements are in a living-to-inorganic-to-living cycle.

When a leaf falls to the ground, for example, and

the carbon, in the form of carbon dioxide, is absorbed by water instead of being reused by a plant, some of the carbon atoms eventually may be used in oyster shells or limestone, forming inorganic calcium carbonate. The same calcium carbonate is used in composts (and fertilizers), so when you apply them to your plants, the carbon goes into the plant to be used in the growth process again *(fig. 81)*.

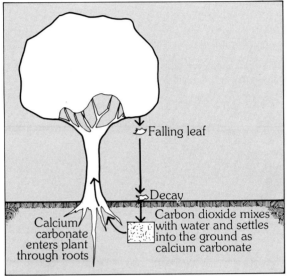

Fig. 81
Living-to-inorganic-to-living cycle

Green manuring

For ground beds, one of the quickest ways to recycle is to sow a crop of domestic or Italian rye grass over the bed, adding ½ pound of actual nitrogen per 100 square feet of bed *(see chapter 11 for details)*. In two or three weeks, the rye grass will be up about 6 inches—you can then turn it over with a spade, and it will decompose in another two weeks to provide organic matter for the soil, which will aid in moisture retention and provide nutrients.

Compost pile
Aerobic

There are almost as many ways of composting as there are people doing it. Each fits into one of two categories, however: aerobic (with aeration), or anaerobic (without air). The typical aerobic compost pile is constructed to allow frequent turning in order to admit air; many of the bacteria that break down organic matter in the compost pile require oxygen.

The mix also must be kept moist to accomplish the decomposition process. For details of construction and maintenance, see the appendix.

Anaerobic

Organisms in the soil that break down organic matter without oxygen are called anaerobic bacteria. These bacteria also are active when we make compost, and during the winter, when it is too cold for outside composting, anaerobic composting in a plastic garbage can or drum can be done in the basement or under a bench in the greenhouse. For instructions on construction and maintenance, see the appendix.

Microorganisms

Also important to the composting process are the fauna of the soil—fungi, bacteria, and protozoans that act upon organic matter to accomplish decomposition. They usually are abundant in good soils or in animal manures if added to the soil. If you wish to add fauna to the soil and prefer not to use manure, you can purchase inert decomposition fungi and bacteria in such products as Gro-zyme and Fertosan (see sources of supply following this chapter). Enriching the soil fauna with inert bacteria usually speeds up the process of decomposition.

SOURCES

General information

CANADA:
Ball Red Book. Twelfth edition. Ball-Superior, Ltd., 1155 Birchview Dr., Mississauga, Ontario L5H 3E1

Chatelaine's Gardening Book. Lois Wilson. McLean-Hunter, 481 University Ave., Toronto, Ontario M5W 1A7

UNITED STATES:
Ball Red Book. Twelfth edition. Geo. J. Ball, Inc., P. O. Box 335, West Chicago, IL 60185

Bedding Plants. Second edition. 1976 Pennsylvania Flower Growers, 103 Tyson Bldg., University Park, PA 16802

Gardening Under Glass. Jerome A. Eaton. MacMillan, 866 3rd Ave., New York, NY 10022

Organic Gardening Under Glass. G. K. Abraham.

Rodale Press, 33 E. Minor St., Emmaus, PA 18049

The U. C. System (Manual #23). Agricultural Publications, University of California, Berkeley, CA 94720

Western Fertilizer Handbook. California Fertilizer Assoc., 2222 Watts Ave., Sacramento, CA 95825

Supplies

Compost shredders

CANADA:
Solo, P. O. Box 464, Burlington, Ontario

UNITED STATES:
Amerind-MacKissic, Inc., P. O. Box 111, Parker Ford, PA 19457

John Bean, Div. FMC Corp., 1305 S. Cedar St., Lansing, MI 48910

Fruit & Produce Packaging Co., P. O. Box 1851, Indianapolis, IN 46231

Gilson Bros. Co., P. O. Box 152, Plymouth, WI 53073

Lundin & Milner, P. O. Box 1146, Los Altos, CA 94022

Osborne Mfg. Co., P. O. Box 29, Osborne, KS 67173

Roper Sales Corp., 1905 W. Court St., Kankakee, IL 60901

Simplicity Mfg. Co., 500 N. Spring St., Port Washington, WI 53074

Winona Attrition Mill, 1009 W. 5th St., Winona, MN 55987

W-W Grinder Corp., 2957 N. Market, Wichita, KS 67219

Inert bacteria

CANADA:
Fertosan, Vancouver, British Columbia

UNITED STATES:
Enzyme Industries of U.S.A., 895 Shawnee Rd., P. O. Box 466, Lima, OH 45802

Soil sterilizers

UNITED STATES:
Dillon, E. C. Geiger, P. O. Box 285, Harleysville, PA 19438

Famco, Inc., 300 Lake Rd., Medina, OH 44256

Lindig Mfg. Corp., 1877 W. Country Rd. C, St. Paul, MN 55113

Soil testing equipment

UNITED STATES:
Beckman Instruments, Inc., Cedar Grove Operations, 89 Commerce Rd., Cedar Grove, NJ 07009

Edmund Scientific Co., 555 Edscorp Bldg., Barrington, NJ 08007

Empire Corp., 8777 Brighton Rd., Adams City, CO 80022

Highsmith Co., Inc., P. O. Box 25, Fort Atkinson, WI 53538

Hydroponics Chemical Co., Inc., 3489 Sawmill Rd., Copley, OH 44821

Kel Instrument Co., Inc., P.O. Box 1118, Pompano Beach, FL 33061

LaMotte Chemical Products, Chestertown, MD 21620

Sanders, Ray and Co., 396 S. Pasadena Ave., Pasadena, CA 91105

Soilmoisture Equipment, P.O. Box 30025, Santa Barbara, CA 93105

Soil Sampler Co., P. O. Box 555, Downers Grove, IL 60515

Taylor Chemicals, Inc., 7300 York Rd., Baltimore, MD 21204

Trans-Sphere Trading Corp., P. O. Box 1564, Mobile, AL 36601

Vaughan-Jacklin Corp., Seed Div., 8803 Sprague Ave., Dishman, WA 99213

Soil testing laboratories

CANADA:
Alberta: Alberta Soil & Feed Testing Laboratory, 801 O. S. Longman Bldg., P. O. Box 8070, Edmonton, Alberta T6H 4P2

British Columbia: Soil, Feed and Tissue Testing Laboratory, Field Crops Branch, 1873 Spall Rd., Kelowna, British Columbia V1Y 4R2

Manitoba: Manitoba Provincial Soil Testing Laboratory, Dept. of Soil Science, University of Manitoba, Winnipeg, Manitoba R3T 2N2

New Brunswick: Soils Laboratory, New Brunswick Dept. of Agriculture, Fredrickton, New Brunswick E3B 5H1

Newfoundland: C. D. A. Research Station, P. O. Box 7018, St. John's West, Newfoundland A1E 3Y3

Nova Scotia: Provincial Soils Laboratory, Nova Scotia Dept. of Agriculture and Marketing, Truro, Nova Scotia B2N 5E3

Ontario: Soil Testing Laboratory, Dept. of Land Resource Science, Ontario Agricultural College, University of Guelph, Guelph, Ontario N1G 2W1

Prince Edward Island: Soils Advisory Laboratory, Research Station, P. O. Box 1600, Charlottetown, Prince Edward Island C1A 7N3

Quebec: Quebec Soil Testing Laboratory, La Pocatiere, Quebec

Saskatchewan: Saskatchewan Soil Testing Laboratory, University of Saskatchewan, Saskatoon, Saskatchewan S7N 0W0

UNITED STATES:
The Edwards Laboratory, P. O. Box 318, Norwalk, OH 44857

Harris Laboratories, Inc., 624 Peach St., Lincoln, NE 68502

Prescription Soil Analysis, S. R. Sorenson, P. O. Box 80631, Lincoln, NE 68501

Soil and Plant Laboratory, P. O. Box 1648, Bellevue, WA 98009

Most states also have soil testing laboratories associated with the state agricultural college.

Hydroponics
General information
UNITED STATES:
Beginner's Guide to Hydroponics. James S. Douglas. Drake Publishers, 381 Park Ave. S., New York, NY 10016

The Complete Guide to Soilless Gardening. W. F. Gericke. Prentice-Hall, Englewood Cliffs, NJ 07632

Hydroponic Gardening. Raymond Bridewell. Woodbridge Press, 1149 Acacia St., Loma Linda, CA 92354

Hydroponics as a Hobby (Circular #844). University of Illinois, College of Agriculture, Urbana, IL 61801

Nutriculture—A Guide to the Soilless Culture of Plants (Extension Service Bulletin #41). Maynard and Barker. University of Massachusetts, Amherst, MA 01002

The Water Culture Method of Growing Plants Without Soil. D. R. Hoagland and D. I. Arnon. University of California at Davis, Davis, CA 95616.

Supplies
Equipment
CANADA:
City Green Hydroponics, Ltd., 6471 Northam Dr., Mississauga, Ontario L4V 1J2

UNITED STATES:
Burwell Geoponics Corp., P. O. Box 125, Rancho Sante Fe, CA 92076

Ecoref, P. O. Box 1600, Palo Alto, CA 94302

Hydroponic Specialties, P. O. Box 1013 PA, Carlsbad, CA 92008

Water Works Garden Houses, P. O. Box 905B, El Cerrito, CA 94530

Nutrient mixes
UNITED STATES:
Robert B. Peters Co., 2833 Pennsylvania St., Allentown, PA 18104

Plant Marvel Laboratories, 624 W. 119th St., Chicago, IL 60628

Ra-Pid Gro Corp., 88 Ossian St., Dansville, NY 14437

This palm has brown tips — on closer inspection, you can also see small, light blotches throughout the green portion of the leaf, both top and bottom — what is wrong?

DIAGNOSIS

WHAT'S WRONG WITH YOUR PLANT?

When you first suspect there is something wrong, don't panic! Pick up the pot and examine it. Take your time. You can find out what's wrong by careful and patient observation and examination.

Place the plant in front of you—good diagnosis begins with observation of the whole plant as it sits in the pot, then proceeds to the examination of all parts of the plant under a hand-lens magnifier (4x, 8x, and 20x). Observe the following:

1. *The whole plant wilts*

    The entire plant is wilted or drooping. Possible causes:

    (a) Soil insects or nematodes that are attacking the root system—tap the plant out of the pot, wash the root system free of soil, and check against symptoms in the disease table *(chapter 14)*

    (b) Fungi that are inside the plant and blocking the transport tubes — check the stem (using 20x lens) for the presence of spores or mycelia of fungi *(chapter 14)*

    (c) Too much water in the soil is limiting the oxygen supply to the roots, thus permitting root rot *(chapter 7)*

    (d) An excess of salts in the soil does not permit proper uptake of water and nutrients into the plant *(chapter 11)*

2. *The whole plant is stunted*

The entire plant is not wilted or drooping —but is small, stunted, and lacking in vigor:

(a) Soil insects or nematodes are attacking the root system—proceed as in question one, part (a)

(b) The water balance of the soil mix is improper *(chapter 7)*

(c) The plant is potbound and full of roots—transplant to the next size larger pot

(d) There is a nutritional deficiency *(chapter 11)*

(e) The plant has a virus or bacterial disease *(chapter 14)*

(f) There are excess salts in the soil— see question one, part (d)

(g) The pH of the soil mix is improper— test for pH *(chapter 9)*

3. *Parts of the plant are abnormal*

If an inspection of the entire plant does not give you a diagnosis, examine flowers, leaves, stem, and roots (use a 10x hand lens); when you find something that looks abnormal, check the diagnosis table *(plates 17-23)* to see what is wrong (treatment is given in the chapter indicated)

DIAGNOSIS CHECKLIST

Often the detective game of diagnosis is a matter of eliminating the things that are *not* wrong with the plant in order to discover what *is* wrong. The following check list should help:

- [ ] 1. Insect or pest   *(chapter 13)*
- [ ] 2. Disease   *(chapter 14)*
- [ ] 3. Watering practices   *(chapter 7)*
- [ ] 4. Nutritional problems   *(chapter 11)*
- [ ] 5. Pollution   *(chapter 8)*
- [ ] 6. Humidity   *(chapter 8)*
- [ ] 7. Excess cold or heat   *(chapter 4)*
- [ ] 8. Light conditions   *(chapter 3)*
- [ ] 9. Chemical damage   *(chapter 8)*
- [ ] 10. Relative acidity pH   *(chapter 9)*

For a list of sources for professional help, see the appendix.

See Diagnosis table
Plates 17-23
between pages 84-85

SOURCES

General information

UNITED STATES:
Basic Book of Organic Gardening. Robert Rodale. Random House, 201 E. 50th St., New York, NY 10022

Diseases and Pests of Ornamental Plants. P. P. Pirone. Ronald Press, 79 Madison Ave., New York, NY 10016

Diseases of Ornamental Plants. J. L. Forsbert. College of Agriculture, University of Illinois, Urbana, IL 61801

Handbook on Garden Pests. Vol. 22, No. 1. Plants & Gardens Series. Brooklyn Botanic Gardens, 1000 Washington Ave., Brooklyn, New York, NY 11225

How to Control Plant Diseases. M. C. Shurtleff. Iowa State University Press, Ames, IA 50010

Insect Pests. Davidson and Pairs. John Wiley & Sons, 605 3rd Ave., New York, NY 10016

Insect Pests. G. S. Fichter. Golden Nature Series Guide. Golden Press, Western, 220 Mounde Ave., Racine, WI 53404

Yearbook of Agriculture, 1952 (insects). U. S. Dept. of Agriculture, Superintendent of Documents, Washington, DC 20250

Yearbook of Agriculture, 1953 (plant diseases). U. S. Dept. of Agriculture, Superintendent of Documents, Washington, DC 20250

Supplies

UNITED STATES:
College Biological Supply Co., P. O. Box 1326, Escondido, CA 92052

College Biological Supply Co., P. O. Box 25017, Northgate Station, Seattle, WA 98125

Edmund Scientific Co., 555 Edscorp Bldg., Barrington, NJ 08007

The Nature Co. (hand lenses—20x pocket microscope), P.O. Box 7137, Berkeley, CA 94707

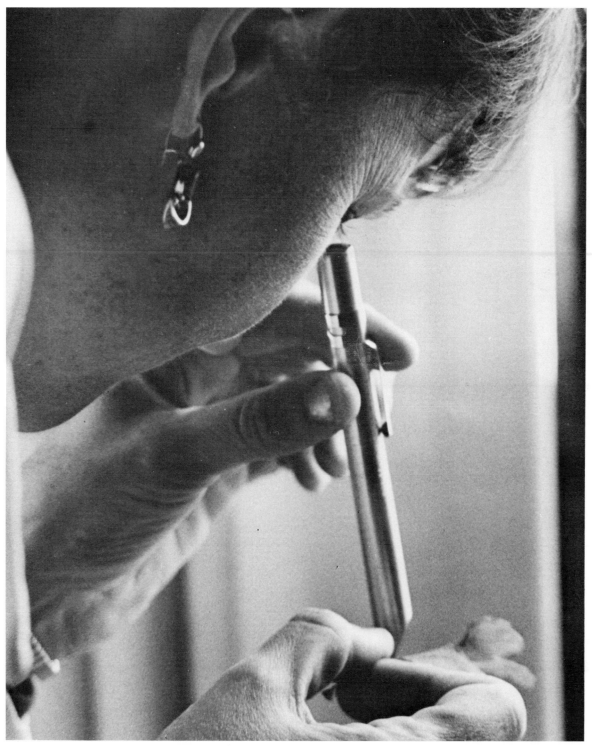

Inspecting plants closely or even portions of leaves lets you eliminate some problems and focus on the real source of trouble

Good nutrition results in healthy, vigorous plants

Chapter

11

NUTRITION

CONSTITUENTS OF FERTILIZER

When you go to the store to buy fertilizer, you find a bewildering array of brands and types on the shelf. The best way to get the fertilizer you need is to understand some of the basics about fertilizer.

Because the elements are supplied by nature, we tend to forget that carbon (C), hydrogen (H), and oxygen (O) are fundamental components of the plant structure. These and other elements normally considered essential for growth are detailed with their deficiency symptoms in the tables that follow.

Carbon, as carbon dioxide from the air, is in the cell wall, in the sugars manufactured, in the chlorophyll, and is a part of most chemical activities. By dry weight about 50 percent of the plant is carbon.

Hydrogen is necessary for the formation of sugars and starches, and in combination with oxygen—as water—is the fluid that keeps the cells turgid and the plant structurally rigid. The leaf, in fact, is a hydraulic system in which internal water pressure (turgor pressure) is essential to avoid wilting.

Oxygen plays its role in forming sugars, starches, and cellulose. It is necessary for the process of respiration, which provides the energy for growth. Excess oxygen is given off into the air.

FERTILIZER FORMULAS

Fertilizer at your local nursery will carry a number formula on every package, such as 8-3-1, 5-10-5, or 12-6-6. These figures represent, in order, the percentage of nitrogen (N), phosphate (P), and potash (K), usually written NPK for short. (See table of major nutrients at the end of the chapter).

Thus if you purchase 1 pound, or 16 ounces, of a 20-20-20 formula you have 20 percent, or 3.2 ounces, each of NPK for a total of 9.6 ounces of actual fertilizer. The other 6.4 ounces in the package is filler, often composed of organic material, chelating compounds, or other materials to assist the nutritional process.

There are also manufacturers or formulators of plant food that include some or all of the minor or trace elements in their product (see table of minor nutrients at the end of the chapter). Inspect the label for an NPK formula and the minor element content of the package. It is also possible to buy minor elements singly or in mixes to add to any fertilizer that you may be using.

ORGANIC FERTILIZERS

If you are planning to use *all* organic materials, the following list of percentage content of N (nitrogen), P (phosphate), and K (potash) may be of some help:

ORGANIC MATERIALS	FERTILIZER CONTENT		
	N	P	K
Urea formaldehyde (synthetic organic)	38.0	0.0	0.0
Activated sludge	5.0	3.0	0.5
Apple pomace	2.0	0.0	0.0
Blood meal	13.0	1.5	1.0
Bat guano	13.0	5.0	2.0
Bone meal: raw	4.0	18.0	0.0
Bone meal: steamed	3.0	25.0	0.0
Coffee grounds	2.0	5.0	5.0
Cotton seed meal	6.0	3.0	2.0
Manure: beef	0.8	0.3	0.7
Manure: goat	3.0	2.0	3.0
Manure: steer	2.0	0.5	2.0
Manure: horse	0.7	0.3	0.5

ORGANIC MATERIALS	FERTILIZER CONTENT		
	N	P	K
Manure: hog	1.0	1.0	1.0
Manure: sheep	2.0	1.0	3.0
Manure: rabbit	2.0	1.5	1.5
Manure: poultry	1.5	1.5	1.0
Straw	1.5	0.3	1.5
Fish meal	10.0	5.0	0.0
Tankage (steamed refuse animal matter)	7.0	8.0	2.0
Liquid seaweed	1.0	2.0	3.0
Wood ashes	0.0	1.5	7.0
Winery pomace	2.0	1.5	1.0

Role of microorganisms in nutrition

Directly or indirectly, microorganisms are involved in the breakdown of nitrogen, carbon, sulfur, phosphorus, potassium, calcium, magnesium, and iron. Any change in activity of the microorganisms in the soil has an effect on plant nutrition. Organic nitrogen is a good example of an element that must be broken down by microorganisms before it can be utilized by a plant. Following are the three steps breaking down organic nitrogen to nitrate, which can be readily absorbed by the plant:

Step 1: Microorganisms such as bacteria, fungi, and actinomycetes (related to bacteria), break down the organic nitrogen—the first product is ammonium—very often the ammonium is "tied up" in the soil, however, and not available to the plant without further action by other microorganisms

Step 2: The ammonium is broken down by a particular bacteria, Nitrosomonas, to produce nitrite nitrogen; nitrite is toxic to plants, and once again action by microorganisms is required before the nutrient can be used

Step 3: The nitrite nitrogen is broken down by another specific bacterium, Nitrobacter, to produce nitrate nitrogen; nitrate is the principal form of nitrogen available for plants and can be absorbed readily with no further breakdown by microorganisms

Summer growing conditions often mean more active microorganisms in the soil mix and, thus, quicker conversion of organic nitrogen to nitrate. With winter conditions, on the other hand, and less active soil microorganisms, it is necessary to provide nitrate that is available to the plant without the action of microorganisms. In fact, many growers recommend using a fertilizer that is half nitrate year round in order to get a quick response from the plants—the percentage of nitrate is noted on the fertilizer package.

SYNTHETIC-ORGANIC FERTILIZERS

The term "synthetic organic" refers to a manufactured non-protein organic nitrogen, such as urea, which is soluble in water. In most "natural" organic materials, the nitrogen is initially in an insoluble form not readily available to the plant. Although some organic gardeners make the distinction between nitrogen that is organic and that which is not, the plant uses nitrogen without regard to its source, whether it is from the air, a factory, or a dead fish! In fact, the elements—carbon, hydrogen, oxygen, nitrogen, and others—are used by the plant regardless of the form in which they are applied to the soil.

FERTILIZERS FROM THE SEA

There is some evidence that plants are more resistant to cold temperatures as well as insect and disease problems when the feeding program includes plant food products from the sea. Most nurseries and garden shops carry a fish fertilizer, the best of which are made by grinding up whole fish, such as herring, and making a soluble emulsion that contains major nutrients as well as the necessary minor elements. The emulsion can be applied to all kinds of plants at the rate of 1 tablespoon per gallon of water.

There are products marketed as fish fertilizer that are really only part fish fortified with chemical solubles. Read the label to make certain that at least 50 percent of the fertilizer content is fish emulsion. If the fortified fish fertilizer contains nitrate nitrogen, you will get rapid response as well as all the minor elements in the fish emulsion. Liquified seaweed fertilizer products also supply a full complement of the minor elements and are widely available under many brand names.

Plate 17
DIAGNOSIS

Symptoms	Insect Causes and Treatments (Chapter 13)	Disease Causes and Treatments (Chapter 14)	Other Causes	Chapters for Treatments
LEAF				
 **Brown tips, edges, or areas**			Overwatering Cold air Sun scorch Pollution Nutrition deficiency	7 8 3 8 11
 **Curled**	Alphis Leaf curler	Crinkle	Ethylene or other chemical	8
 **Discolored**			Nutrition deficiency Pollution	11 8
 **Gall**	Aphis Midge	Fungus Exobasidium		
 **Holes**	Beetle Sawfly Slug Weevil	Shot hole	Chemical	8

Plate 18
DIAGNOSIS

Symptoms	Insect Causes and Treatments (Chapter 13)	Disease Causes and Treatments (Chapter 14)	Other Causes	Chapters for Treatments
LEAF (cont.)				
Leaf drop		Wilts	Soil salts Improper watering Ethylene	11 7 8
Malformed	Aphis Mite Nematode	Peach leaf curl Downy mildew	Nutrition deficiency	11
Notched	Ant Cutworm Earwig Leafcutter Slug Weevil	Shot hole		
Silver leaf with glazed underleaf			Pollution: Pan and hydrocarbons	8
Skeletonized	Beetle Sawfly			

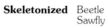

Plate 19
DIAGNOSIS

Symptoms	Insect Causes and Treatments (Chapter 13)	Disease Causes and Treatments (Chapter 14)	Other Causes	Chapters for Treatments
LEAF (cont.)				
Spittle	Spittlebug			
 **Spots: black powdery**		Sooty Mold		
Spots: brown, tiny and dark	Mite	Blight Bacterial disease		
Spots: red, yellow, black, brown		Rusts Anthracnose		
Spots: white powdery	Mealybug	Powdery mildew		

Plate 20
DIAGNOSIS

Symptoms	Insect Causes and Treatments (Chapter 13)	Disease Causes and Treatments (Chapter 14)	Other Causes	Chapters for Treatments
LEAF (cont.)				
 **Stippled: tan to white on new leaves**			Ozone damage	8
 **Tunnels**	Leaf miner			
 **Webs**	Caterpillar Mite Webworm			
 **Yellowing**	Mite	Wilts	Salts in soil Ethylene Nutrition deficiency	11 8 11
STEM				
 **Cankers**		Anthracnose		

Plate 21
DIAGNOSIS

Symptoms	Insect Causes and Treatments (Chapter 13)	Disease Causes and Treatments (Chapter 14)	Other Causes	Chapters for Treatments
STEM (cont.)				
 **Discolored, soft, rotten**		Damping off	Overwatering	7
 **Eggs**	Caterpillar Many others			
 **Holes**	Beetle Borer Carpenter worm Fly larvae			
 **Lumps: hard or soft**	Scale			
 **Malformed: fasciation**		Crown gall	Ethylene	8

Plate 22
DIAGNOSIS

Symptoms	Insect Causes and Treatments (Chapter 13)	Disease Causes and Treatments (Chapter 14)	Other Causes	Chapters for Treatments
ROOTS				
 **Anti-gravity**			Ethylene	8
 **Lumpy**	Nematode			
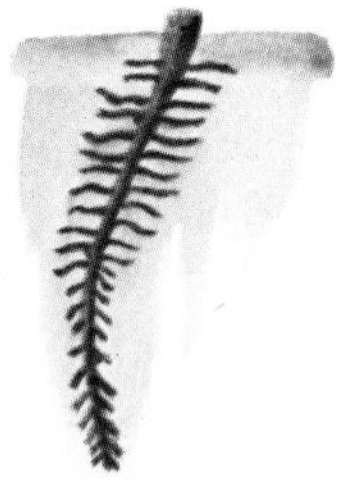 **Short stubby, few root hairs, larvae inside**	Aphis Bulb fly Fungus gnat Millipede Nematode Sowbug Weevil		Calcium deficiency	11
 **Soft, rotten**		Root rot Damping off		
FLOWER AND FRUIT				
 **Bud drop**	Mite		Overwatering Low humidity Ethylene Cold	7 7 8 4

Plate 23
DIAGNOSIS

Symptoms	Insect Causes and Treatments (Chapter 13)	Disease Causes and Treatments (Chapter 14)	Other Causes	Chapters for Treatments
		FLOWER AND FRUIT (cont.)		
Deformed	Thrips	Blight Botrytis Anthracnose		
Failure to Flower			Low light Ethylene Phosphate deficiency	3 8 11
Holes or notched	Aphis Beetle Earwig Weevil			

Plate 24
NUTRITION DEFICIENCY SYMPTOMS

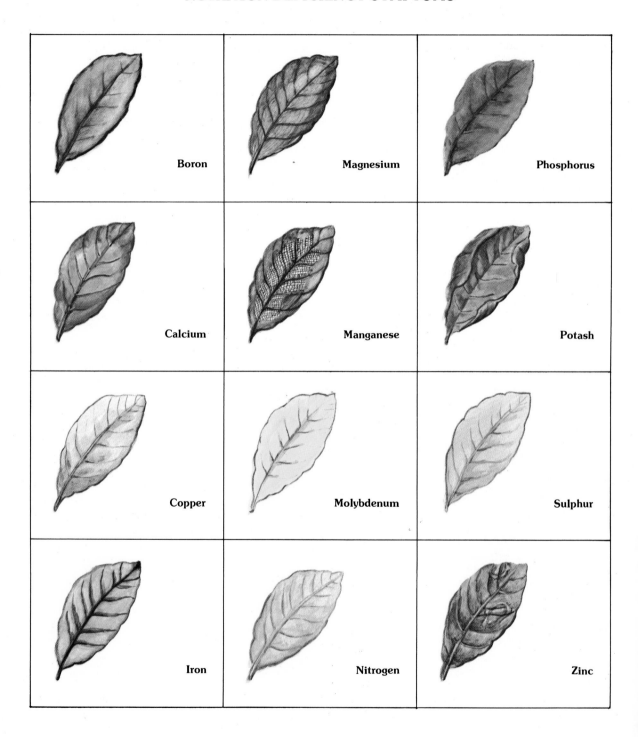

Boron

Magnesium

Phosphorus

Calcium

Manganese

Potash

Copper

Molybdenum

Sulphur

Iron

Nitrogen

Zinc

COMPOSTING HUMAN WASTE

Trying to compost or treat human waste at home is dangerous. Species of salmonella and pseudomonas may well survive the composting process to infect again, particularly if used on food crops. A modern, commercial version of the oriental "honey pot" is the specially processed and packaged activated sewage sludge such as that marketed by the city of Milwaukee as Milorganite. The commercial product is safe and contains minor elements and microorganisms that are beneficial in the soil mix.

FEEDING

Quantity and timing

The menu at the old folks' home would hardly suffice for the high school football team, and it is the same with plants. You learn by experience that when the plant is in an active stage of growth, it needs more food, and when it is getting ready to go dormant, it needs less. During the dark days of winter, for instance, there is less utilization of fertilizer materials. When growing conditions require more water, usually more plant food is needed as well. Water the plant well before feeding if it is dry; otherwise, the fertilizer can burn the fine root hairs through which the nutrients are absorbed into the plant.

If you are starting a feeding program with a fertilizer such as Peters 20-20-20, a general formula is to use 1 tablespoon per gallon of water, an amount found to be correct for most plants by commercial growers and researchers. Apply the fertilizer every seven days to two weeks as the growing conditions indicate. The home greenhouse is one way of maintaining a good growing environment year round. So, in a greenhouse, feeding once every seven days would be appropriate all year.

There is, of course, a wide range of specific fertilizer requirements among the plants commonly grown in the home greenhouse. The literature in books and magazines such as *Plants Alive* is replete with specific data on feeding various kinds of greenhouse plants. For African violets, begonias, and other soft plants, for example, ½ tablespoon in a gallon of water every seven to ten days usually is adequate. For woody plants, use 1 tablespoon per gallon. Cacti, on the other hand, do very well with ½ tablespoon

per gallon of water applied every four months, while tomatoes may require a constant bath of liquid nutrients several times a day when grown hydroponically.

Each greenhouse environment is unique, however, and the best way to establish sound feeding practices for your particular greenhouse is to get lots of experience! Maintaining records on the growth of your plants will help—noted on a 3 by 5 file card, they can be kept in the greenhouse for ready reference. A sample record follows:

Name (of plant)	African Violet
Date	1/15/76
Fertilizer applied	20-20-20, ½ Tbs., 1 gal.
Size of plant (in centimeters)	3 cm. (young leaf)
Date + one month Growth response (in centimeters)	2/15/76 3.5 cm., good color
Comments	Try 1 Tbs., 1 gal.

Liquid feeding

Some of the better ways of providing frequent feedings are soluble-liquid or controlled-release fertilizers. Dry fertilizers must dissolve in the soil solution before they get into the plant.

For many years we thought plants required food infrequently and assumed that fertilizing once a month or less provided adequate nourishment for growing plants. More recent research emphasizes the fact that plants are much more like people and will grow better with food available more often. More and more people are using the controlled-release fertilizers to keep nutrients constantly available for the growth process.

Solubility

Before you purchase a large quantity of an unknown fertilizer, test it to see what degree of solubility it has: put a teaspoon of the soluble fertilizer in a quart of water and let it sit for eight to ten hours. If you have undissolved or crystalline material in the bottom of the bottle at the end of that time, you have an inferior product. In the inferior grades of soluble fertilizer, the residue in the bottom may well be minor elements vital to plant growth.

The better grades of soluble fertilizer, such as

Peters, Rapid-Gro, Plant Marvel, and others, dissolve completely and give a crystal-clear solution that stays clear and will not precipitate. If you are using a Chapin spaghetti tube watering system or a fertilizer injector, it is important to have a completely soluble fertilizer to prevent clogging. See chapters 7 and 15 for more information on these systems.

Slow-release feeding

Many fertilizers move with the water through the soil, or are dissolved and leached out of the soil in a pot rather rapidly, but there are some now marketed as slow, or controlled-release, fertilizers. The slow-release fertilizers are especially useful with the peat-lite or soilless mixes because they do not leach out as rapidly as other fertilizers.

"Osmocote," for example, comes in a wide variety of formulas. It is a soluble fertilizer encased in a polymer resin coating that acts as a semi-permeable membrane to meter out the nitrogen, phosphate, and potassium in relation to temperature. The release rate increases in warm soils, decreases in cool soils, and stops completely in cold soils. The type and thickness of the coating can be varied to create tailor-made formulas and products for a wide range of growing requirements. Products similar to Osmocote are now marketed as Precise, Ortho, and Rainbird time-release fertilizers.

Urea-formaldehyde is another controlled-release nutrient—a synthetic-organic compound that is used in a wide variety of products. Like all other organic materials, however, it must be broken down by soil bacteria before it becomes available to the plant. In this case, the release rate depends upon the conditions of moisture, temperature, and oxygen supply that are necessary for bacterial activity. If the decomposed bacteria count of the growing medium is high, release is fairly rapid and gradual; if the bacteria count is low, release is limited.

Foliar feeding

When plant food is sprayed on the leaves, stem, blossoms, and fruits of most plants, it is absorbed to provide raw materials for the growth process; but it is important to choose the proper fertilizer, one that is designed for foliar application. A plant food that is not intended for foliage use will cause leaf burn or other damage. The safest procedure is to buy a product that states "safe for foliage feeding" plainly on the label!

Foliar feeding is not yet a substitute for feeding through soil or media, but it can be a helpful adjunct. A plant that is damaged or under stress, for example, may recover with foliar feeding, and it is one of the best ways of supplying the minor elements (check to be sure the foliar fertilizer you are using contains these in soluble form). Ra-Pid Gro is one of the oldest brands available, and there are many others at garden shops and nurseries.

Some growers prefer to mix their own foliar fertilizer in order to supply the proper nutrient at the critical time. Before bloom, in the early stages of growth, nitrogen is in highest demand. Just prior to blooming, the phosphates are most useful. And as fruit and seed develop and the plant matures, potash is particularly necessary.

Hydroponic feeding

Exact dilutions and programming are critical for hydroponic feeding. For the beginner, in fact, the best procedure is to purchase a commercial hydroponic formula from one of the manufacturers listed at the end of the chapter. If you want to try mixing your own formula, check the appendix for procedures.

Soluble salt damage

To many of us "salt" means the sodium chloride we put on our eggs at breakfast. This common salt is a compound made up of an acid-forming component, or chloride, and a basic or alkaline-forming component, or sodium, which combine to form a neutral compound called a salt.

Fertilizers also contain both the acid-forming and the alkaline-forming elements. Calcium, sodium, ammonium, potassium, and magnesium are basic, or alkaline, components of many fertilizers; sulphate, phosphate, nitrate, and bi-carbonate are examples of acid-forming components. They combine to form salts. Growth problems arise when there are more salts than the plants can use. The salts accumulate in the soil, causing damage to the roots, and accumulate in the leaf tips and margins, causing burn.

Symptoms of salt damage

The first symptoms of excess salts may be slow growth, yellowing of the leaf, or wilting. As the salt concentration increases, symptoms also can include leaf scorch, shedding of leaves, or even collapse of the entire plant (fig. 82). In all cases, however, it is the damaged root system that results in some of the above-ground symptoms.

Fig. 82
When the root system is destroyed by excess fertilizer salts, the entire plant collapses—watering thoroughly so water flushes through the pot helps solve the problem

Avoiding excess salt problems

The following suggestions can help you prevent salt problems:

1. Avoid single, heavy applications of fertilizer—try using some of the slow-release materials such as Osmocote or Precise time-release plant food

2. Water thoroughly and not too often (when the soil dries out, the concentration of salts in the remaining soil moisture increases, which can kill young seedlings); a thorough watering will leach excess salts down through the pot

3. Thoroughly soak old clay pots before re-using them because salts accumulate in the porous walls

4. Make certain the pot drains well; check it by setting it on a surface that permits good drainage

5. Be careful with feedlot manure as it is often high in urine residues and salt grain residues

6. If you are using sterilized soil, leach it thoroughly before using it for a potting mix

7. Check your water supply; in many areas there is a high concentration of salts in the natural water—you may have to use rainwater, distilled water, or even treat the water to remove excess salts before using it on plants (water softeners usually will not reduce the amount of salt content in the water, and deionizing equipment is too expensive for home use)

If you discover an excess salt problem, you should leach out the excess salts by the following process:

1. Flush out the pot using about 2 quarts of water for a 6-inch pot

2. Wait one hour and repeat

3. Wait another hour and repeat (for a total of three flushings)

4. Fertilize to replace the soil nutrients lost in the leaching process

One way of watering and feeding a single plant

Table 16
PLANT NUTRIENTS
Major Inorganic Elements

Inorganic Elements	Role in Plant	*Deficiency Symptoms	Correction Materials	N-P-K	Teaspoons per Gallon	Comments
Nitrogen (N)	Vegetative growth, primarily leaf and stem; green color and protein; food for soil micro-organisms	Stunted, yellow-ing from bottom up and leaf tip back to petiole	Ammonium sulfate	20-0-0	2	Heavy application may cause leaf tip burn; excess causes the plant to grow all leaf and stem, no flower and fruit (nitrates are available to plant without being broken down by bacteria)
(Acidic reaction)			Ammonium nitrate	33-0-0	1	
			Urea**	42-0-0	1	
(Alkaline reaction)	Same	Same	Sodium nitrate	16-0-0	2	
			Calcium nitrate	17-0-0	2	
			Potassium nitrate	12-0-44	1	
			Formulated products			
Phosphorus (P)	Flower and fruit production, root growth, seedling growth, seedling hardiness	Stunted short internodes, purple or dark green foliage; old leaves die back; flowers and fruit poor	Formulated soluble fertilizers	13-13-13 15-30-15 23-19-17 20-20-20	4 4 4 3	For soil mixes use 20% superphosphate, 2 oz. per bushel of soil (list of formulated fertilizers at end of chapter)
			Slow-release fertilizers (encapsulated liquids with metered release)	14-14-14 19-6-12 18-6-12 18-5-11	— — — —	Apply to top of pot as di-rected on package; slow release will feed from 3 months to 1 year or more
Potassium (K	Hardiness, root growth, manu-facture of sugar and starch, cell membranes	Older leaves scorched on margin; weak stem; fruit shrivelled	Muriate of potash	0-0-60	1	Most plants require large amounts of potash
			Potassium sulfate	0-0-48	1	
			Potassium nitrate	13-0-44	1	
			Formulated products	—	—	

Minor Inorganic Elements

Inorganic Elements	Role in Plant	*Deficiency Symptoms	Correction Materials	N-P-K	Teaspoons per Gallon	Comments
Boron (B)	Necessary for plant's use of calcium for cell-wall formation	Tip of growing plant dies; bud becomes light green; roots are brown in center; fruit is corky; flowers do not form	Boric acid H_3BO_3, 17% B		1 tsp. in 10 gal. water ($1/_{10}$ tsp. per gallon of water)	Amount needed is critical—excess will kill plant quickly
Calcium (Ca)	Necessary for cell-wall formation and division; is enzyme catalyst	Young leaves turn yellow then brown; growing tip bends; weak stem; short, dark roots	Calcium nitrate 37% Ca		2	Dry sources are lime and dolomite; used in soil mix 3 oz. per bushel

*See color table of symptoms in plate 24, between pages 84-85

**Urea—Biuret is a by-product of the manufacture of commercial urea preparations; it is toxic to plants and causes stunting, leaf scorch, yellowing of the leaves — look for a label that says "Biuret-free"

—Data not available at time of publication

Inorganic Elements	Role in Plant	Deficiency Symptoms	Correction Materials	Teaspoons Per Gallon	Comments
Copper (Cu)	Activates enzymes; necessary to photosynthesis and respiration; regulates soil nitrogen	Leaves appear bleached; new growth dies back	Copper sulphate 25% Cu	.001 oz. per gallon of water	Liquified seaweed and manures contain minute quantities — enough for home greenhouse use
Iron (Fe)	Chlorophyll formation; respiration of sugars to provide growth energy	Young leaves are yellow between veins first, top to bottom; veins, margins, and tips stay green	Sequestrene 330+ 10% Fe	.004 oz. per gallon of water	Read labels carefully to be sure you get all trace elements
Magnesium (Mg)	Chlorphyll production; enzyme manufacture	Leaves are thin, lose green color from between veins from bottom of plant up; tend to curve upward	Magnesium sulphate 10 Mg (epsom salts)	2	Available in some formulated products; strong light causes magnesium deficiency
Manganese (Mn)	Catalyst in growth process; formation of oxygen in photosynthesis	Tissue between veins turns white; leaves have dead spots; plant is dwarfed	Manganese sulphate 25% Mn	.001 oz. per gallon of water	Same
Molybdenum (Mo)	Nitrogen metabolism and fixation	Plant is very stunted and yellowed out	Sodium molybdate 22% Mo	.0001 oz. per gallon of water	Same
Sulphur (S)	Protein synthesis; water uptake from soil; fruit and seed maturity; speeds up decomposition; good fungicide	Lower leaves yellow; stem and root small in diameter; stems hard and brittle	Ammonium sulphate 24% S	2	Dry sources are powdered agricultural sulphur (1 oz. per bushel) or wood ashes
Zinc (Zn)	Chlorophyll formation, respiration, nitrogen metabolism	Terminal leaves are small; bud formation is poor; leaves have dead areas	Zinc sulphate 20-30% Zn	.001 oz. per gallon of water	Use a complete fertilizer including all minor or trace elements

For some plants there are other minor elements that play a part in the growth process, such as:

Chelating Agents:	Chemicals used principally with the minor elements to prevent "tie up" in the soil mix; this is why chelated iron, for example, is used to green up plants that have yellowed out
Chlorine:	Catalyst for oxygen production in photosynthesis, and chlorophyll production and water retention by plant cells
Cobalt:	Involved in nitrogen fixation in root nodules
Fritted Trace Elements:	Sprayed with hot ceramic material and then ground to a fine powder, making them insoluble but slowly available to the plant
Iodine:	Role unknown, but it seems to be necessary for some seaweeds
Sodium:	Affects the manner in which the plant uses potassium; it is needed by plants in a salty habitat and certain vegetable crops such as celery, beets, turnips, and chard

SOURCES

General information

CANADA:

Ball Red Book. Twelfth edition. Ball-Superior, Ltd., 1155 Birchview Dr., Mississauga, Ontario L5H 3E1

Chatelaine's Gardening Book. Lois Wilson. McLean-Hunter, 481 University Ave., Toronto, Ontario M5W 1A7

Gardening Under Glass. Jerome A. Eaton. Collier-MacMillan, Ltd., 1125 B Leslie St., Don Mills, Ontario

UNITED STATES:

Ball Red Book. Twelfth edition. Geo. J. Ball, Inc., P.O. Box 335, West Chicago, IL 60185

The Care and Feeding of Garden Plants. National Fertilizer Institute, 1015 18th St. N.W., Washington, DC 20036

Dictionary of Fertilizer Materials and Terms. American Fruit Grower Publishing Co., 37841 Euclid Ave., Willoughby, OH 44094

Gardening Under Glass. Jerome A. Eaton. MacMillan, 866 3rd Ave., New York, NY 10022

Ohio Florist's Association Bulletin. 2001 Fyffe Ct., Columbus, OH 43210

Soil Conditions and Plant Growth. E. W. Russell. John Wiley & Sons, 605 3rd Ave., New York, NY 10016

The U. C. System (Manual #23). Agricultural Publications, University of California, Berkeley, CA 94720

Western Fertilizer Handbook. California Fertilizer Assoc. 2222 Watts Ave., Sacramento, CA 95825

Supplies

UNITED STATES:

Controlled-release fertilizers

S & D Products, P.O. Box 66, Prairie du Chien, WI 53821

Sierra Chemical Co., 1001 Yosemite Dr., Milpitas, CA 95035

3M Co., 3M Center, AC & S Div., St. Paul, MN 55101

There are also many others.

General purpose dry fertilizers

Brantwood Publications, 850 Elm Grove Rd., Elm Grove, WI 53122

Home and Garden Supply Merchandiser, P.O. Box 67, Minneapolis, MN 55440

Intertec Publishing Co., 1014 Wyandotte St., Kansas City, MO 64105

There are several other buyer's guides that also have complete lists of manufacturers.

Soluble fertilizers

Alaska (Atlas) Fish Fertilizers, 865 Lind Ave. S.W., Renton, WA 98055

Robert Peters Co., 2833 Pennsylvania St., Allentown, PA 18104

Plant Marvel Laboratories, 624 W. 119th St., Chicago, IL 60628

Ra-Pid Gro Corp., 88 Ossian St., Dansville, NY 14437

See Nutrition Deficiency Symptoms
Plate 24, facing page 85

You can foliar feed hanging plants overhead with an extension mist sprayer

Bonsai is the most refined art of plant growth control

Chapter 12

GROWTH REGULATION AND CONTROL

FACTORS LIMITING GROWTH

We usually grow plants in a greenhouse with a specific objective in mind. Many options are possible in regulating plant growth; for example, you can seek to produce only foliage, or flowers with foliage, or fruit with foliage. You also could wish to dwarf the growth of a plant, as in bonsai, or to accelerate the growth, as with a vine. You may simply want to eliminate unwanted growth. Whatever the objective, by using growing practices that vary the growth-limiting factors, you can achieve a proper balance for optimal growth.

The factors that limit growth are water, light, temperature, humidity, nutrition, soil quality, and pruning. In general, when you increase or decrease any one of the growth factors, you should increase or decrease them all proportionally.

On the following pages, the first table indicates how the growth factors affect plants, including further references for requirements of specific plants. A second table delineates the hormones or chemicals that regulate growth. Please note that the dilutions of hormone-growth regulators and chemicals are very precise—the materials are manufactured in different strengths and under many brand names. Read the labels carefully and follow the manufacturer's directions for each product.

ACCLIMATIZATION

Plants you buy from a commercial greenhouse have been grown under optimal conditions. If you take them home to your greenhouse, you can continue the same treatment. If you plan to use them in your home, however, they should be "acclimatized" first, or gradually adjusted to the new environment, since growing conditions will be less than ideal (especially for foliage plants). Acclimatize the plants in your greenhouse using the following three steps:

1. Shade the plant to reduce the light intensity during part of each day—some plants put out new leaves that are structurally different in order to survive in the low light available in most homes (see diagram in the appendix)

2. Water heavily and often to leach the fertilizer salts out of the soil mix

3. For the first year, feed lightly once every three months with an organic, low-in-nitrogen fertilizer, such as fish emulsion—increase the feeding to once a month as the plant grows

ALLELOPATHY

Many plants produce inhibitory or toxic by-products that act to regulate the growth of other plants. The discovery of this phenomenon has led to a new field of study called allelopathy. The plants produce tanins, terpenes, phenolic compounds, and alkaloids, which are released from the roots into the soil and from the leaves into the air. Some of the products released into the soil act as growth inhibitors to prevent the germination of seed. Some of the chemicals volatilized into the air may act as insect repellants, which would explain the old idea of "companion planting" (see chapter 13). Gardening literature contains many references to keeping aphis out of the roses, for example, by planting chives or

Table 17
PLANT GROWTH MANAGEMENT

Growth Factor	Optimum	Excess	Deficiency
Water	Amount of water varies with the other factors (see chapter 7)	Plant is yellowed, has soft rot, no flowers or fruit; becomes disease-prone	Plant grows slowly or is stunted; has leaf drop, wilting; bears early but small flowers and fruit
Light	(For specific candlepower needs, see chapter 3)	Leaf becomes scorched; plant has no flowers or fruit	Plant has elongated, pale growth (etiolation); no flowers or fruit
Temperature	(For specific temperature needs, see chapter 4)	Plant has soft rapid growth; becomes leaf scorched; has poor or no flowers and fruit	Plant grows slowly or is stunted; becomes leaf scorched; has poor or no flowers or fruit
Humidity	(For details on humidity control, see chapter 8)	Plant is disease-prone, has soft growth, and poor flowers and fruit	Plant grows slowly; has wilting, leaf drop; bears no flowers or fruit
Fertilizer	High nitrogen for foliage only, high phosphate for flowers and fruit (see chapter 11)	Plant has rapid, soft growth; leaves and roots burn; has no flowers or fruit	Plant is stunted, yellowing, has small or no flowers or fruit
Soil	If the soil is well aerated, well drained, loose and friable, growth will be optimum; if the soil is hard packed, poorly drained and aerated, the plant will be stunted with poor flowers and fruit		
Pruning (for bonsai)	Too much root pruning or top pruning may kill the plant; a balance between both must be maintained		

garlic among the plants in the rose bed. These natural repellants also may well account for why, in some instances, Peruvian Ground Cherry (Nicandra physalodes) planted in the greenhouse controls white fly.

BONSAI

Perhaps the ultimate in growth control is the art of bonsai. Bonsai began with plants collected from mountain and rock habitats where nature produced gnarled and dwarfed growth forms. Just as early man domesticated animals and brought them into his dwelling, so he collected dwarf plants and kept them. In the Orient, bonsai became an art reflecting the aesthetic and spiritual rapport people felt with living things. A hundred-year-old ficus passed down from one generation to another exemplifies the intertwining of the lives of plants and people.

Growth control in bonsai consists of pruning both the top of the plant and the roots to create a minimum-growth balance between top and bottom. This means pruning on a regular schedule to suit the specific plant. By managing the following growth factors, you can keep the plant small and growing well in a small container.

1. Light: except for new growth, which should be shaded, light usually is not restricted —use an upper shelf in the greenhouse

2. Temperature: in general, keep the temperature on the cool side for the particular plants you are growing—hardy plants will take temperatures down to freezing; tender plants need higher temperatures

Table 18
PLANT GROWTH RESPONSE

Growth Regulators	Flowers and Fruit	Stem	Leaf	Other
Abcisic acid (ABA)	Suppresses bud growth; induces dormancy; inhibits germination	No effect	Promotes stomatal closure, leaf drop, defoliation	
Amo-1618	No effect	Reduces height	No effect	Persists in soil for 10 years; experimental, not widely tested on many varieties
A-Rest	Increases bud count	Shortens internodes	Intensifies color	Best bet for foliage plants; aids rooting; lasts 1 year
Auxins Indoleacetic Acid (IAA) Indolebutyric Acid (IBA) Naphthalene Acetic Acid (NAA)	Induces flowering; is an artificial pollinator	Inhibits bud development; increases internode length; stimulates cell division	Delays leaf drop	Initiates roots; accelerates callus in tissue culture; acts as plant tonic
B-Nine	No effect	Shortens internodes	Darkens foliage	Aids rooting azaleas, mums; lasts 3-4 weeks
Cycocel	Increases bud set	Shortens internodes	Intensifies color	Use on azaleas, hydrangeas; lasts 3-4 weeks
Cytokinins Kinetin Zeatin 6-benzyl adenine (PBA)	Promotes seed germination	Promotes cell division	Promotes leaf expansion; slows leaf aging	Promotes bud formation and cell division in tissue culture
Ethylene Ethephon Florel	Induces flowering; speeds ripening	Inhibits cell elongation; stunting; swelling	Promotes leaf drop	Promotes germination, aids rooting (see chapter 17)
Gibberellins Gibrel (26 known kinds)	Induces flowering in long-day plants; increases % of seed germination; increases size of fruit; produces seedless fruit	Increases shoot growth; elongates inter-nodes	Increases ratio of leaf surface to internode length	Breaks dormancy of seed (see chapter 17)
Phosfon-L	No effect	Shortens plant	No effect	Persistent in the soil
Phytochrome	Regulates pig-ments, flowering time, germination, ripening	Regulates stem elongation	Regulates leaf expansion, chlorophyll production	Accelerates cell division

Dilutions for Experimental Use:
Research is in progress on the specific uses and dilutions for growth control. The dilutions indicated here are for test purposes and should not be used on choice specimen plant material

(See "Tables and Measures" in the General Appendix for ppm* data)

A-Rest
(ancymidol)

4 ppm or 2 oz. of .0264% ancymidol in 1 gal. water; apply 4 oz. of the diluted solution to one 6-inch pot

B-Nine

5,000 ppm or 12 oz. B-Nine in 1 gal. water; apply 8 oz. of the diluted solution to one 6-inch pot

Cycocel

2,000 ppm or 2 oz. of 11.8% cycocel in 1 gal. water; apply 6 oz. of the diluted solution to one 6-inch pot

Florel
(ethephon)

300 ppm or 1 oz. in 1 gal. water

Gibrel
(.5% potassium gibberellate)

5 ppm or 1 tsp. in 1 gal. water

*ppm = parts per million

---

3. Water: water usually is applied often, sometimes several waterings per day, because the soil mix for bonsai has perfect drainage and all the water goes through the pot (amount varies with the type of plant)

4. Fertilizing: fertilizing is best done with low nitrogen, organic fertilizers—apply as indicated on the package about three times per year during the growing season for each particular plant

Recently, selected cultivars of dwarfed chrysanthemums have become available. Perennial bonsai with chrysanthemums and other indoor plants offers some new challenges for experimentation that might well include experimenting with growth retardants such as Amo-1618, which has a ten-year residual period. A list of plants for bonsai is in the appendix.

REGULATING GROWTH TO PRODUCE VITAMINS

A green plant is an efficient organic chemical factory that manufactures or synthesizes an enormous number of products, one of which is vitamins. In order for plants to be self-sufficient producers of vitamins, however, they must be fed the minor elements from which they manufacture the vitamins. This means that if you are growing food plants in a hobby greenhouse, your feeding program should provide not only nitrogen, phosphate, and potash, but all the trace or minor elements listed in chapter 11 as well.

VITAMIN	SOURCE
Vitamin A	The materials from which Vitamin A is formed are found in all parts of the plant—they become Vitamin A in the animal body
Vitamin B	
B$_1$ thiamine	Chiefly in leaves
B$_2$ riboflavin	In all parts of the plant
Niacin (nicotinic acid)	Chiefly in grains and fruits
B$_6$	In all parts of the plant
Pantothenic acid	Chiefly in grains and fruits
Biotin	In all parts of the plant
B$_{12}$	In most plant parts, especially seaweed
Folic acid	Chiefly in leaves and mushrooms
Vitamin C	In all parts, highest in leaves and in certain fruits
Vitamin D	Found only in animals—plants contain precursors converted to Vitamin D by ultraviolet light—they become Vitamin D in the animal body
Vitamin E	Leaves and fruits, some grains
Vitamin K	Chiefly in leaves

One of the best sources of these raw materials from which the plant makes vitamins is fertilizer from the sea, such as whole fish emulsion or seaweed. If you are in doubt as to minor element content of your fertilizer, apply a separate minor element in addition to the fertilizer you are using. The preceding list indicates vitamins that are synthesized by plants.

STIMULATING GROWTH

Both vitamins and hormones are used in making products that are marketed as plant tonics. These mixtures can be used profitably in growing situations that require stimulation of the natural plant processes. Following are some examples of circumstances in which a plant tonic could be useful. Sources of tonics are listed at the end of the chapter.

1. Transplanting or repotting a plant: whenever you do anything to a plant that damages or destroys the fine root-hairs system, the plant suffers a setback—tonics will trigger new root growth

2. Wilted plant: sometimes you receive badly wilted plants in the mail—tonics often will help get fluids back into the plant tissue

3. Sickly plant: there are times when a plant just does not grow well, but you can find nothing clearly wrong—tonics may well trigger natural growth processes to start the plant on the road to recovery

CONTROL OF WEED GROWTH

Why should you worry about weeds in and around the greenhouse? Because weeds are not only aesthetically offensive, but also rob your plants of water, light, and nutrients. In addition, they provide the optimal environment for insects and disease, both of which can spread to your own choice plants.

Inside the greenhouse, along the walls and under the benches, and outside, bordering the greenhouse, weeds find the ideal conditions for growth. Control measures are not difficult—and not only can save considerable expense for fungicides and insecticides, but will give you extra growing space under the benches as well.

Mechanical control

You can clean out the under-bench area in a small greenhouse with a good scuffle hoe. Because weed seed blows in, or is carried in on your feet, cleaning must be done frequently. Weeding the area outside thoroughly also will help reduce the incidence of weeds inside the greenhouse.

Chemical control

If you weed by hand, there will still be weed seed and perhaps spores of fungi and bacteria in the soil under the benches. After weeding, it, therefore, is worthwhile to spray the ground with a compound to reduce disease and pest residues. Some compounds available are formulated with vegetable oils, copper oleate, pyrethrins, rotenone, cube resins, ethylene compounds, iron, zinc, and manganese from soybean oil. Apply according to package instructions, and let the soil sit for forty-eight hours before you plant or place flats of growing material on it.

If you prefer to keep only clean earth under the benches, a long residual spray such as Karmex is necessary. Karmex contains diuron, which kills by absorption through the root system as well as the leaves; it is consequently more effective on young weeds than on older growth. Apply Karmex at the rate of 1 ounce (6 teaspoons) per gallon of water to cover 400 square feet. Karmex does not volatilize readily and will not damage plants on the benches; but to be certain, remove choice plants for a couple of days after applying the chemical. To control older growth, also use a wetting agent, which will increase the effectiveness of the weed killer as much as 50 percent.

Cautions

There are many compounds that should not be used in the greenhouse because they volatilize and will damage plants on the benches. Avoid any 2- or 4-D and 2-, 4-, or 5-T compounds; Casoron used under the benches will defoliate the plants on the bench, and such things as kerosene and diesel oil give off fumes that also will damage plants.

Outside the greenhouse

For clean, bare soil outside the greenhouse, use Karmex as directed above. Even more profitably, the areas around the greenhouse might be weeded and then planted to herbs, vegetables, or ornamentals.

SOURCES

General information

CANADA:
Commercial Flower Forcing. Laurie, Kiplinger, and Nelson. Seventh edition. McGraw-Hill, 330 Progress Ave., Scarborough, Ontario M1P 2Z5

The Living Plant. Peter M. Ray. Holt, Rinehart and Winston, 55 Horner Ave., Toronto, Ontario

UNITED STATES:
Commercial Flower Forcing. Laurie, Kiplinger, and Nelson. Seventh edition. McGraw-Hill, 1221 Ave. of the Americas, New York, NY 10020

Control Mechanisms in Plant Development. A. W. Galston and P. J. Davies. Prentice-Hall, Englewood Cliffs, NJ 07632

Cornell Recommendations for Commercial Floriculture Crops. Dept. of Floriculture, Cornell University, Ithaca NY 14850

The Experimental Control of Plant Growth. F.W. Went. Ronald Press, 79 Madison Ave., New York, NY 10016

Plant Propagation. Hudson T. Hartman and Dale E. Kester. Prentice-Hall, Englewood Cliffs, NJ 07632

Plant Propagation. John P. Mahlstede and Ernest S. Haber, John Wiley & Sons, 605 3rd Ave., New York, NY 10016

Bonsai

UNITED STATES:
Bonsai, Sakei, Bonkei. R. L. Behme. William Morrow, 105 Madison Ave., New York, NY 10016

Bonsai for Americans. G. F. Hull. Doubleday, 277 Park Ave., New York, NY 10017

Bonsai Handbook. Brooklyn Botanic Gardens, 1000 Washington Ave., Brooklyn, New York, NY 11225

Bonsai Techniques. John Yoshio Naka. Bonsai Institute of California, P.O. Box 78211, Los Angeles, CA 90016

WORLD:
Kanuti: A New Way in Bonsai. W. E. Bolleman. Faber & Faber, 3 Queen Square, London, WCIN 3AU, England

Supplies

Chemicals

See the General Appendix, Sources of Supply, for a list of suppliers.

Plants

UNITED STATES:
Sunnyside Gardens (chrysanthemums for bonsai), 8638 Huntington Dr., San Gabriel, CA 91775

Tonics

UNITED STATES:
Brooker Chemical (Hormex vitamin hormone concentrate), P.O. Box 9335, North Hollywood, CA 91606

Vitamin Institute (Superthrive), 5411 Satsuma Ave., North Hollywood, CA 91603

A pyramid greenhouse—capitalizing on the theory that plants grow better due to concentration of energy brought about by the form of the structure

©Copyright, David Scharf, 1975

Red spider mite magnified nearly 700 times through the use of an electron microscope

INSECTS AND PESTS

For years the standard procedure for pest and disease control has been frequent and generous applications of chemicals—until it was evident that pests become immune to chemicals and that the environment is sensitive to toxic pesticides. With the changing ecological awareness, most growers have turned to integrated pest management through a combination of cultural, biological, ecological, mechanical, and chemical control methods *(figs. 83, 84,* and *85).*

Fig. 84
White fly is another major insect problem (magnified three times)

One of the most serious pests, red spider mite, infesting a plant (magnified 2½ times)—when webbing is this severe, major plant damage has already occurred
Fig. 83

Left unchecked, mealybug builds to a major destructive force (magnified two times)
Fig. 85

CULTURAL CONTROL

Cultural control begins with careful sanitation. Use good disinfectants such as LF-10 and Clorox (*see chapter 14*). The following annual sanitation checklist should help you get your greenhouse in a state of cleanliness that discourages insects, pests, and diseases alike.

Annual sanitation checklist

☐ Take all the plants out of the greenhouse, then spray everything inside with LF-10 or Clorox

☐ Remove all debris, dead plants, flats, pots, etc.

☐ Remove weeds from under the benches (*see chapter 12*)

☐ Install several hooks on which to hang the hose

☐ Make sure you have a can of Clorox solution in which to dip all hand tools

☐ Put new plants in a separate quarantine case or room before moving them into the greenhouse

☐ Clean up the potting shed or adjacent structures

☐ Make sure you have plenty of air circulation (*see chapter 8*)

☐ Clean up all outside weeds adjacent to the greenhouse

Once you have the facility cleaned, here are some cultural procedures that can help keep it sanitary:

1. Buy pre-sterilized soil mix or pasteurize your own (*see chapter 9*)

2. Keep the temperature constant to avoid shock from rapid changes of temperature

3. Space the plants on the bench to allow good air circulation

4. Try to avoid wetting the foliage; water in the early morning, so the sun can dry off any water you spill on the leaves

5. Check your plants often with a good hand lens for early signs of pests or diseases

6. Use resistant varieties! Go over the seed catalogues carefully (*see seed sources in chapter 17*), and you will find many new varieties of both flowers and vegetables that are resistant to a wide range of diseases and pests

BIOLOGICAL CONTROL

As mentioned, considerable interest has developed recently in controlling insects and other forms of life with materials from nature. There are many species of plants that contain alkaloids with insecticidal properties. Following is a partial list of these natural chemicals, all of which are available in formulations at most nurseries and garden centers.

NATURAL CHEMICALS	SOURCE	CONTROLS
Nicotine	Tobacco	Aphis, thrips, white fly, spider mite, leafhopper
Pyrethrum	Chrysanthemum	Aphis and other soft-bodied insects
Ryania	Ryania speciosa (South America)	Corn borer
Rotenone	Derris cube	Many common insects
Sabadilla	Lily family (Venezuela)	Leaf feeders
Dimboa	Corn	Borers
Basic H	Soybean	Thrips, aphis, red spider
Quassia	Ailanthus	Aphis, others not known
Oak leaf	Smoke	Aphis
Wilt-pruf	Liquid polyethylene	Aphis, spider mite

Recipes for home-grown remedies

Following are some recipes for concoctions used by various growers for control of soft-bodied insects, such as flies, aphis, and mites. Perhaps these recipes will suggest some experimenting at home with other plant brews that might control common insects.

1. Put in a blender: 8-10 spearmint leaves, 6 onion tops, 2 Tbs. of horseradish, 3-4 red hot peppers

Add just enough water to make an emulsion

Pour the emulsion into a gallon jug with 1 Tbs. of detergent, and fill with water

Apply undiluted

2. Put the juice from one garlic clove in a pint of water

Add 1 Tbs. of cayenne pepper, 2 tsp. of mineral oil, 1 tsp. of detergent

Mix well or blend

This pint makes a stock solution — apply by diluting 2 Tbs. of stock in 1 qt. of water

3. Steep 1 tsp. of tobacco in 1 qt. of water

Apply undiluted with a small hand sprayer

4. Mash 1 c. of turnip

Add 2 Tbs. of corn oil and 1 pt. of water

Apply undiluted

Predators

There are well over 300 species of insects that prey upon other insects. Some of these currently are available for use at home. A gallon of ladybugs costing $7.00 or $8.00, for example, is one way of getting rid of aphis, mites, and scale. Following are some common available predators that are safe to handle.

PREDATOR	PREY
Lace wing	Aphis
Praying mantis	Aphis and others
Spider	Flying insects
Wasp (Encarsia) (Macrocentrus) (Aphelinus)	Aphis and others
Beetle (Vedalia Lady) (Ground-Calosoma)	Aphis, scale, mealybug Caterpillars
Fly (Syrphid)	Aphis

Parasites

There is a host of parasitic microorganisms that feeds on insects; for example, 250 kinds of virus, 80 bacteria, 460 fungi, 250 protozoa, and 20 rickettsia are all organisms that live in or on an insect.

Parasites presently available for insect control are Bacillus thuringiensis, which is used to control caterpillars of moths and butterflies, and Milky spore bacteria (B. popilliae), which controls Japanese beetle. No doubt, with continuing research there will be more parasites available for control of other destructive insects.

Plants that repel insects

There are many species of plants that repel insects by volatilizing chemicals into the air or by exuding chemicals through the root system. The classical example of the phenomenon is the Peruvian Ground Cherry (Nicandra physaloides), which, as mentioned, usually will keep an 8-by-8 or 8-by-12-foot greenhouse free of white fly. Other plants that apparently have repellant properties are tansy, sage, rosemary, mint, basil, osage orange, coriander, anise, and others.

This, again, is a fertile field for experimentation by home greenhouse owners. If you try plants that repel insects with success, report your findings to magazines like *Plants Alive*, so that everyone can profit from your experiments.

ECOLOGICAL CONTROL

Wherever your greenhouse is located, it is part of an ecosystem — a complex of relationships between a particular environment and the life forms in it. There are several things you can do to manage your ecosystem so it becomes a better place in which to grow greenhouse plants.

1. Remove or destroy all the pest and disease habitats around the greenhouse; clean up any debris, old flats, pots, branches, leaves, etc.; remove weeds and grass in the greenhouse area

2. Use species that repel insects for landscape plantings around the greenhouse

3. Keep pets out of the greenhouse — they are carriers of weed seed, fungal spores, bacteria, and other organisms that can cause problems for the grower

4. Install screens on the door and on the air intake louvres to prevent airborne pathogens from entering the greenhouse

5. Encourage birds to take up residence in your ecosystem—a single brood of young sparrows, for example, may consume as many as 2,000 insects or larvae in a single day—birds need trees and nesting materials such as dried grass, hair, moss, string, straw, rootlets, and mud (robins, sparrows, nuthatches, brown creepers, chickadees, warblers, finches, crows, bluejays, towhees, juncos, and woodpeckers are among the species of birds that will help control the insect population)

CHEMICAL CONTROL

About a hundred years ago, when there was a major grasshopper infestation, the only chemicals available for control were Paris green, kerosene, coal oil, and soap. At the turn of the century, however, chemical companies began to formulate and manufacture special products for agricultural as well as home use. Now, we have thousands of chemicals and laws to govern their use. In situations where biological controls are not rapid enough to save choice plants, you must rely on chemicals for quick control. See *table 19* (p. 106) for a list of commonly used pesticides.

Rating toxicity

When you go to the store to purchase chemicals, pick up the product and read the label. It will be marked with one of the following three designations: danger, poison; warning; or caution. (For details of toxicity, see the appendix.)

The words DANGER, POISON, and a skull-and-crossbones symbol mean a highly toxic compound with LD50 rating of 0-50 mg./kg.; this includes chemicals such as Systox, Di-Systox, Parathion, Temik, Zectran, and others that are formulated for commercial use—in most states a permit is required (home and garden products containing these chemicals have been formulated at low concentrations to reduce the hazard to the user and do not require the DANGER or POISON designation)

Moderately toxic materials have the word WARNING on the label—with an LD50 range of 50-500 mg./kg., an ounce to a pint is a lethal dose for humans—some of the familiar controls fall into this group, such as Chlordane, Diazinon, Meta Systox-R, Pyrethrum, Vapona, and others.

The word CAUTION appears on the label of slightly toxic chemicals with an LD50 rating of 500-5,000 mg./kg.; this includes any of the other chemicals you may find available, such as Captan, Malathion, Kelthane, Ferbam, Fixed Coppers, and others (these compounds are properly labeled CAUTION and should be used with care; depending upon the chemical, an ounce to a pint could be fatal, especially for children)

Precautions

With all chemicals, it is essential to observe proper precautions.

1. Don't inhale or swallow chemicals; be careful not to spill them on your skin

2. Store all chemicals in a locked cabinet away from children

3. Don't smoke while handling pesticides

4. Dispose of used cans or bottles properly—if you don't know how, call the State Health Department, or the nearest Poison Information Center (if you need help locating either of these, call your county agricultural extension agent)

5. Please take the one to three minutes necessary to read the label!

Insect growth regulators

Chemicals that arrest the life cycle of an insect in the larval stage or earlier are called juvenile hormones. Hormonal control, unlike other pest controls, reduces insect population gradually. Chemicals that act to influence the life cycle or behavior of the insect, such as sex attractants, are called pheremones. Sources of insect growth regulators are listed at the end of the chapter.

Combination sprays

Don't try mixing your own pesticide chemicals. Combining chemicals incorrectly may arrange the molecular structure so that two safe compounds become toxic to humans as well as to plants, or so that the mixture becomes a crystalline precipitate, a lumpy solution, a gelatinous mass, or simply a useless compound incapable of controlling anything!

Most nurseries and garden centers carry combination insecticide sprays that the manufacturer has formulated and found safe as well as effective. These will control most of the ills encountered by the average home greenhouse grower. If your hobby has expanded into a sizable operation, you may want to use controls listed in *table 19* (p. 106) or have a licensed pesticide applicator come in and spray for you.

Phytotoxicity

Phytotoxicity is plant injury caused by application of chemicals. Greenhouse pesticides generally have been selected to prohibit injury to foliage or flowers, but there are some sensitivities that should be avoided. Read formulation labels carefully for phytotoxicity information. If you are in doubt, try the chemical on one leaf before treating the entire plant. Following is a phytotoxicity list:

CHEMICAL	CAUSES INJURY TO
Diazinon	Gardenia, Poinsettia, Schefflera, ferns, Stephanotis, Hibiscus, Cordyline
Dimethoate (Cygon)	Many tropical foliage plants, ferns, Gloxinia, Yucca, Norfolk pine, Begonia, Geranium
Kelthane	Pepermoia, Schefflera, Cordyline, Codiaeum (do not use if temperature is over 75°F)
Malathion	Ferns, Orchid, African violet, Gloxinia, Rieger begonia, Aralia, Ficus, Peperomia
Meta-Systox R	Geranium, Rieger begonia, ivies, Peperomia, lillies
Nicotine	Ferns, Gardenia, Kalanchoe, lilies
Sevin	Pilea, Schefflera, Boston ivy, Peperomia, Syngonium
Tedion	Schefflera, roses

Wetting agents

Besides their role in water absorption, as explained in chapter 7, wetting agents, or surfactants, can be added to spray solutions to lower the surface tension and allow the liquid to flow over leaf surfaces. These chemicals spread the pesticide into the folds and crevises of the plant to improve the "wetting" of materials as diverse as powdery mildew and peat moss.

Most pesticides and fungicides are formulated with a wetting agent or spreader-sticker; with those not so formulated, you can increase the effectiveness of the spray by adding a wetting agent. There are many brand names of surfactants such as X-77, Triton B 1956, and Brand X Spreader-sticker. Application and dilution directions are on the labels.

Control of pests

Control of any severe problems with rats, mice, moles, and other vertebrate animals involves the use of extremely toxic chemicals that are best applied by a licensed professional applicator. In most major cities they are listed in the yellow pages. Extension agencies also have this type of information available.

MECHANICAL CONTROLS

Baits

Slugs and snails usually are controlled with metaldehyde formulated in baits with cereal grains and molasses. Earwigs can be controlled with baits containing sodium fluoride or sodium fluosilicate.

Pheremones, or chemicals volatilized by insects, can also be used as bait. One method, for example, involves placing a female insect in a simple box trap with a sticky substance to restrain the captive male insects. Zoecon Corporation now has such pheremone baits for coddling moth, oriental fruit moth, some leaf rollers, maggot fruit fly, white fly, and spruce budworm. In addition, synthetic pheremones have been found effective on over thirty species of insects and may well replace many other types of insect and pest control.

Traps

It is sound ecological procedure to use traps to control the insect population in a home greenhouse. Traps using a sticky substance have been in use for many years. There also are traps available that control insects by drowning them in soapy water or by electrocution. In both cases, the insects are attracted by black light, and most of the control is accomplished during evening and night hours. Daylight traps seem to attract more insects if they are painted yellow.

Table 19
PESTICIDES
Danger, Highly Toxic:
Oral or Dermal LD50 Rating of 0-100°

Chemical Trade Name	Chemical Common Name	Type	Use	LD50 Rating Oral	Dermal	Teaspoons per Gallon Dilution
Aldrite (4 EC)	Aldrin	Hydrocarbon	Weevils	39	98	8
Azodrin (4 EC)	Monarotophos	Organic phosphate	Mites	20	342	1½
Bidrin (2 EC)	Dicrotophos	Organic phosphate	Leaf miner	22	225	2
Dieldrite (50 W)	Dieldrin	Chlorinated hydrocarbon	Weevils	46	90	2½
Di-Syston (15%)	Disulfoton	Organic phosphate, 15% granular systemic	Leaf miner, aphis, mites, white fly	7	15	2½ oz. per inch of stem diameter
Guthion (2 EC)	Azinphosmethyl	Organic phosphate	Aphis, mites, leaf feeders	13	220	3
Lindane (25 W)	Lindane	Chlorinated hydrocarbon	Aphis, borers, fungus, gnat	88	1,000	1
Lannate	Methomyl	Carbamate	Caterpillars	17	1,500	¼ - ½
Meta-Systox (R 2 EC)	Oxydemeton-methyl	Organic phosphate, systemic	Aphis	65	250	½
Nicotine (40 EC sulphate)	Same	From tobacco, commercial varieties	Aphis	83	285	1 - 4
Systox (2 EC)	Demeton	Organic phosphate	Aphis, white fly, mealybug, scale	6	14	1 - 2
Temik (10% granular)	Aldicarb	Carbamate	Nematodes, aphis, white fly, mites	1	5	See label for application
Thimet (15% granular)	Phorate	Organic phosphate	Seed treatment	4	630	See label for application
Trithion (25W)	Carbophenothion	Organic phosphate	Bagworms, mites, scale	32	1,270	1 - 2
Vapona (4E)	Dichlorvos	Organic phosphate	Many insects	56	107	1
Zectran	Mexacarbate	Carbamate	Slugs, scale, mites, white fly, aphis	19	2,500	2 - 3

Warning, Moderately Toxic:
Oral or Dermal LD50 Rating of 100-500°

Chemical Trade Name	Chemical Common Name	Type	Use	LD50 Rating Oral	Dermal	Teaspoons per Gallon Dilution
Baytex (4 EC)	Fenthion	Organic phosphate	Aphis, leaf feeders, mites	310	330	1 - 2
Chlordane (45 EC)	Same	Chlorinated hydrocarbon	Bagworms, soil insects	335	840	2
Cygon (2 EC)	Dimethoate	Organic phosphate	White fly, leaf miner, scale	215	400	2
Diazinon 4 (Spectracide)	Same	Organic	Aphis, leaf miner, roaches	466	900	3
Dibrom (8 EC)	Naled	Organic phosphate	Mites, aphis, white fly	430	1,100	1
Dursban (2 EC)	Chlorpyrifos	Organic phosphate	Mites, leaf hoppers, aphis	500	1,000	2
Dylox (4 LS)	Trichlorfon	Organic phosphate	Bagworms, webworms	500	2,000	2

Chemical Trade Name	Chemical Common Name	Type	Use	LD50 Rating Oral	Dermal	Teaspoons per Gallon Dilution
Ethion (.15 + oil)	Fenthion	Organic phosphate	Scale	119	915	16
Entex (3 EC)	Same	Organic phosphate	Aphis, mites	310	330	1 - 2
Furadan (10% granular)	Carbofuran	Carbamate systemic	Weevils, many insects	132	10,000	See label for application
Heptachlor (20% granular)	Same	Chlorinated hydrocarbon	Weevils	100	195	See label for application
Imidan (50W)	Chloraniform-methane	Organic phosphate	Caterpillars	216	3,000	
Pirimor (50 W)	Same	Carbamate	Aphis	—	—	½
Pyrethrum	Same	From plants (Derris)	Aphis, white fly, webworms	200	1,800	See label for application
Resmethrin	SBP-1382	Synthetic phrethroid	White fly, others	—	—	1
Rotenone	Same	From plants (Derris)	Aphis, leaf eaters	145	940	See label for application
Thiodan (50 W)	Endosulfan	Chlorinated hydrocarbon	Aphis, white fly, mites, borers	110	359	3

Caution, Slightly Toxic:
Oral or Dermal LD50 Rating of 500-5,000 or More[°]

Chemical Trade Name	Chemical Common Name	Type	Use	LD50 Rating Oral	Dermal	Teaspoons per Gallon Dilution
Acaraban (4 EC)	Chlorbenzilate	Chlorinated hydrocarbon	Mites	1,220	5,000	½
Cythion (57 EC)	Malathion	Organic phosphate	Aphis, scale, mealybug, thrips	1,375	4,500	2
Kelthane (1.6 EC)	Dicofol	Chlorinated hydrocarbon	Mites	1,100	1,230	1 - 2
Marlate	Methoxychlor	Chlorinated hydrocarbon	Beetles, webworms, leaf eaters	5,000	6,000	4
Morestan (25 W)	Oxythioquinox	Organic carbonate	Mites	1,800	2,000	1
Orthene (75 W)	Acephate	Organic phosphate	Aphis, caterpillars	945	866	1 pkg./2 gal.
Pentac (50W)	Same	Chlorinated compound	Mites, two-spot	—	3,200	2
Plictran (50 W)	Same	Organic tin	Mites	1,676	—	1
Sevin (50 W)	Carbaryl	Carbamate	Leaf eaters	850	4,000	3
Tedion (1 EC)	Tetradifon	Sulfone	Mite eggs	14,700	—	2

Exempt: Non-Toxic[°]

Chemical Trade Name	Chemical Common Name	Type	Use	LD50 Rating Oral	Dermal	Teaspoons per Gallon Dilution
Dormant oil	Same	Highly refined oil	Scale, mites, aphis eggs	Exempt	Exempt	See label for application
Thuricide	Bacillus thuringiensis	Bacterial spores	Moth larvae, lepidoptera	Exempt	Exempt	See label for application

[°] Check for restricted use regulations
Abbreviations: EC = emulsified concentrate
　　　　　　　LS = liquid solution
　　　　　　　W = wettable powder
　　　　　　　— = no figures available

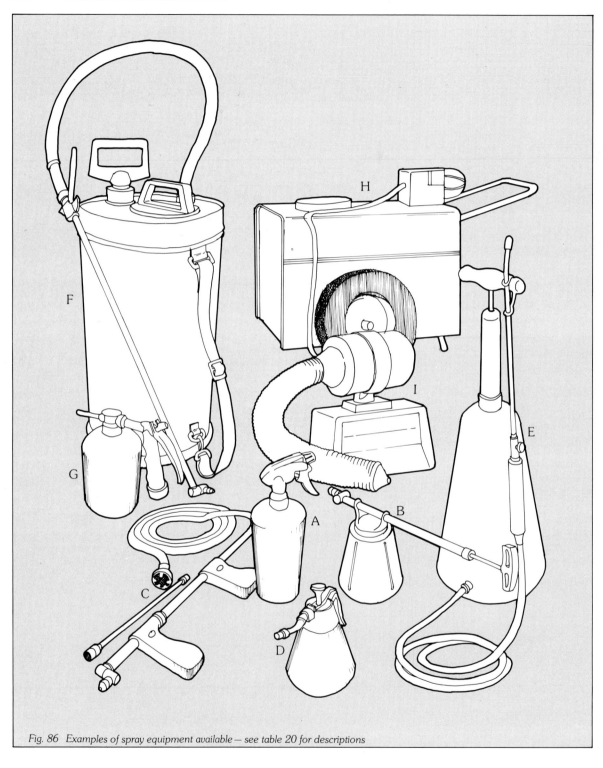

Fig. 86 Examples of spray equipment available — see table 20 for descriptions

IDENTIFYING INSECTS AND PESTS

The illustrated insect and pest control table *(plates 25-28)* should help you to identify and treat pest problems. If you are stumped and need further help, however, try your local nursery or garden center first. If your problem is not one they can solve, go next to government or university extension agencies, where you will find highly trained personnel and the necessary equipment for dealing with the more difficult problems. See also *table 16* for more information on insect identification.

See Pest Control Basics table
Plates 25-28
between pages 116-117

SPRAYING EQUIPMENT

Most stores sell a bewildering array of devices for spraying plants. One of the quickest and easiest ways to spray is the aerosol can. Aerosols contain an insecticide chemical mixed with a liquified gas, which acts as the propellant. The can is airtight, with a tube leading from the solution to a valve with a pinhole nozzle. When the valve is depressed, the liquid gas rushes out through the nozzle taking the insecticide with it. Hold the can 18 inches away from a plant to avoid damage to the foliage.

Care of spray equipment

Many of the problems people have with sprayers are a result of failure to clean equipment after use —most nozzles are very fine and clog easily. The best way to keep a sprayer functioning properly is to rinse it out thoroughly with water and to spray plain water through the nozzle before putting the sprayer away. Avoid leaving spray materials in the sprayer; mix only what you need for the job, and then clean the sprayer. In addition, if you have used oil or other materials that may form gum in the nozzle, use a cleaning solvent such as Nutrasol, which is available in many garden stores or from greenhouse suppliers. The following spray equipment table should help you to select the equipment you need for your particular situation. Besides the ones illustrated, there are many other brands available.

Table 20
SPRAY EQUIPMENT

Hand Sprayers

Type	Capacity	Type of Spray	Approximate Cost
Hand squeeze (A)	1 pt. or 1 qt.	Fine mist adjustable to stream	$ 2.00
Hand pump (B)	1 qt.	Adjustable: mist to stream	$10.00
Slide action (C)	Use in any size bucket or barrel	Adjustable: mist to stream	$20.00
Compressed air, (D) pump up, trigger action; plastic container	2 pt.	Fine mist	$10.00

Type	Capacity	Type of Spray	Approximate Cost
Same (E)	1½ gal.	Adjustable: fine mist to 30 ft. stream	$15.00
Compressed (F) air, pump up, hand-squeeze valve; stainless steel container	4 gal.	Adjustable: fine to coarse	$60.00

Hose-End Sprayer			
Water-pressure (G) powered; mixes undiluted insecticide and water in the sprayer at rate of 1 gal. per 50 seconds at 40 lbs.; automatically measures 1 to 10 tsp. with adjustable dial; all brass	100 gal.	Adjustable: fine mist to solid spray	$15.00

Gasoline-Powered Sprayer			
Centrifugal pump; (H) fiberglass, steel tank—porcelain lined; 3 HP	10 gal.	Adjustable: mist to jet stream	$300.00

Atomizer Sprayer			
Electric-powered (I) airblast; polyethylene tank; weight 12½ lbs.	25+ gal. from 1½ gal. tank (e.g., for 1 tsp. per gallon, put up to 25 tsp. or, 4 oz., in tank, fill with water, and spray) 25x standard dilution for hydraulic sprayers	Adjustable: mist to watering; 1.5 to 14 gph (gallons per hour); up to 100 ft. throw	$90.00

SOURCES

General information

UNITED STATES:

Diseases and Pests of Ornamental Plants. P. P. Pirone. Ronald Press, 79 Madison Ave., New York, NY 10016

Gardening Without Poison. Beatrice T. Hunter. Houghton Mifflin, 2 Park St., Boston, MA 02107

Insect and Mite Control on Ornamentals. Richard L. Miller. Extension Entomologist, Ohio State University, 1735 Neil Ave., Columbus, OH 43210

Insect Control by Chemicals. A. W. Brown. John Wiley & Sons, 605 3rd Ave., New York, NY 10016

Insect Pests of Farm, Garden, and Orchard. Davidson and Pairs. John Wiley & Sons, 605 3rd Ave., New York, NY 10016

Insect Sex Attractants. Martin Jacobson. John Wiley & Sons, 605 3rd Ave., New York, NY 10016

The Organic Way to Plant Protection. Organic Gardening, 33 Minor St., Emmaus, PA 18049

Principles of Biological Control. H. L. Sweetman. W. C. Brown, Dubuque, IA 52001

Yearbook of Agriculture, 1952 (insects). U.S. Dept. of Agriculture, Superintendent of Documents, Washington, DC 20402

Supplies

Specialty biological controls or insect growth regulators

UNITED STATES:
Bio-Control Co., 10180 Ladybird Dr., Auburn, CA 95603

Fairfax Biological Laboratory, Clinton Corners, NY 12514

Zoecon Corp., 975 California Ave., Palo Alto, CA 94304

Traps

CANADA:
Air Electrix, Inc., 3333 deSouvenir Chomedey, Laval, Quebec

UNITED STATES:
Automatic Radio (Flowtron), 2 Main St., Melrose, MA 02176

Fred C. Gloeckner & Co., 15 E. 26th St., New York, NY 10010

See the General Appendix, Sources of Supply, for a more complete list of companies that have both chemical and biological controls as well as spray equipment available.

Diseased or healthy? In this case, it's a variegated bromeliad and is quite normal—viruses in certain plants can cause similar striping

Chapter 14

PLANT DISEASES

PREVENTION OF DISEASE

The best approach to disease problems is to use good growing practices that prevent disease. Following are some guidelines to disease prevention; if they sound more like hospital hygiene than greenhouse maintenance, don't despair. Once the greenhouse is clean, good habits will keep it clean and save you from spending money on chemical remedies. It takes less time to prevent disease than it does to control and cure.

1. Keep plants healthy—vigorous plants are less susceptible to trouble

2. Keep the greenhouse clean—pick up and decontaminate plant debris, old flats, and pots

3. Keep hose nozzles off the ground

4. Get rid of diseased plants—quarantine or burn infected material before the infection spreads

5. Apply disinfectants to benches, walks, tools, and pots (use the following application table)

DISINFECTANT	APPLICATION RATE	COMMENTS
LF-10 65%	1 tsp. per gal. of water	Dip tools 30 minutes, pots 1 hour
Clorox 10%	10 tsp. per 1 pt. of water	Dip tools and soak pots in undiluted clorox; use diluted solution for benches, walks, etc.

TYPES OF DISEASE

Bacteria caused
Bacteria are very small one-celled microorganisms that do not have chlorophyll and, hence, cannot manufacture food. Instead, they are parasitic and live on the organic compounds manufactured by a host plant. Bacteria multiply rapidly, often three times per hour, and can spread throughout a small greenhouse in a day.

Control of bacteria
Bacteria find it difficult to survive under conditions of high temperature, dryness, strong sunlight, and cleanliness. Since many of them are in the soil, pasteurization is one of the standard preventive practices (see chapter 9). Chemical controls are listed in the plant disease section (plates 29-32). Unless you have very choice plants that cannot be replaced, however, it is better to burn bacterial disease-infected plants and to replace them.

Effects of botrytis on a chrysanthemum
Fig. 87

Fungus caused

Fungi are many-celled organisms that are more plantlike, but still do not manufacture their own food. Fungi cause the majority of diseases in the greenhouse *(figs. 87, 88)*. Use the plant disease section to look for symptoms of fungus diseases with the unaided eye.

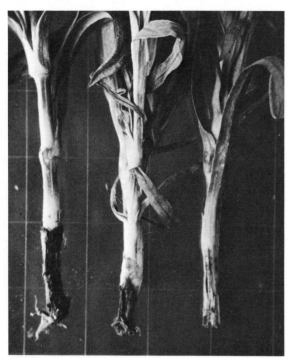

Fig. 88
Effects of fusarium on carnations

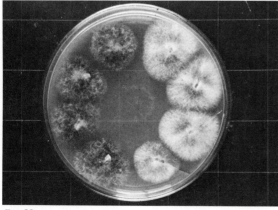

Fig. 89
Fusarium mycelia growing on pieces of carnation

If fungi are present, hyphae (individual strands), mycelium (mass of hyphae), or spore structures *(fig. 89)* are visible with a hand lens (10x or 20x). Many times you also can see the colored spore pustules on the underside of the leaf or on the stem, and shaking the plant may loosen a fine cloud of spore dust. If untreated, the spores develop a hard outer case for the resting period and become resistant to heat or chemicals. Small pieces of hyphae also develop a hard outer coating to overwinter and are then called "sclerotia."

See Plant Diseases table
Plates 29-32
between pages 116-117

Control of fungus

The same good growing practices mentioned under control of bacteria usually will control fungus diseases. Unlike bacteria-caused diseases, however, these diseases can be controlled readily with the chemicals listed in the disease section *(plates 29-32)*.

In addition, every year new fungicides come on the market as manufacturers constantly develop chemicals that are more effective and safer to use. The fungicide reference table that follows lists most of the chemicals used in formulas made for home and garden use. The table includes many of the names to ask for at greenhouse supply companies. When only the common name is listed, the formulation is used by government agencies and universities who prefer not to recommend brand names. Read the labels of the fungicides carefully to select the chemical you need to treat your particular problem. (For an explanation of the toxicity ratings, such as LD50, see the appendix.)

Virus caused

Viruses are extremely small infective agents— they are visible only with an electron microscope. The symptoms are complex but, in general, appear as abnormal growth of leaf, root, or flower.

Control of virus

Since chemical control is not satisfactory for most viral diseases, unless the plant is irreplaceable, it should be discarded and replaced with virus-free stock. Growing procedures outlined for control of bacteria apply as well to preventing viruses. Many

Table 21
FUNGICIDES

Chemical Trade Name[*]	Chemical Common Name	Type	Use	LD50 Rating Oral	Dermal	Teaspoons per Gallon
Actidione PM .5%	Cyclohexamide	Antibiotic	Powdery mildew	2	Severe skin irritation	2½
Agrimycin	Streptomycin	Antibiotic	Bacterial diseases	9,000	600	See label
Banrot 40%	—	—	Water molds, damping off	—	—	½
Benlate 50W	Benomyl	Carbamate systemic	Powdery mildew, damping off rots	9,950	—	3 - 4
Botran 50W	Dichloran	Chlorinated benzene	Botrytis, soil fungi	10,000	—	1
Bravo 75W	Daconil chlorothalinol	—	Botrytis, leaf spot on vegetables	—	—	2 - 3
Captan 50W	Same	Dicarboxymide	Leaf spots, soil insects on vegetables	9,000	—	3 - 4
Copper	Tri-basic micronized	Fixed metallic	Shot hole, leaf curl	5,000	—	4 - 5
Cyprex 65W	Dodine	—	Scab	1,000	—	½
Dexon 35W	Same	Sulfonate	Soil organisms, rots	60	—	1 - 3
Dithane M45	Manzate 200 mancozeb	Maneb manganese and zinc	Leaf spots, rusts	7,500	1,000	2 - 3
Dyrene 50W	Same	Chloroanilo group	Botrytis, damping off	2,700	—	2
Fermate 76W	Ferbam	Iron carbamate	Rusts, leaf spots on vegetables	17,000	1,000	2
Karathane 25W	Dinocap	Dintrophenol	Powdery mildew	980	1,190	2 - 3
Nurelle 5EC	Pyroxychlor	Pyridine systemic	Foliage plant diseases	—	—	1 - 2
Parnon LC	Darinol	Chlorophenyl pyridinemethanol	Powdery mildew prevention	—	—	½ - 1
Parzate	See Zineb					
Phaltan 75W	Folpet	Dicarboximide	Leaf spots, powdery mildew	10,000	—	1
Pipron LC	Piperalin	Dichlorobenzoate	Powdery mildew treatment	—	—	½ - 1
Polyram 80W	Metiram	Zinc carbamate	Blights, leaf spots	6,400	—	2
Spergon	Chloranil	Quinone	Seed treatment	4,000	—	Dust
Terraclor 75W	PCNB	Penta-nitrobenzene	Root and stem rot fungi	1,750	—	½ - 1 - ½
Truban 25EC	Ethazol	Thiadiazole	Pythium, phytopthera	—	—	¼ - ½
Truban 30W	Ethazol	Thiadiazole	Water molds, damping off	—	—	1 - 2
Zineb 75W	Parzate	Zinc carbamate	Rusts, gall leaf spots	5,200	1,000	3

[*] Check for restricted use regulations
— Data not available at time of publication

viruses are carried by insects, so it is especially important to keep the greenhouse insect-free, thereby reducing the incidence of virus infection.

Physiologically caused

There are many symptoms of poor growth that are caused, not by a disease organism, but by faulty cultural practices. Some of the physiological diseases in the following list resemble the symptoms of disease or insect damage, however, so in diagnosis, it is best to check the physiological diseases before blaming plant ills on an infectious disease.

1. *Improper planting:* many plants will not stand being planted too deeply, for example; the oxygen at greater depths is inadequate for the root system, and the whole plant declines in vigor, turns brown, and dies

2. *Packed soil:* again, this shuts off oxygen and water, which will stunt and eventually kill the plant

3. *pH reading is too high;* pH acid-loving plants will turn yellow and eventually die; most plants do well at pH 6-7, and if grown at lower pH they also will be yellowed and stunted *(see chapter 9)*

4. *Improper feeding:* too much or too little of some fertilizers produces symptoms resembling disease infection *(see chapter 11)*

5. *Too much or too little water:* either practice means a plant reduced in vigor and readily susceptible to disease *(see chapter 7)*

6. *Oedema:* high humidity and poor air circulation will cause some plants, such as geraniums, to form water blisters on the foliage

7. *Pollution:* these symptoms bear some resemblance to disease, but can be distinguished *(see chapter 8)*

DISEASE IN SEEDS AND SEEDLINGS

Prevention

Young seedlings are particularly vulnerable to attack by disease organisms. You can protect both seeds and seedlings as follows:

1. Purchase and sow treated seed

2. Treat the seed yourself before planting:

   Pathogens on the seed surface—soak the seed in Clorox at a dilution of 1-to-9, or 1 tsp. of Clorox to 9 tsp. of water, for five minutes

   Pathogens in the seed—put the seeds in a cheesecloth bag and immerse in hot water, 120°F (49°C) up to 128°F (53.3°C) for twenty minutes (both time and temperature must be accurate to avoid damage!)

   Pathogens in the soil—use Spergon, Captan 50W, Truban 30W, or Benomyl 50 percent; put the seed in a paper bag with a small amount of dust and shake

3. Purchase a pre-sterilized planting mix

4. Sterilize or pasteurize your own mix

5. Practice good sanitation

Control of seedling diseases

The following list notes the most common of the damping off and rot diseases with the chemicals for control. Dilutions are given under specific diseases in the disease table *(plates 29-32)*.

DISEASE	CONTROL[*]
Cylindrocladium	E
Fusarium	C,D,E
Phytophtora	A,C,D
Pythium	A,C,D
Rhizoctonia	B,C,D,E
Sclerotina	B,E
Thielaviopsis	D,E

[*]A = Dexon 35%
B = Terraclor 75%
C = Banrot 40%
D = Truban 30% or 25EC
E = Benlate
    Benomyl 50%

A combination of Truban 50W and Benomyl 30W will control all of the listed diseases, and with Captan 50W, should control most of the diseases likely to be encountered in a home greenhouse. Captan 50W is one of the older fungicides; while it can control or repress some of the listed diseases,

Plate 25
PEST CONTROL BASICS

	Pest	How to Identify	Control	Teaspoons per Gallon	Comments
	**Ant**	Nest underground or in litter; black, red, or brown; some are leaf cutters; adult .1 to .4 in.	Chlordane 5%, Chlordane 70%	Dust, 2-3	Some ants domesticate aphis and pasture them—they pick up aphis on one plant and move them to another
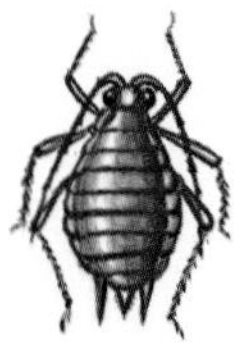	**Aphis**	Nymph feeds by sucking; green, yellow, pink, or brown; .04 to .2 in. long	Enstar 5E, Cygon 2E, Meta-Systox R, Zectran 2E, Vapona 2E, Pirimor, Nicotine sulphate,	1, 1-4, 1-2, 2-3, 1, ¼, 2	Over 300 kinds; reproduce rapidly, born alive in the greenhouse or move into greenhouse for the winter; excrete honeydew, which promotes black mold
		Pyrethrum, and Rotenone in formulated sprays (see label), predators: ladybug, wasp, lace wing			
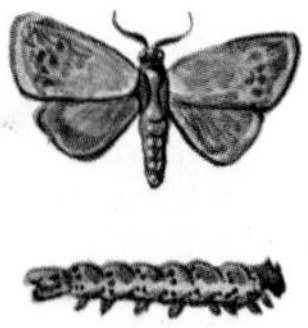	**Cutworm**	Coiled up in a ball during the day in soil; greenish-brown larvae, adult dull brown; larva 2 in.	Dipel, Thuricide, Zectran 2E, Sevin 50W	1-2, 1-2, 2-3, 3	Moths attracted to light at night; other lepidoptera such as army worms, corn ear worms, leaf rollers, can be treated as indicated here
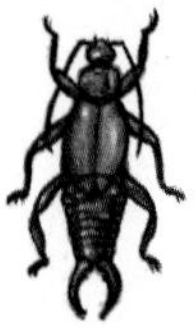	**Earwig**	Easily identified by the pincers at the back end of the abdomen	Sevin 50W, Malathion 50EC, Chlordane 45EC; biological: baits containing sodium fluosilicate or Baygon; predator: bantam hens	6, 2, 2	Feed on plant flowers, leaves, fruit, and decaying organic matter; night feeders, hide in cracks and crevices by day
	**Fungus gnat**	Cloud of tiny black or gray flies on surface of soil; move very quickly— running on the soil; larva .5 in.	Diazinon 50W: drench soil thoroughly; prevent fungal growth	½-1	Feed on tender roots, like organic matter such as peat moss, larvae of some species feed on fungi
	**Leaf miner**	Look for the tunnel tracks in the leaf where the miner has been feeding on the epidermal layers; larva 1 in.	Vapona 4E; systemic insecticides: Meta-Systox R, Systox	1, 1-2, 1-2	Eggs laid in leaf, and larvae tunnel and burrow inside leaf; not a single species, includes larvae of moths, flies, or beetles

Insects are shown for clarity but not for scale

Plate 26
PEST CONTROL BASICS

Pest	How to Identify	Control	Teaspoons per Gallon	Comments
Leaf roller	Rolls up leaf edge and fastens it with a silky web	Sevin 50W; biological control: Dipel	3 1-2	On dwarf fruit in the greenhouse
Mealybug	White cottony mass on leaf; female white, nymph orange; sucks plant juices; adult .2 to .3 in	Malathion 50%, Diazinon 50%, Cygon 2E, Zectran 2E; predator: Australian lady beetle	1-2, 2, 1-4, 2-3	Ants sometimes domesticate mealybugs
Millipede	Hard, cylindrical, brown, shiny; moves slowly and coils into ball; found in soil or debris under benches; adult 1.0 to 1.5 in.	Malathion 50 EC, Chlordane 45 EC	1-2 2	Arthropod relative of the spiders; move into greenhouse to escape cold in the fall; usually feed on decaying organic matter, but will feed on roots, especially of seedlings
Nematode	Pie-shaped brown areas on stems and leaves or scarred and distorted, between veins turns brown; decline in vigor, roots weak and distorted, swollen; adult .008 to .05 in.	Cygon 2E, Nemagon 70 EC, Methyl Bromide, Nemagon 10G (can be used with living plants); sanitation: hot water 109°-110°, sterilize soil in oven 1 hour at 350°	1-4, 6, ½ lb. per 100 sq. ft., 1 lb. to 250 sq. ft.	Invisible to unaided eye (use 20x hand lens), parasite on particular plants and insects; live on cell contents, enter through wounds; controls must be applied to bare soil with no plants present—minimum soil temperature 50°F required for Methyl Bromide application—or consult nearest nematologist at experimental station or university
Pine shoot moth	Lives in the new young candles that bend over; larva brownish-red with black head, .75 to 1 in. long	Diazinon 50W	3	Often found on Mugho pine, which is used for bonsai

Plate 27
PEST CONTROL BASICS

Pest	How to Identify	Control	Teaspoons per Gallon	Comments
 **Sawfly**	Larva green and white, brown pupa in the soil, adult bronze; larva .5 in.	Meta-Systox R, Cygon 2E, Rotenone 5%	1-2, 1-4, dust	Larvae often called a rose slug when feeding on rose leaves
 **Scale**	Semi-round, motionless scales; brown, gray, white on the underside of leaf and stem; adult .1 to .4 in.	Malathion 50%, Diazinon 50% Cygon 2E; dormant oil; predators: Vedalia beetle, junco, sparrow	1-2, 2, 1-4 8-16	Soft scale in the greenhouse, hard outdoors; insect lives under a shell like a limpet
 **Slugs and snails**	Slimy trails on soil or benches; leaves eaten or whole plants defoliated; adult 2 to 5 in.	Zectran; biological: baits of metaldehyde, bran molasses, and water, Mesurol (bait), Sanil Snare (dehydrates)	2-3; as directed	Mollusks that feed on foliage; found under flats, debris, and benches
 **Sowbug**	Usually brown or gray crawlers that coil up in a ball when disturbed; found under boards, in leaves and debris, under benches; adult .6 in.	Diazinon AG 500; hot water on benches	2	Land dwelling crustaceans related to crab and lobster; feed on decaying vegetation and tender roots; poultry and some birds eat sowbugs
 **Spider mite (red)**	Use hand lens— underside of leaf, sometimes webbing; feeds by sucking; red to purple; .006 to .04 in.	Morestan, Kelthane EC, Meta-Systox R, Chlorobenzilate, Pentac 50W; dormant oil; predators: other mites, Phytoseiulus persimilis	1-2, 1, 1-2, 1, 2; as directed	Keep greenhouse cool; up to 200 eggs per mite every 7 days, takes 3 days to kill

Plate 28
PEST CONTROL BASICS

Pest	How to Identify	Control	Teaspoons per Gallon	Comments
 **Spittlebug**	Foamy spittle on stem or leaf; nymph .3 in.	Diazinon 50W, Rotenone 25W	3, 5	Insect sucks the juices of the plant; use a sticker-spreader for control
 **Thrips**	Silver-gray clusters of fringed-wing insects on leaf tips and flower; nymph white or cream, adult black or brown, some orange or white; petals of flowers banded without color; nymph .04 to .06 in.	Malathion 50, Diazinon Ag 500, Zectran 2E, Vapona 4E	1-1½, 2, 2-3, 1	Larvae burrow into soil to pupate, carriers of disease; common in greenhouse and on onion plants and gladioli; repeat spray at 7-day intervals
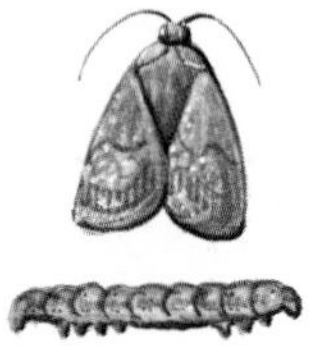 **Tomato fruitworm**	Larvae eat flowers and fruit when green; larva 1 to 2 in.	Diazinon 50W, Sevin 50W; predator: wasp (Trichogramma minutum)	3, 3	Found on tomato, corn, and peppers; one moth may deposit up to 1,000 eggs
 **Webworm**	Webs on leaf and stalk; larvae are leaf chewers; larva .5 to 1 in.	Dylox 80%, Diazinon 50W, Sevin 50W; biological: Dipel	2-3, 3, 3; 1-2	Night feeders common on vegetables
 **Weevil**	Adult feeds on leaves, notched at margin or almost entirely eaten away; larvae on roots or bark—sometimes girdled; larva .2 to .5 in.	Chlordane 45EC, Diazinon AG 500, Sevin 50W; Lysol, miscible oil on soil	2, 2, 6; 6, 8-16	Snouted beetles are in soil at night, feed in the day, larvae feed inside carrots, beets, etc.; some hibernate in debris during winter; some species difficult to control, try several chemicals
 **White fly**	Greenish white nymph; larvae feed by sucking juices; larva .08 in., adult .1 in.	Resmethrin (SBP-1382), Diazinon 25%, Meta-Systox R, Vapona 4E, Enstar 5E (controls egg nymph, adult); predators: wasp (Encarsia formosa), Peruvian ground cherry (Nicandra physaloides, adult repellant only)	1, 3-4, 1-2, 1, 1	Likes chickweed; excrete honeydew, which promotes black mold; 3 applications per week until controlled

Plate 29
PLANT DISEASES

	Disease	How to Identify	Control and Prognosis	Teaspoons per Gallon	Plants Affected
			HOLES IN LEAF		
	**Shot-hole fungus**	Spots on leaves; leaves drop early	Captan 50W; micronized or fixed copper; repeated applications will control	3-4; 4	Almond, apricot, cherry, peach, plum
			MALFORMED LEAF		
	**Crinkle mosaic virus**	Young leaves crinkle or curl and spot yellow to brown; early leaf drop	No good control— destroy infected plant	—	African violet, begonia, coleus, geranium, tomato
	**Leaf curl virus**	Leaves leathery, distorted, curled; orange-red turning black	Ferbam 76%, fixed copper 53% with sticker; fritted trace elements will suppress the disease (see chapter 11)	2, 5; 1 (apply dry to 6" pot)	Azalea, ferns, maple, peach
	**Leaf gall**	Leaves thick, pale green to white; bladder-like fleshy swelling	Zineb 75%; hand pick and burn infected parts	3	Azalea, apricot, ferns, peach
			SPOTTED LEAF		
	**Downy mildew fungus**	Pale green to yellow spots on upper leaf, downy white or purple spots on underside	Bravo 75WP, Zineb 75%; easily controlled	2, 3	Grapes, rose, vegetables, Virginia creeper

Plate 30
PLANT DISEASES

Disease	How to Identify	Control and Prognosis	Teaspoons per Gallon	Plants Affected
SPOTTED LEAF (cont.)				
 **Alternaria fungus**	Brown to black spots with a yellow edge ⅛ to ½ in.	Bravo 75WP, Daconil 75%, Captan 50W; good control with sticker-spreader	3, 1½, 3-4	Carrots, citrus, melons, schefflera, tomato
 **Cercospora fungus**	Small brown to red spots; tiny pin-point swellings on underside of leaf	Daconil 75%, Benomyl 50%, Captan 50W; good control	1½, ½-1, ¾	Cordyline Ficus, Peperomia, vegetables
 **Dactylaria fungus**	Small spots on underside of leaf, 2 mm, yellow with brown center; they collapse and appear sunken (use hand lens)	Captan 50W, Benlate 50W, Manzate 200/80W; keep leaves dry— good control	2, ½-1, 1	Philodendron and related genera
 **Fusarium fungus**	Young growing tip spotted yellow or red, sunken red-brown lesions	Daconil 75% Bravo 75%, Benomyl 50%; good control	1½, 1½, ½	Dracaena, chrysanthemum, cyclamen, pleomele, sansevieria
 **Powdery mildew fungus**	White powdery spots or coating on leaf surface	Benomyl 50%, Actidione PM .5%, Karathane 25%, Daconil 2787 75%; short life cycle, spray every 3 days; good control	½-1, 2½, 12, 1	Almost all plants except resistant varieties

Plate 31
PLANT DISEASES

Disease	How to Identify	Control and Prognosis	Teaspoons per Gallon	Plants Affected
SPOTTED LEAF (cont.)				
 **Pseudomonas bacteria**	Irregular brown or black spots with yellow margin	Tribasic copper sulfate; control difficult	4	Ferns (some) gardenia, monstera, pothos
 **Xanthomonas bacteria**	Yellowing along leaf tip and margin, brown to red; leaves drop	Combination of Kocide 101 and Dithane M45; control difficult	1½, 1½	Anthurium, begonia, dieffenbachia, gardenia, geranium, ivy, philodendron
LEAF BLIGHT				
 **Erwina bacteria**	New leaves yellow; leaf spots brown to black, mushy; rapid rot and collapse of entire plant	Try Streptomycin; control difficult	1	Aglaonema, chrysanthemum, dieffenbachia, philodendron, poinsettia, syngonium
ON LEAF, STEM, OR FLOWER				
 **Anthracnose fungus**	Leaf tips yellow then turn dark brown, scorching all along edges first; pink spots along the veins; cankers on the stem	Bravo 75%, Benomyl 50%, Daconil 75%, Dexon 35%; control difficult	3, ½-1, 1, 1-3	Araucaria, aucuba, azalea, ivy, vegetables
 **Rust fungus**	Orange to red or brown spots of spore masses (⅛ in. and larger) on the leaf surface	Zineb 75%, Manzate 200/80%, Plantvax 75%; good control	3, 2-3, 3	Aralia, azalea, ferns, fuchsia, geranium, pine

Plate 32
PLANT DISEASES

Disease	How to Identify	Control and Prognosis	Teaspoons per Gallon	Plants Affected
ON LEAF, STEM, OR FLOWER (cont.)				
 **Sooty mold fungus**	Black spots or coating on leaf, stem, or flower	Control insects that secrete "honey dew," such as aphis, scale, white fly		Gardenia, geranium, ivy, lemon, orange, philodendron
 **Botrytis fungus**	Gray spore masses cover leaf, stem, and flower; parts become soft and rotten	Daconil 75%, Benomyl 50%, Captan 50W; keep humidity low, ventilate; good control	1, 1, 3-4	Almost all plants, some vegetables
 **Wilts, bacteria and virus**	Lower leaves yellow, drop off— progesses from lower leaves up to top	Burn infected plant; no good control		Asparagus fern, cyclamen, orchids, vegetables
ROOT AND STEM ROTS				
 **Crown gall bacteria**	Stem blackens and rots; roots become stubby, rotten; plant collapses	Truban 30%, Benomyl 50%, Banrot 40%, Nurelle, Dexon 35%	½, 1½, ½, 1-2, 1-3	Practically all plants, especially seedlings and cuttings
 **Damping off, collar rot- caused by Pythium, Rhizoctonia, Fusarium, Phytphthora, Selerotina, Cylindrocladium, fungi**	Swollen tumors or lumpy growth near soil line on roots and stem	Burn infected plant; no good control		Azalea, chrysanthemum, citrus, geranium, kalanchoe, peach, tomato

no data on specific control is available. Recent chemicals such as Truban and Benomyl, however, are very specific; for example, Truban will not control sclerotinia, and Benomyl will not control Pythium.

DISEASE DIAGNOSIS

The illustrations of plant diseases *(plates 29-32)* should help you recognize some of the common plant diseases. In addition, consult the diagnosis table (plates 17-23) for other causes of plant ills that may appear similar to disease; for example, brown tips and edges on the foliage might be a bacterial or fungal disease, but you could have similar symptoms from overwatering, cold air, sunscorch, pollution, or a potash deficiency.

If you find it difficult to decide just what your plant problem is, consult your local garden center or nursery. Many retailers have highly trained or licensed personnel who are glad to be of assistance to you.

If you have a particularly choice plant with a disease problem, you may wish to have it diagnosed by a plant pathologist at a university or experiment station. The following procedure is recommended:

1. Remove diseased leaves or pieces of stem and wrap in foil or a plastic bag

2. Seal the bag tightly and put it in a crush-proof carton for mailing

3. On an enclosed piece of paper, give the plant pathologist all the information you can, including the name of the plant, size, where purchased, and names of sprays and fertilizers applied

4. Enclose a self-addressed envelope for return of the diagnosis

SOURCES

General information

UNITED STATES:
"Common Diseases of Tropical Foliage Plants." J. F. Knauss. *Florist's Review.* 11 October 1973 and 17 May 1973. Florist's Publishing Co., 310 S. Michigan Ave., Chicago, IL 60604

Diseases and Pests of Ornamental Plants. P. P. Pirone. Ronald Press, 79 Madison Ave., New York, NY 10016

Diseases of Ornamental Plants (Special Publication #3). J. L. Forsberg. University of Illinois, Urbana, IL 61801

How to Control Plant Diseases. M. C. Shurtleff. Iowa State University Press, Ames, IA 50010

Insects, Mites and Disease Control on Commercial Greenhouse Floral Crops (Bulletin #538). C. C. Powell and R. K. Lundquist. Cooperative Extension Service, Ohio State University, Columbus, OH 43210

The Plant Doctor. R. Nichols. Running Press, 38 S. 19th St., Philadelphia, PA 19103

Rx for Ailing House Plants. C. M. Evans and R. L. Pilner. Random House, 201 E. 50th St., New York, NY 10022

Yearbook of Agriculture, 1953 (plant diseases). U. S. Dept. of Agriculture, Superintendent of Documents, Washington, DC 20402

Supplies
See the General Appendix, Sources of Supply.

See Diagnosis table
Plates 17-23
between pages 84-85

Cantaloupes prefer warm temperatures and high humidity, a perfect match for growing in a fully-automatic greenhouse

AUTOMATION

Automating the environmental control system in a hobby greenhouse gives you more time for the fun of growing by eliminating the time spent adjusting the environmental conditions by hand. The basic needs of the plant—water, nutrition, light temperature, and humidity—can be automated by the average grower who is handy with tools. Installation diagrams for automatic systems are included in the appendix.

If you are not mechanically inclined, most areas have greenhouse contractors listed in the yellow pages who can automate for you. Complete environmental controls for all of the functions discussed in this chapter also can be regulated by one properly engineered master control panel. For companies that provide this service, see the sources at the end of this chapter.

CONTROLLING WATER

Water in the greenhouse is used for two purposes: first, to soak the soil in pots or ground beds so the plants can take up water through the root system, usually called "watering"; and second, to coat the surface of the plant material, often cuttings, with a film of moisture that reduces transpiration and slows metabolism to preserve energy for root growth, at the same time adding moisture to the air to increase the humidity—this is called "misting."

Because watering and misting require different equipment, we will consider them separately. In both instances, automated simply means installing equipment that waters or mists when you are not there. Such a system involves a control device that turns water on and off by activating a valve.

Automatic misting systems

Mechanical

The misting mechanism shown in *figure 40* in chapter 7 is a counter-balance device that operates on the principle of water evaporation. The stainless steel screen rises as the water evaporates from it, and when it is high enough, the mercury-tilt switch closes the circuit, which opens the electric valve and turns the water on. The water falls on the screen and accumulates enough to depress the screen to the down position, tilting the mercury switch to break the electrical current and shut the water off. The counter-balance weights permit adjusting the time interval for short-burst misting or longer watering.

The mercury tilt switch costs $5.00 or less, and if you are handy, you can build your own screen-leaf device using a 2-pound coffee can for a cover. For detailed instructions, see the appendix.

Electrical

Misting of cuttings, seed germination, and humidity control require cycle timers *(fig. 90)* that permit brief bursts of mist at frequent intervals. Cycle timers look like time clocks *(fig. 91)*, but can be set only to regulate the length of intervals between bursts. To regulate misting to come on in the morning and off in the afternoon, for example, on at 8:00 A.M. and off at 4:00 P.M., a twenty-four-hour clock is needed (or you will have to turn the cycle timer on and off by hand). You would set the twenty-four-hour clock for "on" at 6:00 A.M. and "off" at 6:00 P.M. This would turn on the cycle timer at 6:00 A.M., and it would water according to the cycle you choose on the cycle-timer chart, for instance, one second every minute or six seconds every six minutes. It will keep repeating the cycle until the twenty-four-hour clock shuts it off at 6:00 P.M. Cost of installation is $40.00-

Fig. 90
Cycle timer

Fig. 92
Light sensor

Fig. 91
Time clock

$50.00, depending on set-up. A table on automatic watering systems, which includes a list of misting cycle timers, appears later in the chapter. See the appendix for further details.

Electronic

Cycle timers also can be turned on and off by devices other than twenty-four-hour clocks, such as

electronic light sensors and tensiometers. See the appendix for more details.

Light sensors
There are at least three systems available in which the cycle timer is turned off and on by a light sensor (fig. 92) and a control. Water Wizard, for example, senses the light intensity with a photoelectric cell (A on the figure), which activates a cycle timer (B), through a controller (C). The mist automatically goes on in the morning when there is sufficient light intensity, and off when the light intensity decreases —on a cloudy, rainy day or in the evening. The sensitivity to light is adjustable at the controller. The MacPenny Solar Mist and the Solatrol are similar complete misting systems. For further information, see the sources of supply at the end of the chapter.

Tensiometers
Water for misting can also be turned on and off by ceramic blocks that sense the amount of moisture in the soil or the air and make or break an electrical current. MacPenny Mist Propagation System, for instance, has a porous ceramic block connected to a solenoid valve through a controller. When the moisture content of the block is low, a solenoid valve will control either spray mist or watering. Placed in the air or on the soil, the block simulates the transpiration or evaporation rate and provides moisture as needed.

Automatic watering

Mechanical

The Mist-A-Matic discussed under misting also can be adjusted to water with sprinkler nozzles. The Chapin Moist Scale is another watering system. It weighs the amount of soil moisture, turns the water on when the pot gets dry and light, and off when it is watered and heavy. The scale is adjustable to provide the proper amount of water.

Electrical

For a small greenhouse with one or two valves or stations, the time clocks in the following table are suitable for watering. Each clock is adjustable for the length of time the water is on and for the number of times per day that you water. For most watering situations, twelve operations is adequate.

There also are many brands of electric controllers that will activate several valves or stations for the larger greenhouse. The table also lists examples of the systems available for watering.

Hydraulic

There are control systems that keep time by an electric clock but operate on hydraulic valve by water pressure. The valves and controls look similar to those of the electrical system, but the hydraulic control is accomplished by alternately maintaining and removing water pressure on the top of the valve.

Electronic

Electronic control watering equipment is used in many commercial greenhouses where the size of the operation warrants the expense. The Dean automatic watering controller, for example, handles

Table 22
GREENHOUSE AUTOMATIC WATER SYSTEMS

Electric Cycle Timers for Misting

Cycle Timer	Revolution of Dial	Length of Misting	Approximate Cost
Gloeckner Supermist #7260 B*	Adjustable: cycle every 3¾ to 120 minutes	Adjustable: 2 to 220 seconds	$150.00
Plant Products Horticultural Mist Timer	Adjustable: cycle every 0 to 120 minutes; turned on and off by 24-hour clock	Adjustable: 0 to 30 seconds	275.00 (in Canada)
Tork 800 Series**	Not adjustable, separate clock for each cycle; cycle every: 1 min. 6 min. 12 min. 30 min. 60 min. 24 hr.	Not adjustable, length of misting corresponds to cycle: 1 sec. 6 sec. 12 sec. 30 sec. 60 sec. 15 sec.	50.00
Tork 4100**	Cycle every: 24 hours	Adjustable: 2 to 55 minutes	65.00
Intermatic 88 Series**	Adjustable, cycle every: 5 min. 10 min. 30 min. 1 hr. 2 hr. 4 hr.	Cycle every: 2½ sec. 5 sec. 15 sec. 30 sec. 1 min. 2 min.	25.00

* Has a self-contained 24-hour clock

** Requires a 24-hour clock such as the Dayton 2E025 to turn the cycler on in the morning and off in the late afternoon

Electric Time Clocks
(for small greenhouse)

Adjustable Tripper Time Clocks	Dial Duration	"On" Time		"Off" Time		Operations per Day	Approximate Cost
		Minimum	Maximum	Minimum	Maximum		
Dayton Short Range 2E025	24 hrs.	5 min.	60 min.	5 min.	23 hrs. 55 min.	1-12	$ 25.00
Intermatic T180	24 hrs.	10 min.	60 min.	10 min.	23 hrs. 55 min.	1-12	$ 25.00
Tork 4100	24 hrs.	2 min.	55 min.	5 min.	23 hrs. 55 min.	1-23	$ 60.00
Intermatic V4700	24 hrs.	5 min.	55 min.	5 min.	23 hrs. 55 min.	1-23	$ 75.00

Electric Time Clocks
(for large greenhouse)

Controller	Number of Stations	"On" Time per Station Minimum	Station Maximum	Approximate Cost
Bresser	11 20	12 sec. 30 sec.	12 min. 30 min.	—
Toro	8 11, 22, 33	0 min. 0 min.	30 min. 1 hr.	$100.00 $250.00
H₂O	5-11	7 ½ min.	23 hrs.	—
Moody	6 10-30	5 min. 0 min.	1 hr. 1 hr.	$400.00- 900.00
Rainbird	3	5 min.	1 hr.	$ 75.00- 100.00
	12-23	2 min.	1 hr.	$600.00- 800.00
Intermatic	3	5 min.	1 hr.	$25.00- 50.00

— Data not available at time of publication

twelve stations for approximately $400.00 or forty stations for about $700.00. For a hobby greenhouse, mechanical, electrical, or hydraulic controls are adequate and less expensive.

Valves

Mechanical

For spaghetti tube systems, Chapin makes a device that measures or weighs the amount of water going to each pot, then shuts itself off when the proper amount of water has been dispensed. The quantity of water used is controlled automatically, but the "on" or "off" status of the water supply is controlled by a time clock or other device.

Another system is manufactured by Humex Limited called a Levelmatic Capillary Bench Controller, which is a mechanical float valve. This device permits you to supply a capillary bench at two levels without flooding the lower level.

Electrical

Electrical valves are of two types: diaphragm for watering and piloted piston for misting, the pilot responds faster and is better for short bursts of mist (for example, one to five seconds). You can purchase 110-volt or 24-volt electric valves, but for the home greenhouse the latter is probably better. All that is required is a transformer to reduce 110-volt house current to 24 volt.

CONTROLLING NUTRITION

Automatic feeding

Most commercial growers feed their greenhouse plants through the watering system by means of an injector or proportioner. The proportioner is a device that automatically meters a predetermined amount of soluble fertilizer into the flow of water. Fertilizing in this fashion is a great time saver whether you are using a hose or a more sophisticated distribution system such as spaghetti tube or sprinkling heads.

Automatic feeding also has the advantage of supplying the plant food more regularly—recent research indicates that plants grow better when they are fed small amounts at frequent intervals. Many of the plants that you buy have been grown on a daily feeding schedule by commercial growers, and it is often worthwhile to continue this procedure in your own greenhouse.

There are many kinds of feeding devices that act on different principles. Following is a closer look at several of them.

Siphon system

The simplest system is the Syphonex, or Hozon, which has been widely available and in use for many years. This is a siphon device that attaches to a hose and siphons the fertilizer solution out of a bucket into the hose (fig. 93). The proportion is approximately 1-to-15. This means that for every 15 gallons of water that comes out the end of the hose, there has been 1 gallon of fertilizer solution taken from the bucket. Actually, the ratio varies from 1-to-12 to 1-to-18 depending upon the pressure, a variation that is characteristic of siphon devices.

Even though the Hozon is not as accurate as other systems, it has done a satisfactory job for many years. It costs less than $5.00—which means if you have more than one hose outlet, you can afford to

Fig. 93
Hozon fertilizer proportioner

put a Hozon on each faucet. Capacity of the Hozon is about 3 to 4 gallons per minute, or the carrying capacity of the average hose. If you have never done proportioner feeding, this is a good place to start. The Hozon is available in most garden centers or greenhouse supply houses.

A word of caution about keeping the Hozon clean, however: this device will not function properly if particles of dirt become lodged in the orifice that regulates the siphon action. It is a good idea to remove the Hozon after use, check it, and flush it out before using it again.

Injector system

Piston pump

The Hydrocare Injector is a water-operated piston pump that injects fertilizer solution into the water stream at a pre-set dilution ratio of 1-to-24 (1 gallon of concentrate in the tank to every 24 gallons dispensed). It is quite accurate over a wide range of pressures and flow rates and will dispense pesticides and disinfectants as well as fertilizers.

The Hydrocare pump connects to the faucet with ordinary garden hose fittings and can be used anywhere along the hose that is convenient. The cost is about $100.00, and for the degree of accuracy, this is a bargain. In a small greenhouse, the Hydrocare can be set up as a permanent installation to take care of all the watering. The capacity is about 5 gallons per minute, which will take care of a greenhouse in the 10-by-12 foot size for spaghetti watering, or any size of greenhouse that is hand-watered. The Hydrocare also has a sprayer attachment, which permits application of insecticides, fungicides, and other chemicals.

The accuracy factor is within a range of 1 percent under normal usage. The only time you have trouble with this type of injector is when the water pressures are excessively high. The pump is made of plastic and requires reasonable care to function properly. In this price range, however, the Hydrocare is probably one of the best of the small injectors.

At a slightly higher price (approximately $150.00), is the Merit Commander Injector, which functions about the same as the Hydrocare. It has an output of 6.6 gallons per minute and an accuracy factor within a range of 1 percent. It is not as easily portable nor does it have the sprayer conversion capacity of the Hydrocare, but it is very well constructed and should give years of trouble-free performance.

The top quality injector is Smith Measuremix *(fig. 94)*, which is used widely by commercial green-

Fig. 94
Smith injector

house growers. It is a precision-made brass and bronze water-powered motor that injects at the ratio of 1-to-100, regardless of the rate of water flow or pressure. The smallest model is made to plumb into ¾-inch pipe and has a maximum output of 12 gallons per minute. It also can be fitted with hose connections and put on a cart or hand truck for portability. At 90 "plus" pounds, you won't carry it far by hand! The reason commercial growers use the Smith extensively is that it is very reliable, accurate, and almost service-free. It sells for between $600.00 and $800.00.

Tank with liner

The injectors we have discussed thus far have had no internal bag or liner, but there are two types with liners that might be worth considering. In the M-P and the Gewa injectors, the water enters the metal chamber outside a plastic or rubber bag and exerts pressure on the bag, which forces the fertilizer solution into the water stream.

The MP comes in models sized from ½ to 15 gallons *(fig. 95),* with adjustable proportions from

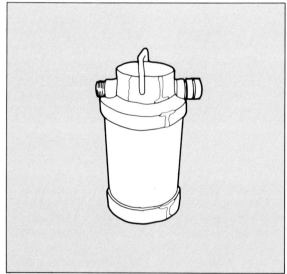

Fig. 95
M-P injector for hobby greenhouse

1-to-30 to 1-to-5,000 at a cost from $50.00 to $300.00. The plastic bag liner does break or crack after use, and unless you are mechanically inclined, it is difficult to replace. The cost of the bag is about $1.00 for the ½-gallon model. The M-P is available at most of the greenhouse supply centers.

The Gewa also has some features that are worth

considering. The 4-gallon model is on wheels, hence readily portable to connect to faucets. It has a set 1-to-100 proportion, and the liner bag is a neoprene rubber compound that holds up longer than plastic. The replacement bag is about $8.00 and the 4-gallon model sells for about $200.00. The Gewa is widely used in Europe.

Diluter

The Cameron Bucket *(fig. 96)* is a 2-gallon diluter with variable ratio proportion, which is set by turn-

Fig. 96
Cameron diluter

ing the dial on the top of the diluter. The Cameron comes supplied with hose fittings for easy installation. Cost is approximately $100.00.

Fertilizer solutions

For general feeding purposes, you probably will use a 20-20-20 soluble fertilizer. Following are some guidelines in preparing the fertilizer solution, which will be dispensed into the water stream.

Eight ounces in 25 gallons of water is the normal application dilution that you would mix for most plant material if the mix were dispensed from a tank. Using only 1 gallon of mix, then, you would use 2 teaspoons of 20-20-20 fertilizer in a gallon of water.

For the Hozon 1-to-15 ratio you would put 4¾ ounces of fertilizer in 1 gallon of water in the bucket to make the concentrate. When this is diluted to the 1-to-15 ratio, the solution that arrives at the plant via the hose is equivalent to 8 ounces in 25 gallons of water.

For the Hydrocare 1-to-24 ratio, use 7¾ ounces per gallon in the concentrate solution, which will give you a dilution of 8 ounces in 25 gallons at the end of the hose.

For the Gewa, Smith, M-P 2-gallon, and the Cameron Bucket, use 2 pounds of soluble fertilizer per gallon of stock solution, set the proportioner at 1-to-100, and it will dispense approximately 8 ounces per 25 gallons.

CONTROLLING TEMPERATURE

Automatic heating and cooling

Mechanical

A mechanical device for raising and lowering the roof ventilators is shown in *figure 97*. The cylinder contains a material that expands when a given

Fig. 97
Mechanical ventilator opener

temperature is reached, driving the piston to activate a lever system and open the ventilator, and of course, the reverse happens when the temperature drops. There is no way to tie this into a controlled system for the complete climate control used in most modern cooling and ventilating systems, but in an older house it might be useful.

Electrical

Controlling the temperature electrically is a matter of having the proper thermostat for the soil and the air, which will automatically start the cooling, the ventilating, and the heating systems. It is best to have thermostats, as well as other electrical devices, installed by a competent electrician so you conform to local codes and avoid injury.

Electronic

More sophisticated control equipment is now available to control heating, cooling, ventilating, humidity, carbon-dioxide content, and other functions. The Acme Team I four-stage unit, for example, controls heating, cooling, ventilating, air circulation, and humidity. It costs about $200.00. For the larger (8-by-12-feet and up) greenhouse, this equipment will give proper temperature and climatic conditions automatically.

Roper-Ickes Braun (IBG) Step Systems (fig. 98) are also multiple function electronic controls. An

Fig. 98
Heating-cooling controller

eight-stage Step System is in the $500.00 to $600.00 range and is used primarily in commercial greenhouses. Recently, Roper-Ickes Braun has introduced the Step 50, a five-stage system costing about $350.00. It controls heating, cooling, air circulation, ventilation, humidity, and other optional functions such as automatic watering. Both of these units can be custom engineered to suit your partic-

ular problems of environmental control. (See addresses under sources at the end of the chapter.)

CONTROLLING HUMIDITY

Humidity is measured by the expansion and contraction of human hair, nylon, or other materials that are moisture sensitive. The expansion of the sensing element completes an electric circuit that turns on a humidifer or mist. When the sensing element is moist enough to contract, the circuit breaks and the mist shuts off.

The Acme Team I and the IBG Step 50 systems can both be engineered with humidity, temperature, light, and water controls. Fine mist nozzles as well as humidifiers can be used for increasing the moisture content of the air. Mist nozzles cost $1.00 to $3.00 each and humidifiers from $100.00 up.

To automate humidity control, use a suitable humidistat installed as indicated in the appendix. Humidistats and humidifers are discussed extensively in chapter 8.

CONTROLLING LIGHTING

Lighting can be controlled by the time clocks or the cycle timers listed under electrical automatic misting systems and electrical automatic watering systems. Photoelectric controls also are available that will switch on the lights when daylight intensity drops to three footcandles. The lights will stay on until daylight increases to nine footcandles—or until they are turned off by a time clock. See details of photoelectric controls in the appendix.

GROWTH CHAMBERS

Most research facilities in experiment stations and universities, as well as many private commercial greenhouses, are using growth chambers in which to germinate seeds and grow plants. A growth chamber is the ultimate controlled environment. Not only light, but all the other growth factors can be controlled: moisture, humidity, temperature, nutrition, carbon dioxide content, and air circulation. In some cases, these systems are highly sophisticated and expensive, but there are smaller units that perform well if you wish to experiment.

SOURCES

General information

CANADA:
Ball Red Book. Twelfth edition. Ball-Superior, Ltd., 1155 Birchview Dr., Mississauga, Ontario L5H 3E1

UNITED STATES:
Ball Red Book. Twelfth edition. Geo. J. Ball, Inc., P.O. Box 335, West Chicago, IL 60185

Commercial Flower Forcing. Laurie, Kiplinger and Nelson. Seventh edition. McGraw-Hill, 1221 Ave. of the Americas, New York, NY 10020

Greenhouse Handbook for the Amateur. Brooklyn Botanic Gardens, 1000 Washington Ave., Brooklyn, New York, NY 11225

Complete environmental control

UNITED STATES:
Acme Engineering & Mfg. (Acme Team I), P.O. Box 978, Muskogee, OK 74401

Roper-IBG (Roper-IBG Step 50), Patrick Helly, P.O. Box 100, Wheeling, IL 60090

Rough Bros., P.O. Box 16010, Cincinnati, OH 45216

Supplies

See the General Appendix, Sources of Supply listed by region, for companies that carry automation supplies.

Containers come in many sizes, shapes, and materials

POTS AND CONTAINERS

ROOT SYSTEM

Good root systems are necessary for plant growth, and it does make a difference whether the roots are free to meander through the soil or are confined by the walls of a pot or container. The body of knowledge about growing plants in the ground is old and extensive, but information about growing in containers is new and scanty.

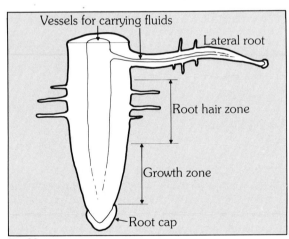

Fig. 99
Root tip enlarged

Functions of a root system
The functions of the root system are to:

1. Support the plant

2. Permit absorption of water and nutrient materials from the soil

3. Serve as a storage area for manufactured materials

4. Give off chemical exudates for growth control *(see chapter 12 for details)*

The absorption of water and nutrient materials takes place near the tip of the growing root through very minute structures called root hairs *(fig. 99)*. These are just behind the growing tip of the root and are usually about a millimeter long. As the root tip grows through the soil, the root hairs die off, and new ones are formed again just behind the growing tip. Root hairs, often an extension of a single root cell, are very fragile. The walls of the root hair are thin to permit ready access to the water and nutrient materials and are, therefore, vulnerable to injury by chemical or mechanical means. Care must be taken when transplanting or when applying fertilizers or chemicals to the soil.

Extent of root systems
In nature, root systems may be very extensive. Alfalfa, for example, has been found with roots over 100 feet below ground level. Studies of a four-month old rye plant showed a combined root length of 387 miles and a total surface of 6,875 square feet. Much of the surface was composed of approximately 14 billion root hairs. That same plant grown in a 6-inch pot would have a much reduced root system.

Thus, when we grow plants in containers, we are introducing new factors and a new environment for the root system. The capacity of a particular plant to adapt to the confinement of a container and the extent of the plant's root system in its native habitat are factors to consider when choosing pot size — plants get potbound and have root systems that spiral around the pot wall. You may have seen an experienced grower pick up a pot, tap it on the bench upside down, and remove the pot to see what the root system is doing. This is the best way to check the condition of the root system.

Diffusion in the pot

Oxygen and water move around and through membranes such as the cell wall in an exchange or intermingling of molecules; this process is known as diffusion. Oxygen from the air goes down into the soil and into the roots. The roots use the oxygen in the growth process and give off carbon dioxide, which diffuses into the atmosphere or is used by soil microorganisms. Water moving rapidly through the soil tends to draw air and, hence, oxygen into the soil.

In most pots or containers, this process happens from the surface of the soil mix down, but in pots that have a porous side wall, there also is diffusion through the wall of the pot *(fig. 100)*. Pots made of

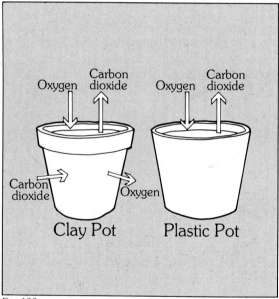

Fig. 100
Diffusion in pots

clay, peat, and fiber all have porous side walls. Some styrofoam formulations also permit air exchange.

Plastic pots, on the other hand, are not porous. If you use these solid-wall pots, you need to adjust your watering practices to accommodate for the lack of diffusion through the wall of the pot. If the soil holds too much water, it holds less air—with growth-retarding results.

Lack of air in the root zone will either kill the root hairs or produce very fragile, thin-walled roots with few root hairs. This, in turn, affects the top of the plant by reducing the leaf area and often produces bud drop and a sickly plant that lacks vigor. With solid-wall pots, you probably will need to water only half as often as with porous-wall pots.

The danger for the home grower is a bench mixing porous and nonporous pots, which should have different watering schedules. Good growers use either all porous or all nonporous pots to facilitate uniform watering. Excellent plants can be grown in either type of pot, but it is difficult to grow healthy plants if you mix both types.

Light transmission

Recent research suggests that light colors in a rigid plastic pot admit enough light to be detrimental to the root system of some plants. It will take more research to know what species have light-sensitive roots, but it is apparent that most plants in their native habitats produce roots in the dark or very low light conditions. Hasek and Sciaroni (University of California at Davis) found white pots admitted as much as 1,000 footcandles; light green pots, 68 footcandles; and dark green opaque pots only .2 footcandles. If you have plants that are not doing well in white pots, try repotting in dark-colored opaque pots.

DRAINAGE

If you are growing on capillary mat, make sure that the pot makes sufficient contact with the mat to permit enough capillary action. Clay pots with one hole in the center of the bottom may not be adequate. Some plastic pots have ridges on the bottom designed to give better drainage on a solid surface. These, also, do not function well for capillary watering.

ALGAE

To remove algae from pot and soil surfaces, use Physan (Consan) at 1 teaspoon per gallon of water applied to the top of the pot. To keep the pot clean, treat once a month.

Regular, careful inspection of plants prevents major insect or disease build-up

SOURCES

General information

CANADA:
Ball Red Book. Twelfth edition. Ball-Superior, Ltd., 1155 Birchview Dr., Mississauga, Ontario L5H 3E1

Commercial Flower Forcing. Laurie, Kiplinger and Nelson. Seventh edition. McGraw-Hill, 330 Progress Ave., Scarborough, Ontario

UNITED STATES:
Ball Red Book. Twelfth edition. Geo. J. Ball, Inc., P.O. Box 335, West Chicago, IL 60185

Commercial Flower Forcing. Laurie, Kiplinger and Nelson. Seventh edition. McGraw-Hill, 1221 Ave. of the Americas, New York, NY 10020

House Plants Indoors/Outdoors. Ortho Books. Chevron Chemical Co., 200 Bush St., San Francisco, CA 94104

Jiffy Pot Technical Bulletin (#100). Jiffy Pot Corp. of America, Town Rd., West Chicago, IL 60185

Supplies

See the General Appendix, Sources of Supply.

Cucumbers are one of the best vegetables to grow in a greenhouse

Seedlings in a seed flat depict man's intervention in nature's most basic method of reproduction

PROPAGATION

One of the most rewarding experiences you can have with plants is finding a choice specimen and reproducing it to give to friends. In this chapter, we will discuss propagation by seed, cutting, grafting, and other specialized methods.

PROPAGATION BY SEED

Probably no one knows how or when men discovered that you could put a seed in the ground and that it would grow into another plant, but I'm sure it goes back to very primitive times. Today, seed is exchanged worldwide by both amateurs and professionals. On a recent trip to Russia, for example, the author made arrangements for seed exchange in Tadjikistan, where many of our common fruits probably originated. Seed catalogues now make it possible to have plants from everywhere growing in your own yard and greenhouse, but we often overlook the seed catalogues from outside North America as a source of interesting plants. Some world seed sources you can try are listed at the back of the chapter.

Conditions necessary for germination

A seed begins as the fertilized egg within the carpel (fig. 101). After fertilization (fig. 102), when the embryo is formed, a tough skin, or coating, develops around the embryo, then growth stops (fig. 103), and the seed is dispersed by the wind, a bird, or a mail order seed catalogue! The seed will begin to grow again, or "germinate" (fig. 104), when the right conditions are present, including a period of dormancy for many seeds, and then becomes a seedling. See the following table (a sum-

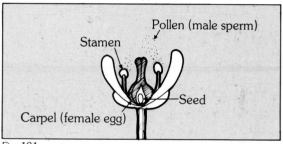

Fig. 101
Parts of flower

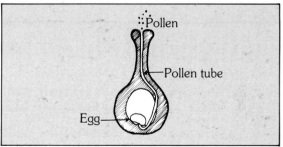

Fig. 102
Fertilization of the seed

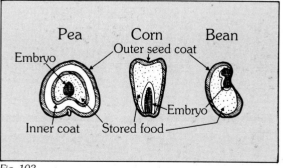

Fig. 103
Cutaway views of pea, bean, and corn seeds

135

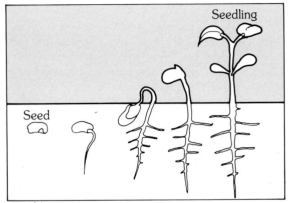

Fig. 104
Germination of a bean

mary from a study published in *Florist's Review,* September, 1969), which shows that there is a wide range of light, dark, and temperature requirements for germination. The conditions necessary for germination include:

1. Adequate moisture
2. Adequate aeration
3. Correct soil temperature
4. Correct light or dark requirement
5. Disease-free medium
6. Correct depth of sowing
7. Period of dormancy
8. Dormancy-breaking treatment

Adequate moisture

Adequate moisture is probably best maintained by using an automatic mist system *(see chapter 15).* With moist germination mixes, a cycle of six seconds every ten to fifteen minutes from morning to evening should be about right, as long as you adjust this to the evaporation rate in your greenhouse. The medium should be moistened thoroughly before you plant the seed *(fig. 105).* If you confine the moisture in a single flat or frame, no watering is necessary until the seeds have germinated. For a small container, bottom watering works well. Remove the cover when germination occurs.

Adequate aeration

Maintaining adequate aeration is a function of the proper medium. As with so many things in horti-

Table 23
GUIDELINES FOR GERMINATION

	Group	Germinate in Light	Germinate in Dark	Temperature (F)
I.	Germinate over a wide range of temperatures	X	X	50°-85°
II.	Germinate only at cool temperatures	X	X	50°-75°
III.	Germinate only at warm temperatures	X	X	60°-70°
IV.	Germinate over narrow range of temperatures	X	X	Specific for variety
V.	Germinate over wide range of temperatures	X		55°-85°
VI.	Germinate over wide range of temperatures (improved results when germinated in light)	X		55°-85°
VII.	Germinate at warm temperatures (improved results when germinated in light)	X		55°-85°
VIII.	Germinate over wide range of temperatures (improved results when germinated in dark)		X	50°-75°
IX.	Germinate at warm temperatures (improved results when germinated in dark)		X	50°-75°

* Data reprinted from "Guidelines for the Germination of Annual, Pot Plant, and Ornamental Herb Seeds" by Henry M. Cathey, *Florist's Review,* 4 September 1969, Vol. 144, No. 3744: 26-29 and 75-77

Fig. 105
Lightly moisten the medium

culture, each grower has his own favorite formula for a seed germination mix.

Perhaps a good solution for most of us is a prepared seeding medium (see list of suppliers at end of chapter). These are uniform mixes, insect- and disease-free, and ready to use out of the bag. Alternatives to a seeding mix are in wide use, including molded cubes and pellets or blocks that are pot and medium in one unit and ready to be seeded. The major variable in these blocks is the water-holding capacity—which means you should become familiar with the block before sowing any quantity of seed. If you enclose the blocks in a poly cover, be sure to remove the cover as soon as the seeds have germinated to prevent etiolation and to provide air circulation. Following are some germination mix formulas you can make yourself:

1. ⅓ vermiculite
    ⅓ perlite
    ⅓ milled sphagnum
      (top-of-bog sphagnum—finely ground)

2. ⅓ soil
    ⅓ sand, perlite, or vermiculite
    ⅓ peat

3. John Innes Seed Compost:
    ½ loam (pH 6.5)
    (clay, sand, humus)
    ¼ peat
    ¼ sand

    To each bushel of mix add:

    1½ oz. superphosphate
    1 oz. chalk (calcium carbonate)

4. University of California mix:

    ¼ fine sand
      (particle size .05 mm to .5 mm)
    ¾ peat moss

    For each cubic yard of this mixture add:

    4 oz. potassium nitrate
    4 oz. potassium sulfate
    2 lbs. superphosphate
    5 lbs. dolomite
    4 lbs. calcium carbonate lime

Correct soil temperature

Correct soil temperature usually means to heat the bottom to keep the soil at about 70°F (21°C). Air temperature should not be below 65°F (18.3°C). The traditional method has been to supply bottom heat with a soil warming cable, but the Famco Mat, which needs no screen or sand, is a much easier device for a small greenhouse. Seed flats can be used directly on top of the mat with the remote bulb of the thermostat inserted in one of the flats. There are various seed germination chambers or boxes available *(fig. 106)*, or you can build your own using plans such as those for the heated bench in the appendix, chapter 4.

Fig. 106
Poly-tents are one good form of propagation box

Correct light or dark requirement

The light and dark requirement refers to the germination period only. As soon as the seed has germinated and begins to show green chlorophyll, light is necessary for growth. The plants that require dark to germinate should have three days of covering with black poly and then be uncovered.

Disease-free medium

Having disease-free medium is a matter of buying sterilized mixes or sterilizing at home with simple equipment. Chapter 9 has a detailed discussion of types of sterilized soil and of the process of pasteurization.

Correct depth of sowing

There are many formulas for determining the proper depth to plant seed, but no formula is as good as your common sense. In order to germinate, the seed must have close contact with the soil particles around it so it can absorb moisture. Very fine seed, for example, need only be sown on the surface —the first misting or watering will "set" it into the medium. Larger seeds should be covered with soil. Remember that it takes oxygen from the air as well as heat and moisture to germinate seeds.

Period of dormancy

Not all seeds germinate readily. The seed coat may be hard and impermeable to water; the embryo may develop only after the seed is dispersed; or there may be an internal, physiological dormancy that requires time, moisture, and chilling before germination takes place.

Dormancy-breaking treatment

In the natural environment seeds are blown about by the wind, alternately frozen and thawed, attacked by soil microorganisms, passed through the digestive tracts of animals and birds, and even preheated or burned by fire. In the stable conditions of a greenhouse, on the other hand, it is often necessary to use artificial means to break dormancy. The types of dormancy and the methods of breaking them are shown in the dormancy table in the appendix.

Nutrients

Most of the prepared seeding mixes are correctly low in fertilizer elements. The energy for germination is stored in the seed, and there is no need for any fertilizer until the seedling shows green indicating that photosynthesis has started; then the young seedling needs a very weak fertilizer solution. Try using 1 teaspoon of 20-20-20 fertilizer in a gallon of water, applied every day as needed for two weeks, then 2 teaspoons in a gallon every two or three days, followed by your regular feeding program *(see chapter 11)*.

PROPAGATION BY CUTTINGS

Conditions necessary for rooting

When you cut off a piece of plant and separate it from its root system, you immediately are facing a specialized problem in plant growth. Having disrupted the normal growth factors of water, humidity, temperature, light, and nutrient supply, you must place the cutting in an environment that is optimum for these factors. Conditions necessary for rooting include:

1. Water and humidity
2. Temperature
3. Light
4. Root feeding
5. Foliar feeding
6. Stock plant feeding

Water and humidity

Normally there is a flow of water into the plant through the root system, up the stem, and into all the plant parts. Some of this water solution is transpired through the leaves into the air, but the intake usually exceeds the output so that water pressure, called turgor pressure, exists in the plant structure and gives it rigidity. When the output through leaves exceeds the input, the plant wilts.

When we cut a leaf bud, leaf, stem, or root to propagate a new plant, the first problem is to prevent

MIST CYCLES		
Mister	Seconds	Per Minutes
Tork 800 series	2	1
	12	6
	24	12
Intermatic 88 series	2½	5
	5	10
	15	30
	30	60
Gloeckner Supermist	Completely adjustable	

water loss, or reduce transpiration, and to maintain turgor pressure. The best way to accomplish this is to water the cutting well and to place it under a regular mist cycle as soon as possible. The misting will provide adequate humidity, but supplementary watering of the medium may well be necessary—remember, however, that the cutting requires oxygen at the cut end in order to produce roots. The mist cycles listed above are commonly used (also see chapter 15).

Temperature

The temperature of the rooting medium is critical—research now indicates that rooting medium temperatures may vary from 65°F-85°F (18°C-29°C) for different kinds of cuttings. Several of the soil cables on the market come with a built-in thermostat set at 70°F (21°C), which limits control of growing medium temperatures. An adjustable thermostat such as the Famco or G.E., which will permit you to vary temperature to suit the material being rooted, is probably preferable. Test the rooting medium temperature in several places to assure uniformity of bottom heat before you plant.

Light

The energy for the growth of new roots comes from light, so when you try to root cuttings, the energy already stored in the cutting is available, plus the energy produced by photosynthesis and respiration in the cutting's leaves. This suggests the need for adequate leaf surface on most cuttings; for example, leave the top two or three leaves on a 4-to-6 inch cutting of gardenia. As in other areas of plant care, with experience, you will learn to judge the amount of foliage to leave on cuttings of various kinds of plants to optimize all available energy.

Root feeding

Increasingly, mixes for seed germination and rooting cuttings contain small amounts of fertilizer. It is apparent that nitrogen (in the form of nitrate) in combination with a complete fertilizer, when made available to the cutting as soon as it has produced the first roots, will enhance continued root production and result in a more heavily rooted cutting. Some research on foliage plant propagation has indicated that surface application of controlled-release fertilizers (such as Osmocote) at the rate of 3 teaspoons per square foot of bench area will improve rooting. If you want to try dry fertilizer in a propagating mix, use small amounts. The U.C.

Soil Mix IC might work for species that root easily. Mix one bushel as follows:

ROOTING MIX	
50%	fine sand
50%	peat moss
1½	tsp. potassium nitrate
1	tsp. potassium sulphate
2	oz. single superphosphate
6	oz. dolomite lime
2	oz. calcium carbonate lime

Foliar feeding

It also makes sense to feed through the leaves when you have a cutting without roots to absorb liquid food solutions. There are many formulas (see the sources following chapter 11) such as Ra-Pid Gro 23-19-7, with a full complement of minor elements that are suitable for foliar feeding. (Use Ra-Pid Gro at the rate of 1 teaspoon to a quart of water or 4 teaspoons to a gallon of water.)

Stock plant feeding

Certainly as important as feeding the cutting is making sure that the stock plant from which you take the cutting has been properly grown and fed so it has adequate carbohydrate storage in the plant tissues. If you have a favorite plant from which you intend to take cuttings, prepare it at least 30 to 45 days beforehand by cutting down on nitrogen and increasing phosphate and potash, and by making sure that you use a fertilizer containing all the minor elements. Take cuttings from side shoots or lower branch tips that are not growing rapidly but have begun to harden off, avoiding any soft, succulent tip growth, which would not have stored carbohydrates.

Types of cuttings

The chances are good that you will use your greenhouse to propagate all kinds of plants to be used outdoors for landscaping your property as well as inside for ornamentals. You may well need more hedge plants or trees, for example, which you want to propagate yourself. Types of cuttings, such as hardwood, softwood, herbaceous, leaf, root, and layering, are described in the appendix including procedures for propagation (illustrations of the techniques used in propagation also are provided).

PROPAGATION BY GRAFTING

Grafting, or budding, is usually done to:

1. Permit a plant with a naturally weak root system to be grown on a vigorous root system, thus producing a larger plant in less time

2. Grow superb flowers, fruit, or foliage on a better root system

3. Rejuvenate an older plant that has lost its vigor

4. Combine several compatible varieties on one plant

Success in grafting is a matter of becoming acquainted with the active growing tissue in woody plants, known as the cambium layer, which divides to the inside to produce wood, or xylem, and to the outside to produce phloem, or conductive tissue *(fig. 107)*. The best way to get acquainted with the

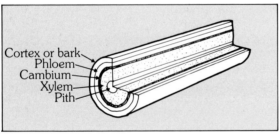

Fig. 107
Layers of tissue in a woody plant

cambium is to take a hand lens (8x power) and go outdoors where you can cut some twigs from woody plants. Cut each twig with a sharp knife and examine the cut end. A twig of maple will show a thin line of bark, then a band of coarse, light green wood, and in the center, pith. A twig of purple plum will have the same sequence of tissues, but it will be various shades of pink.

To graft successfully, the cambium layers of the scion and stock must touch each other so they can grow together *(fig. 108)*. The cambium is such a thin layer of tissue that great care must be exercised to accomplish matching.

Once you are familiar with the cambium, try the cleft graft. After some practice, try the tongue graft,

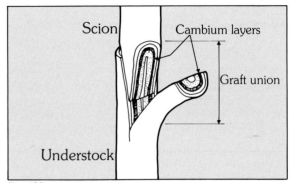

Fig. 108
Example of a graft—the cambium layers of scion and stock must touch

which works well for most evergreens that are used for bonsai. Finally, you might experiment with grafting by budding. The key to success with budding is to do it at the time when the cambium layer is actively dividing so the bark will separate easily from the wood. Roses are good plants on which to practice—small pink buds, or "eyes", are arranged spirally on the rose stem and can be used as scions for the budding. Information on many other kinds of grafting is available in the references listed at the end of this chapter.

PROPAGATION BY TISSUE CULTURE

For the past 50 years, research plant physiologists have been growing small pieces of plant tissue in test tubes to study growth. Given the proper treatment, it has been possible recently to produce an entire new plant from very small pieces of tissue—as little as one cell in a carrot, for example, will produce a new carrot plant.

This development has generated worldwide interest in propagating new plants from little pieces of shoot, root, leaf, pollen grains, seeds, and stems. In fact, at the last meetings of the International Botanical Congress in Leningrad, there were over a hundred research reports from twenty countries relating to propagation by tissue culture. In the United States, there are now a number of commercial plant tissue culture laboratories producing ferns, orchids, gerbera, gloxinias, and other plants using these new methods.

It requires rather specialized equipment and facilities to propagate plants by tissue culture, but it is not beyond the scope of many hobby growers. If you wish further information, there is now a Tissue Culture Association, Box 631, Lake Placid, New York 12946.

SPECIALIZED PROPAGATION

Ferns, orchids, and cacti require specialized propagation methods. Ferns, for instance, have a different life cycle than higher plants and are best propagated by spore germination. (Procedures with illustrations are included in the appendix.)

Orchids, on the other hand, have seeds so small that a single cattleya pod may produce 25 to 35 thousand seeds! There is much written about the difficulties of growing orchids from seed. You do have to wait several years for flowering, but if you wish to try seed, procedures are in the appendix.

The tissues of cacti and succulents are sufficiently different to require special propagation techniques as well. These also are shown in the appendix.

ROOT GROWTH HORMONES

Most plants have natural hormones called auxins that trigger or control root formation and other growth activities. Since the discovery of these natural auxins, four synthetic acids have been developed that are commonly used in the manufacture of rooting compounds:

ROOTING COMPOUNDS
IAA Indole-3 acetic acid
IBA Indole butyric acid
NAA Naphthalene acetic acid
NAD Naphthalene acetamide

There are many compounds on the market, such as Hormodin, Hormex, Rootone, Jiffy Gro, Dip 'N Gro, Seradex, and others, which contain some or all of the previously listed four ingredients. In some brands, a fungicide also is added, or a catalyst such as boron to assist penetration into the root.

When you go to buy a rooting compound, look at the label for the concentration of the chemicals involved. Unfortunately, much of the literature on propagation gives application rates in parts per million (ppm), while the label on the package lists

percentages—both are given in the following lists. You will find most of these products have at least three concentrations, such as those in the first list. Stronger compounds, like that manufactured by Hormex, may be purchased in concentrations as shown in the second list. In general, the harder-to-root plants respond to stronger concentrations, but in excess, these acids will burn or desiccate the cutting tissue, which then turns black at the base.

AVERAGE CONCENTRATION	STRONG CONCENTRATION
.1% acid = 1,000 ppm	1.6% acid = 16,000 ppm
.3% acid = 3,000 ppm	3.0% acid = 30,000 ppm
.8% acid = 8,000 ppm	4.5% acid = 45,000 ppm

Rooting compounds are manufactured dry in talc, liquid ready-to-use, and liquid concentrate. The liquid concentrate is usually a 1 percent or 10,000 ppm solution in which you dip the cuttings for not longer than five seconds. Liquid solutions must be tightly sealed and stored out of the light or they may deteriorate rapidly. Dry powders *(fig. 109)* and

Fig. 109
Treating cutting with a rooting hormone

liquid concentrates will last for many months in storage—but material a year old or older should be discarded.

There is growing research evidence that other chemicals in combination with one or more of the four discussed will enhance rooting. The growth retardants B-Nine and Cycol in combination with IBA, for example, produced more roots per cutting than IBA alone. The literature listed following the chapter should help you if you wish to make your own compounds and experiment with rooting.

SOURCES

General information

CANADA:
Chatelaine's Gardening Book. Lois Wilson. McLean-Hunter, 481 University Ave., Toronto, Ontario M5W 1A7

UNITED STATES:
Greenhouse Gardening. Henry T. and Rebecca T. Northen. Second edition. Ronald Press, 79 Madison Ave., New York, NY 10016

Handbook on Propagation. Brooklyn Botanic Gardens, 1000 Washington St., Brooklyn, New York, NY 11225

Plant Propagation. Hartman and Kester. Prentice-Hall, Englewood Cliffs, NJ 07632

Plant Propagation. John P. Mahlstede and Ernest S. Haber. John Wiley & Sons, 605 3rd Ave., New York, NY 10016

Plant Propagation in Pictures. Montague Free. Doubleday, 277 Park Ave., New York, NY 10017

Plant Propagation Practices. James S. Wells. MacMillan, 866 3rd Ave., New York, NY 10022

Plant Propagation Principles and Practices. Hudson T. Hartmann and Dale E. Kester. Third edition. Prentice-Hall, Englewood Cliffs, NJ 07632

Propagation Handbook (#24). Brooklyn Botanic Gardens, 1000 Washington Ave., Brooklyn, New York, NY 11225

Seeds of Woody Plants in the United States (revised edition of *Woody-Plant Seed Manual*, 1948). U.S. Dept. of Agriculture, Superintendent of Documents, Washington, DC 20402

Organizations

CANADA:
Toronto Civic Garden Center, 777 Lawrence Ave., East Don Mills, Ontario M3C 1P2

UNITED STATES:
International Society of Plant Propagators, W. E. Snyder, Dept. of Horticulture, Rutgers State University, New Brunswick, NJ 08903

WORLD:
The Grafter's Handbook. R. J. Garner. Third edition. Oxford University Press, Oxford, England

Bulletins

UNITED STATES:
Budding and Grafting Fruit Trees (Extension Bulletin #508). Cooperative Extension Service, Michigan State University, East Lansing, MI 48823

Building and Using Hotbeds and Cold Frames (Bulletin #HO-53). Cooperative Extension Service, Purdue University, Lafayette, IN 47907

Home Propagation of Ornamental Trees and Shrubs (Bulletin #80). U.S. Dept. of Agriculture, Agricultural Research Service, Plant Science Research Div., Superintendent of Documents, Washington, DC 20402

Intermittent Mist Propagation (Circular #506). Cooperative Extension Service, North Carolina State University, Raleigh, NC 27607

New Plants by Layering (Bulletin #HO-1). Cooperative Extension Service, Purdue University, Lafayette, IN 47907

These bulletins are just a sampling of many government and botanic garden publications. Ask your county extension agent, state university horticulture department, or local botanic garden for other available bulletins.

Supplies

Cubes, pots, blocks for seeds or cuttings

CANADA:
Plant Products Co., Ltd., 314 Orenda Rd., Bramalea, Ontario

UNITED STATES:
American Can Co. (BR-8 blocks), Greenwich, CT 06830

Floralife, Inc., 4420 S. Tripp Ave., Chicago, IL 60632

Jiffy Pot of America, P.O. Box 338, West Chicago, IL 60158

Pullen Molded Products (Kys-Kubes), New Iberia, LA 70560

Smither-Oasis (foam blocks), P.O. Box 118, Kent, OH 44240

Grafting

UNITED STATES:

Walter Clark & Son, Orange, CT 06477

Alfred Teufel Nursery, 12345 N.W. Barnes Rd., Portland, OR 97215

Hermann Wirth, P.O. Box 25, Saysville, NY 11782

Seeds

CANADA:

C.A. Cruickshank, Ltd. 1015 Mt. Pleasant, Toronto, Ontario

Golden West Seed Co., 1108 6th St. S. E., Calgary, Alberta T2E 5S8

W. H. Perron & Co., 515 Labelle Blvd., Chomadey, Quebec

Ritchie Seed, Ltd., 27 York St., Ottawa, Ontario

Rothwell Seeds, Ltd., P.O. Box 511, Lindsay, Ontario K9V 4L9

Stokes Seed Co., P.O. Box 10, St. Catharines, Ontario L2R 6R6

UNITED STATES:

Allen, Sterling & Lathrop, Rt. 1, Falmouth, ME 04105

Burgess Seed & Plant, P.O. Box 2000, Galesburg, MI 49053

Burnett Bros., 92 Chamber St., New York, NY 10007

W. Atlee Burpee Co., Philadelphia, PA 19132; Clinton, IA 52732; Riverside, CA 92502

Burrell Seed, P.O. Box 150, Rocky Ford, CA 81068

Degiorgi Co., Council Bluffs, IA 51501

Enviro-Gro, Inc., 145 Plant Ave., Hauppauge, NY 11787

Farmer Seed & Nursery (midget vegetables), Faribault, MN 55021

Feader Nurseries (novelty and unusual), P.O. Box 4284, San Fernando, CA 91342

Henry Field Seed & Nursery (hard-to-find items), 407 Sycamore St., Shenandoah, IA 51601

Glecklers Seedsmen (unusual vegetables), Metamora, OH 43540

Fred C. Gloeckner (foliage plants and ferns, wholesale only), 15 E. 26th St., New York, NY 10010

Gurney Seed, 1448 Page St., Yankton, SD 57078

Joseph Harris Co., Moreton Farm, Rochester, NY 14624; P.O. Box 432, Gresham, OR 97030

Charles C. Hart Seed Co., Main and Hart Sts., Wethersfield, CT 06109

H. G. Hastings Co., P. O. Box 4088, Atlanta, GA 30302

Herbst Bros., 1000 N. Main St., Brewster, NY 10905

J. L. Hudson, Seedsman, P.O. Box 1058, Redwood City, CA 94604

Jackson & Perkins (vegetables), Medford, OR 97501

J. W. Jung Seed Co., Station 8, Randolph, WI 53956

Kitizawa Seed Co., 356 W. Taylor St., San Jose, CA 95154

D. Landreth Seed Co., 2700 Wilmarco Ave., Baltimore, MD 21223

Le Jardin de Gourmet (French seed), P.O. Box 119, Ramsey, NJ 07446

Mail Box Seeds, 2042 Encinal Ave., Alameda, CA 94501

Earl May Seed Co., 6032 Elm St., Shenandoah, IA 51601

Meyer Seed Co., 600 S. Carolina St., Baltimore, MD 21231

E. C. Moran (trees, shrubs, wildflowers), Stanford, Montana 59479

Natural Development Co., P.O. Box 215, Bainbridge, PA 17502

Nichols Nursery, 1190 N. Pacific Hwy., Albany, OR 97321

Robert Nicholson Seed Co., P.O. Box 15487, Dallas, TX 75215

L. L. Olds Seed Co., 2901 Packers Ave., Madison, WI 53701

Geo. W. Park Seed Co., Greenwood, SC 29646

Reuter Seed Co., New Orleans, LA 70119

Clyde Robin (unusual), P.O. Box 2091, Castro Valley, CA 94546

Rocky Mt. Seed Co., 1325 15th St., Denver, CO 80217

Roswell Seed Co., P.O. Box 725, Roswell, NM 88201

Seedway, Hall, NY 14463

R. H. Shumway, Seedsman, 628 Cedar St., Rockford, IL 61101

Stokes Seeds, P.O. Box 528, Main P.O., Buffalo, NY 14240

Geo. Tait & Sons, 900 Tidewater Dr., Norfolk, VA 23504

Thompson & Morgan, 401 Kennedy Blvd., Somerdale, NJ 08083

Twilley Seed Co., Salsbury, MD 21801

Wetsel Seed Co., P.O. Box 791, Harrisonburg, VA 22801

WORLD:

Argentina: J. A. Diharce & Co., Buenos Aires, Argentina, South America

Australia: Pacific Seeds, Biloela, Queensland, Australia

Denmark: J.E. Ohlsens Enke, Dk 2630, Taastrup, Denmark

East Africa: Pop Vriend, Ltd., Arusha, Tanzania, East Africa

England: Sutton Seeds, Ltd., London Rd., Earley Reading, Berkshire, England RG6 1AB

Finland: Keskusosuusliiki Hankkila, Helsinki, Finland

France: Tezier Freres, 471 Ave. Victor Hugo, BP 223, 26002 Valence-sur-Rhone, France

Germany: L. C. Nungesser, 61 Darmstadt, Germany (BRD)

Holland: Enkhauser Zaadhandel, G. Weishut, The Hague, Holland Royal Sluis, Box 22, Enkhuizen, Holland

India: Namdeo Umajii & Co., Bombay, India

Japan: Fujii & Sons, Ltd., Osaka, Japan

Mexico: Gordon Ross, Chiapas, Tapachula, Mexico

New Zealand: Peter B. Dow & Co., Box 696, Gisborne, New Zealand

Pakistan: Sheriff Farms, Karachi, West Pakistan

South Africa: Straathof's Seed Co., Johannesburg, South Africa

Spain: Semillas Pacifico, Sevilla, Spain

Sweden: General Swedish Seed Co., Svalov, Sweden

Switzerland: Haubensak-Schollenbrecker Seeds, Ltd., Bottmingen, Switzerland

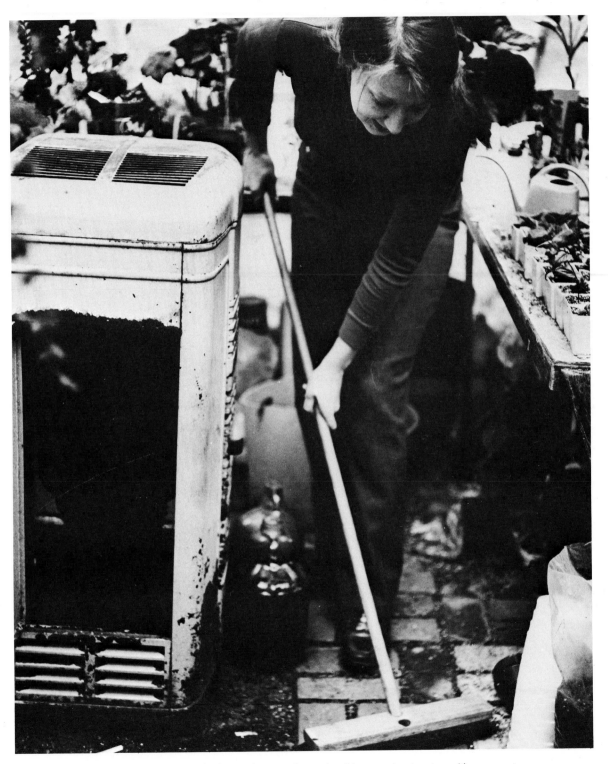

Keeping the greenhouse picked up and storing chemicals safely are major steps toward happy growing

Caution with chemicals is only one of the safety precautions to follow

SAFETY

Greenhouse gardening, like many hobby activities, is a lot of fun as long as there are no accidents. This chapter is designed to help you avoid accidents in the greenhouse—by maintaining an attitude of caution and care—or to deal with accidents should they happen. The following checklist should help you have a safe greenhouse.

PREVENTING ACCIDENTS

Chemicals

☐ Do you read the label?
The manufacturer spends a lot of money creating a label to inform and protect you. Before you purchase a chemical, read the label to find out:

1. If the chemical will do what you need done

2. If the material is too toxic to be used safely

3. If protective clothing is required for application

4. How, when, and in what quantities to apply the chemical

☐ Are your chemicals kept in a locked cabinet? (Children should not have access to toxic materials.)

☐ Do you wrap and mark empty chemical containers for disposal by the garbage collector? Or do you bury empty containers at least 18 inches deep in an area away from water supply?

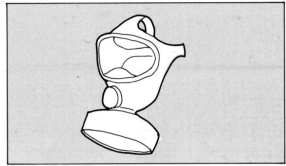

Fig. 110
Gas mask for protection from highly toxic fumes

Fig. 111
Dual-cartridge respirator for protection against harmful chemical dusts and sprays

☐ Where is the respirator or gas mask?
Most home hobby growers will not use the highly toxic chemicals that require wearing a gas mask *(fig. 110)*. The dual-filter respirator *(fig. 111)* should be in the storage compartment with the chemicals, however, to use when applying dusts or sprays of agricultural chemicals. Make certain that the chemical cartridges are changed after eight hours of actual use (or oftener if chemical odor is detected).

147

☐ Where are the protective gloves?
Use rubber gloves—cloth or leather gloves absorb chemicals and increase the injury to your skin from toxic or caustic chemicals. Garden gloves and kitchen gloves, unless they are made of rubber, are not suitable for handling chemicals. Test the gloves for pin holes by filling with water and squeezing—discard those with holes.

Fire

☐ Where is the fire extinguisher?
Mount a fire extinguisher inside or close to the greenhouse. Check to see that the extinguisher is rated for control of electrical fires *(fig. 112)*—most greenhouse fires are electrical in origin. Read the directions for the extinguisher's use immediately—and stay familiar with the instructions so that in case of fire you can grab it and go!

Fig. 112
Fire extinguisher is handy

Heating

As a precaution against fire, have the wiring for the heating system installed by a competent electrician. Often a greenhouse is erected with a 100-volt current for lighting, and later heaters are added that may overload the wire service—the overloading heats up the wire to the point where it can start a fire.

☐ Do you check or have your heating system checked each fall before winter use for the following:

1. Proper venting for oil and gas heaters?

2. Loose stack or stove pipe?

3. Dirty or clogged nozzles?

4. Soot accumulated in stove or flue?

Physical hazards

☐ Do you have tripping or slipping hazards?
1. Are the walks free of flats, pots, boxes, garden hoses, tools, etc.?

2. Are the walks free of slippery algae and moss? (If not, clean them with Clorox or Javex.)

☐ How is your back?
Carrying heavy containers of wet peat moss, soil or compost, fertilizer, etc. can cause back injury.

1. Use a hand truck or wheelbarrow, such as the one shown in *figure 113*

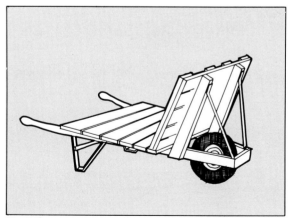

Fig. 113
Wheelbarrow makes moving easier

2. Store materials in plastic garbage cans *(fig. 114)* that are moved easily with a hand truck

Fig. 114
Tightly-covered plastic cans make safe storage

☐ Do you wear shoes?

Bare feet in the greenhouse can step on a sharp or pointed object or come in contact with materials that are injurious, for example, a chemical solution, which may be absorbed through the skin.

DEALING WITH ACCIDENTS

☐ Where are the telephone numbers for aid?

At the least, the following numbers should be permanently posted in a clearly visible spot beside the telephone:

1. Police Department—aid car service

2. Fire Department—aid car service

3. Nearest hospital

4. Nearest Poison Control Center

5. Family physician

☐ Does someone know first aid?

It is a good idea for one member of every family to have some first aid training for emergencies.

☐ Where is the first aid kit?

There should be a first aid kit in the locked storage compartment for chemicals. Put in some salt and milk of magnesia for use

if chemicals are swallowed. The following section outlines first aid steps if an accident occurs that involves a chemical.

First aid for chemical poisoning

We are exposed to toxic chemicals in the medicine chest, in the cleaning closet, and in the garage. But instead of making such materials illegal, we should learn how to use and store the chemicals properly. If an accident does occur, however, the following first-aid measures should be taken.

If you are alone:

1. Check the victim's respiration—if there is no breathing, apply artificial respiration *(fig. 115)*

2. Stop exposure to poison

3. Call a physician

If there is someone with you:

1. Have the other person call a physician

2. Check the victim's respiration— if there is no breathing, apply artificial respiration

3. Stop exposure to poison

Chemicals on the skin

1. Drench the victim's clothing and skin with water

2. Remove clothing

3. Wash skin thoroughly with soap and water

Chemicals in the eye

1. Hold the eyelids open

2. Wash eyes out with a gentle stream of water for at least fifteen minutes

Chemicals swallowed

1. Induce vomiting (EXCEPT in circumstances listed under point 2)

2. DO NOT induce vomiting, instead give milk, water, or milk of magnesia when:

   a. The victim is in a coma or has convulsions

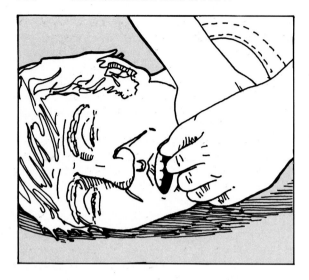
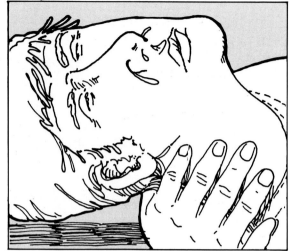
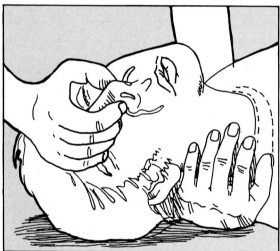
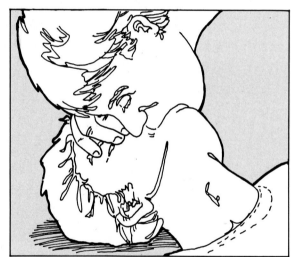

Fig. 115
Mouth-to-mouth resuscitation

1. Place victim on back and clear any foreign material from the mouth

2. Tilt head back by lifting the neck from the back—the jaw must be jutting (this should keep the tongue from falling back and blocking the passage of air)

3. Pinch the nostrils closed with one hand, keeping firm upward pressure on the neck

4. Blow vigorously into the victim's mouth, then raise your head to watch for chest movements and to listen for the movement of air from the victim's nose and mouth. Repeat

twelve times per minute for adults, twenty times for children (caution: it is possible for an adult to rupture a child's lungs if too much force is used; use smaller breaths, depending on the child's size)

A final note: if you anticipate the need for using mouth-to-mouth resuscitation, consider taking a first-aid course (which often is available through the fire department or the Red Cross). The course would give you a chance to practice the procedures as well as inform you of potential problems (such as a tendency for the victim to expel the contents of the stomach)

b. The victim has swallowed a corrosive such as lye

3. Wrap victim in a blanket for warmth until help arrives or you get the victim to a hospital

4. Get medical help:

    a. Call a physician

    b. Drive the victim to the nearest hospital, taking the chemical container with you

POISONOUS PLANTS

We currently are moving plants all over the world —your favorite plant shop may well have foliage plants from Africa, Asia, and South America. For many of these plants, we do not have information available as to their toxic or irritant qualities. The safe procedure, therefore, is not to eat or make a brew of any plant with which you are not familiar. If you have questions about poisonous plants, call or visit the nearest Poison Control Center. If the center is not listed in a phone book, call the nearest hospital for information.

The same also can be said for plants in your greenhouse and on home property. The safe procedure is to exercise good judgment yourself and to instruct your children to follow two simple rules:

1. Do not eat, put into the mouth, or use to make tea or drink, any part of any plant

2. If you see someone else playing with or eating plant parts, tell a parent or another adult at once

SOURCES

General information

CANADA:
The Wild Food Trail Guide. Alan Hall. Holt, Rinehart & Winston, 55 Horner Ave., Toronto, Ontario

UNITED STATES:
Poisonous Plants of the United States. W. C. Munescher. MacMillan, 866 3rd Ave., New York, NY 10022

Also

Physician (your own)

Poison Control Center (your local)

Safety Council (your local)

Supplies

UNITED STATES:
Willson Products (safety equipment), P.O. Box 622, Reading, PA 19603

See the General Appendix, Sources of Supply.

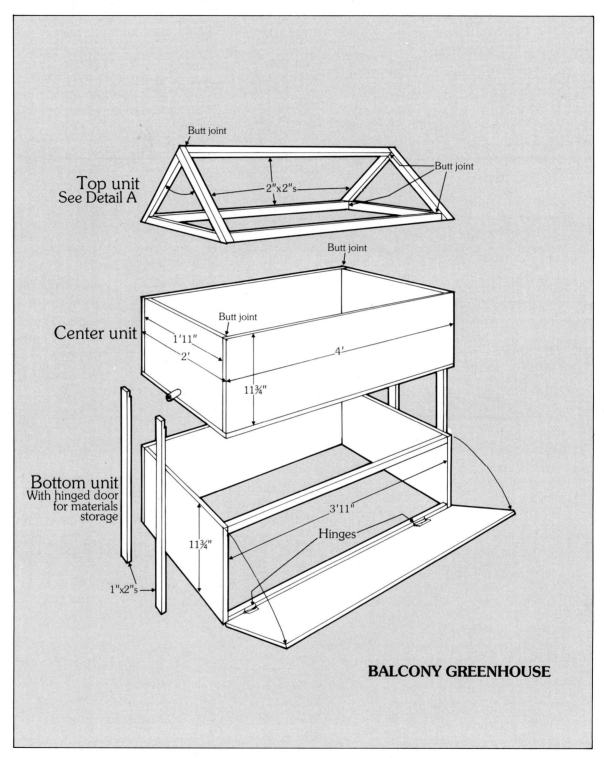

Butt joint

Top unit
See Detail A

2"x2"s

Butt joint

Butt joint

Butt joint

Center unit

Butt joint

1'11"

2'

4'

11¾"

Bottom unit
With hinged door
for materials
storage

3'11"

Hinges

11¾"

1"x2"s

BALCONY GREENHOUSE

APPENDIX
Chapter 1
Structures

BALCONY GREENHOUSE

Materials
One sheet of ½" exterior grade plywood
34' of 2"x 2" lumber (remember, this is usually
    milled to 1½"x 1½")
9' of 1"x 2" lumber
One sheet of ¼" plexiglass 3'x 5'3"
Three 3" chrome hinges with ¾" bolts
Three 3" chrome hinges with wood screws
Roll of 6-mil polyethylene
4" piece of ¾" PVC pipe
1¼" #9 size brass or galvanized screws
2" galvanized nails
Plastic-resin glue
Latch mechanism and handle
Redwood stain, if desired
Waterproof tape

Tools
As a minimum, you will need:
Pencil
Tape measure
Drill and bits (a power drill helps)
Screwdriver
Hammer
Saw
Mitre box
Plastic-resin glue (usually a powder you mix with
    water; do not use white glue!)
Sandpaper
Mitre clamps (sold to help in making picture
    frames; these are not essential, but they help
    make nice, square corners and hold the
    corners steady better than any friend can)

Lumberyards have specialized equipment that takes the hassle out of working with a 4'x 8' piece of plywood. You should be able to find a lumberyard that will cut the plywood for you.

Other greenhouse projects in the appendix require some experience with woodworking (also a bit of masonry). You will notice that the instructions for these structures include more drawings and less descriptions. There are many books available on woodworking; you might wish to start slowly, using the more specialized volumes.

PROCEDURE

Cutting

1. Plywood (see detail A):
   Cut the plywood cross-wise into six pieces
   11¾" wide
   Cut two of these into four pieces 1'11"
   long
   Cut the remainder of the sheet down to
   2' width

2. 2"x 2" lumber:
   Cut three pieces 3'9" long
   Cut two pieces 3'11" long
   Cut the remainder as you construct the
   top, referring to the diagrams (particularly detail A)

3. 1"x 2" lumber
   Cut four pieces 2'1" long

4. Plexiglass (see detail A):
   Cut the piece in two, 4' from one end
   Cut this piece lengthwise to get two pieces
   1'5" wide
   Save the remainder of the sheet for the
   end pieces; cut to fit later

Constructing
Note: apply plastic-resin glue to all wood joints and use screws to secure. Remember not to tighten them too much since plywood side-grain is not very strong.

1. Center unit:
   Construct a box using two 1'11" pieces
   and two 4' pieces, as shown

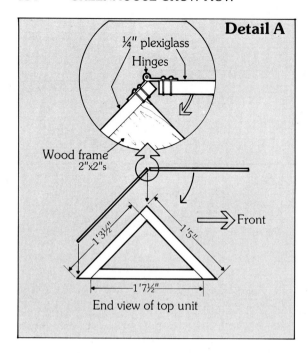

Detail A

¼" plexiglass

Hinges

Wood frame
2"x2"s

Front

1'3½"   1'5"

1'7½"

End view of top unit

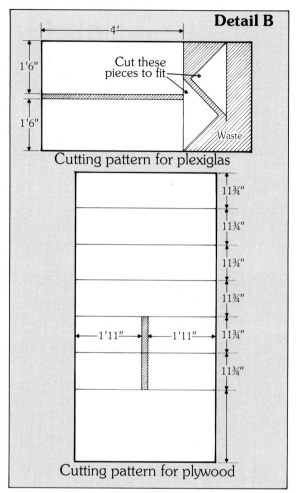

Detail B

4'

1'6"

Cut these
pieces to fit

1'6"

Waste

Cutting pattern for plexiglas

11¾"

11¾"

11¾"

11¾"

1'11"   1'11"   11¾"

11¾"

Cutting pattern for plywood

Attach the 2'x4' piece to the bottom of this assembly

Line the box with 6-mil polyethylene, folding neatly at the corners

Drill a ¾" diameter hole, as shown, and glue the 4" piece of pipe in. Use waterproof tape to attach the polyethylene lining to the pipe for water drainage

2. Bottom unit:
    Take the remaining pieces of plywood and the two 3'11" pieces of 2"x 2"; attach the two shorter pieces to one of the longer pieces in the same fashion as in number 1, but in place of the second long piece, put in the two pieces of 2"x 2" (they go "inside" the box, at top and bottom, as shown)

    Take the remaining piece of plywood and cut ⅝" off so that instead of being 11¾" wide it's now 11⅛" wide; attach the three hinges with wood screws to the lower long edge

Lay this on the ground in front of the box and attach the hinges to the lower end of the 2"x 2"s; now attach the latch (generally there are instructions with these) and the handle

3. Top unit:
    This is the tricky part, so measure, and work slowly and carefully. You may wish to buy several extra feet of lumber for any "contingencies"
    Build one end of the frame at a time. First,

cut one piece of 2"x 2" 1'7½" long; cut both ends to 45° so that both are sloping up (check to be sure the long side remains 1'7½"

Cut two pieces of 2"x 2" so that one end is square and one end is 45°—one piece should measure 1'3½" on the long side and the second piece 1'5"

Assemble these pieces as shown in detail A, starting with the butt joint at the top of the frame

Go through the same procedure for the other end

Finally, attach the three 3'9" cross-pieces to these frames as shown on the two drawings

Now attach the plexiglass to the frame; the back piece is fastened down to the 2"x 2"s, and the front piece is hinged off of it; you also should cut out the two plexiglass end pieces and fasten them to the outside of the frame

4. To attach the units, fasten the four 2'1"x 1"x 2" pieces to the ends of the lower box, as shown, and stack the center box on top. You will need to notch the top portion of these 1"x 2"s to accommodate the thickness of the plexiglass. Finish fastening each unit to these 1"x 2"s and you're done—stain the wood if you wish

COLDFRAME GREENHOUSE

Materials

One sheet of ½" exterior grade plywood
8' of 2"x 2" lumber (remember, this is usually milled to 1½"x 1½"
48' of ½"x 2½" pine lattice (actual size)
3' of 1"x 2"
Two pieces of flat 5-ounce clear fiberglass 5'6"x 4'1"
1¼" #9 size brass or galvanized screws
½" flathead galvanized nails
1" flathead galvanized nails
Three 3" chrome hinges with appropriate size

and quantity hex bolts to mount half the hinge with bolts, ¾" long and the other half 2" long (also need plenty of washers)
Redwood stain, if desired

Tools

See the preceding section, Balcony Greenhouse, for a list of tools

PROCEDURE

Cutting

1. 2"x 2" lumber:
   Cut two pieces 1'6" long, two pieces 2' long, and save scrap; cut the end of each of the four pieces to a point (preferably pyramid shaped)

2. Plywood (see detail A):
   Make first cut 2'6" in from one end; set aside
   Make the lengthwise cuts: first 1'6", then 1'; cut the rest into 3" pieces. Take three of these pieces and cut them to 4'1" long (see detail B for cutting details for *all* of these 3" pieces)
   Now take the first piece you set aside, and make marks 1' in from opposite sides, as shown; draw a line connecting these, and cut the piece in half (try to make these pieces the same size; it makes the fit better)

3. ½"x 2½" pine lattice:
   Don't cut this up until you begin construction; it is easier then

Constructing

Note: apply plastic-resin glue to all wood joints and use screws to secure. Remember not to tighten them too much since plywood side-grain is not very strong.

1. Base:
   Attach one short 2"x 2" and one long 2"x 2" to either end of piece **b** (match short to short, long to long) with wood screws; they should be flush to the top and to the long edge
   Do the same for the opposite piece **b**, re-

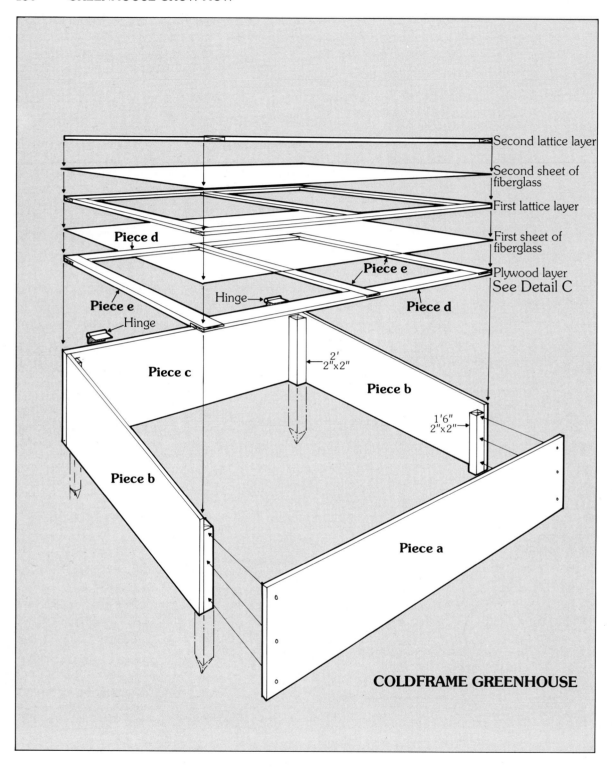

Second lattice layer

Second sheet of fiberglass

First lattice layer

First sheet of fiberglass

Piece d

Piece e

Plywood layer
See Detail C

Hinge

Piece e

Hinge

Piece d

Hinge

Piece c

2'
2"x2"

Piece b

1'6"
2"x2"

Piece b

Piece a

COLDFRAME GREENHOUSE

membering that the 2"x 2"s go on the other side of it

Attach pieces **a** and **c** to the appropriate ends; overlapping the ends of piece **b** with a butt-joint; set aside

2. Lid:

Cut the 3" strips of plywood, as shown, for the lapjoints; this works best if you have access to a radial-arm saw, but a back saw and chisel will work if you go slowly

Assemble the pieces with glue and with the flathead nails (it may help to clamp the joints while they dry)

Now take one piece of the clear fiberglass and nail it down on the plywood, using the ½" nails (see appendix, chapter 2 for working with fiberglass)

Take the ½"x 2½" lattice and lay it over the top of the fiberglass (*now* is when you

want to cut it). Cut it to fit neatly along the plywood frame. Attach with the 1" nails. Now apply another layer of fiberglass and another layer of lattice, and you've got the lid done

3. Assembly:

Attach the hinges to the underside of the lid with the 2" long bolts (see detail C); lay the lid on the base and drill the holes for the hinges in piece **c**

Take the whole thing to the area in which you've decided to set up; using the scrap 2"x 2" and a hammer, "nail" the corner pieces into the ground; work slowly, putting all four corners into the soil at the same time (like tightening lug-nuts, for you auto mechanics)

Now attach the hinges with the ¾" bolts, and you're done

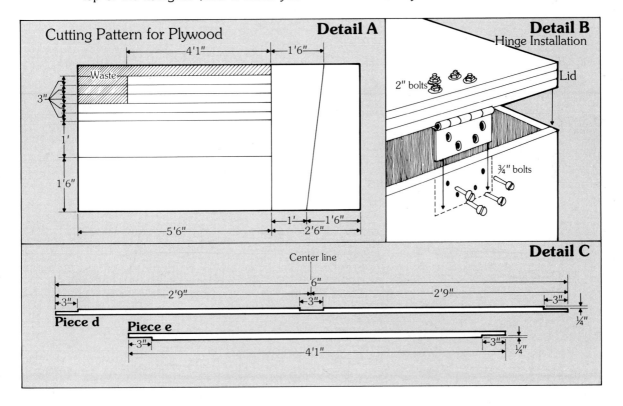

HOTBED

PROCEDURE

Installing

Adding a soil heating cable to the coldframe structure will give you a hotbed for growing at regulated temperatures. The electrical output of heating cable varies with the manufacturer. The cable can be installed from 2 to 4 lineal feet per square foot of bed. Follow the manufacturer's recommendations.

To avoid problems of cable installation and spacing, you can use a propagating mat instead, available in 22"x 60" and 18"x 70" for about $50.00. With a propagating mat there is an adjustable thermostat that allows you to regulate the soil temperature. Cost of the thermostat is about $40.00.

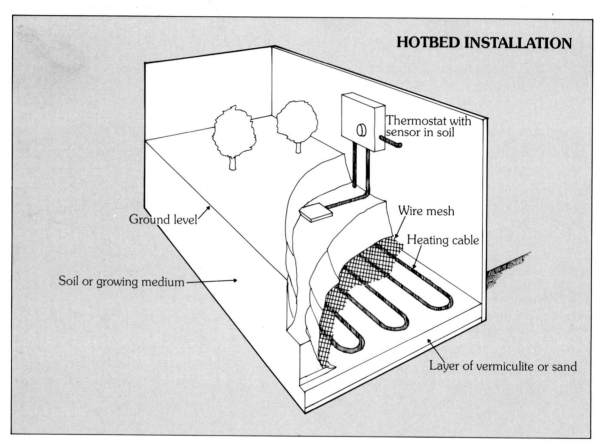

HOTBED INSTALLATION

Thermostat with sensor in soil

Wire mesh

Heating cable

Ground level

Soil or growing medium

Layer of vermiculite or sand

FREESTANDING GREENHOUSE

The freestanding greenhouse requires a good deal of skill and some larger power tools (a radial-arm saw is best at minimum) for construction.

It takes about 250 feet of 2"x 4" lumber, 10 feet of 1"x 2" lumber, 6 feet of 1"x 4", and a piece of 2"x 2" about a foot long. In addition, you may wish to build windows, which can be propped open to gain extra ventilation in very hot country; this needs an addi-tional 120 feet of 2"x 4" lumber. All four sides and the roof are fiberglassed.

The plans shown here are for a greenhouse 8-feet square. If you wish, you can build it 8-feet-by-12-feet or longer. Just work in 4-foot increments; all you do is add more center constructions. You will want to refer to the appendix, chapter 2, on working with fiberglass, both for applying fiberglass and for flashings. You also will want to check the section on foundations that follows.

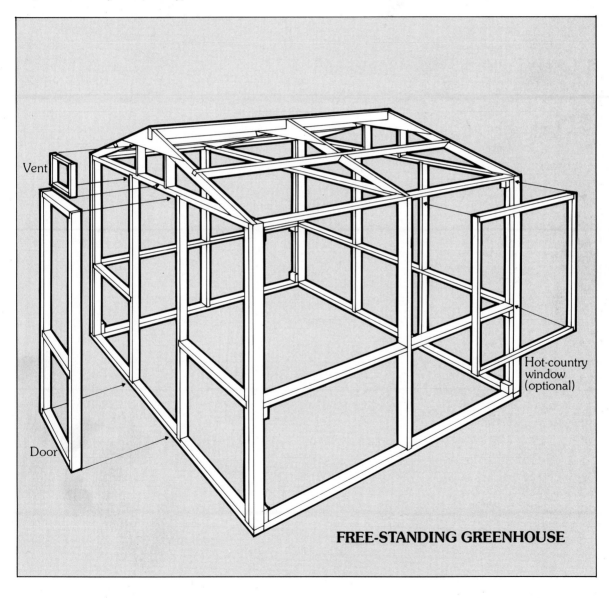

Vent

Door

Hot-country window (optional)

FREE-STANDING GREENHOUSE

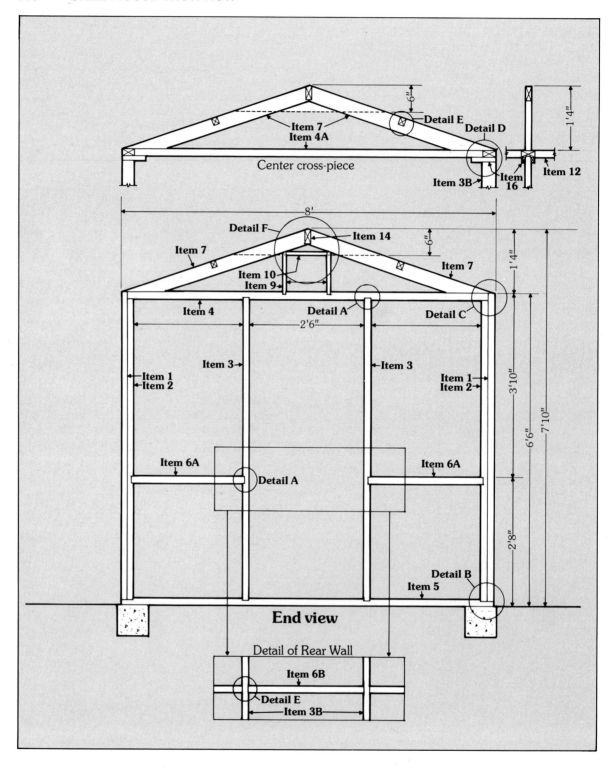

Center cross-piece

End view

Detail of Rear Wall

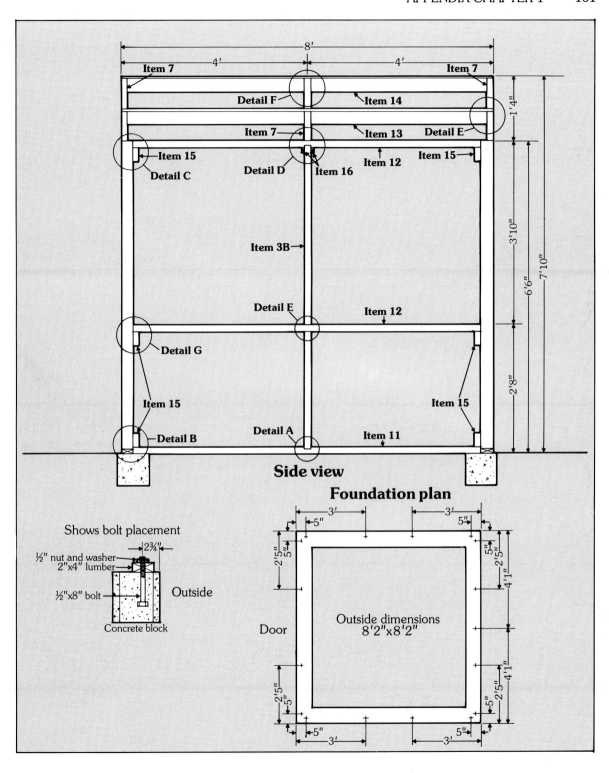

Side view

Foundation plan

Shows bolt placement

½" nut and washer
2"x4" lumber
2¾"
½"x8" bolt
Outside
Concrete block

Door

Outside dimensions
8'2"x8'2"

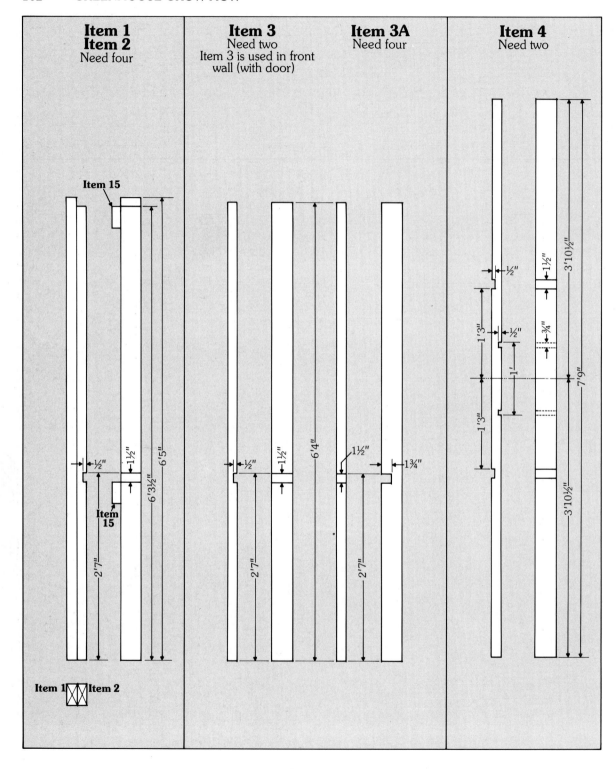

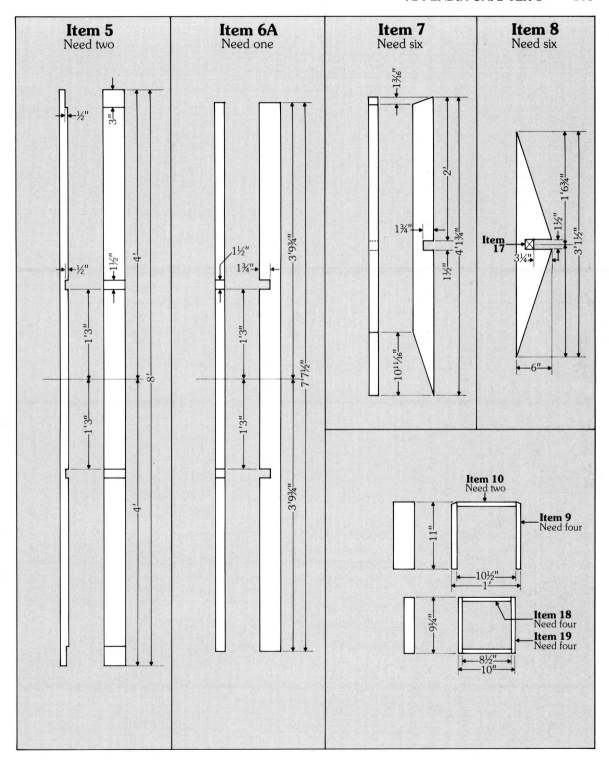

Item 5
Need two

3″ · ½″ · 1½″ · ½″ · 4′ · 1′3″ · 8′ · 1′3″ · 4′

Item 6A
Need one

1½″ · 1¾″ · 3′9¾″ · 7′7½″ · 1′3″ · 1′3″ · 3′9¾″

Item 7
Need six

1³⁄₁₆″ · 2′ · 1¾″ · 4′1¾″ · 1½″ · 10¹¹⁄₁₆″

Item 8
Need six

1³⁄₁₆″ · Item 17 · 3¼″ · ½″ · 1′6¾″ · 3′1½″ · 6″

Item 10
Need two

Item 9
Need four

11″ · 10½″ · 1′

9¼″ · 8½″ · 10″

Item 18
Need four

Item 19
Need four

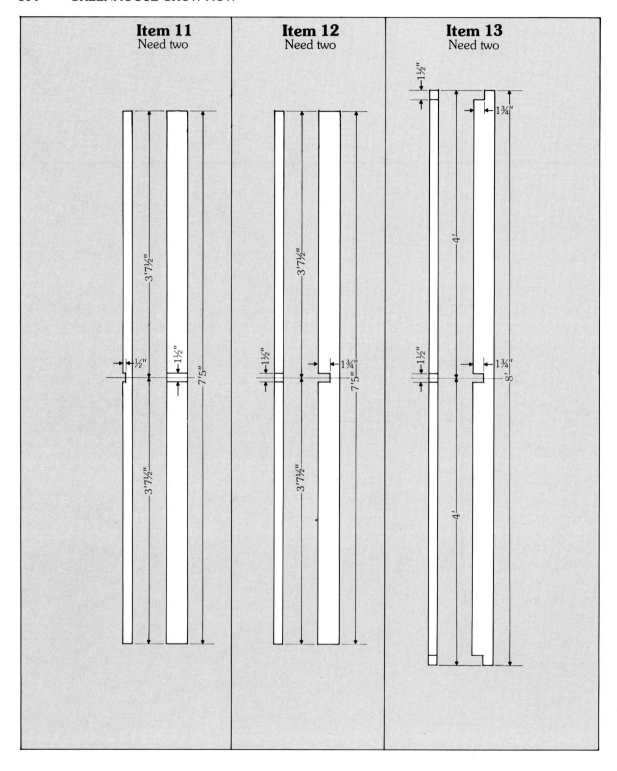

Item 11
Need two

Item 12
Need two

Item 13
Need two

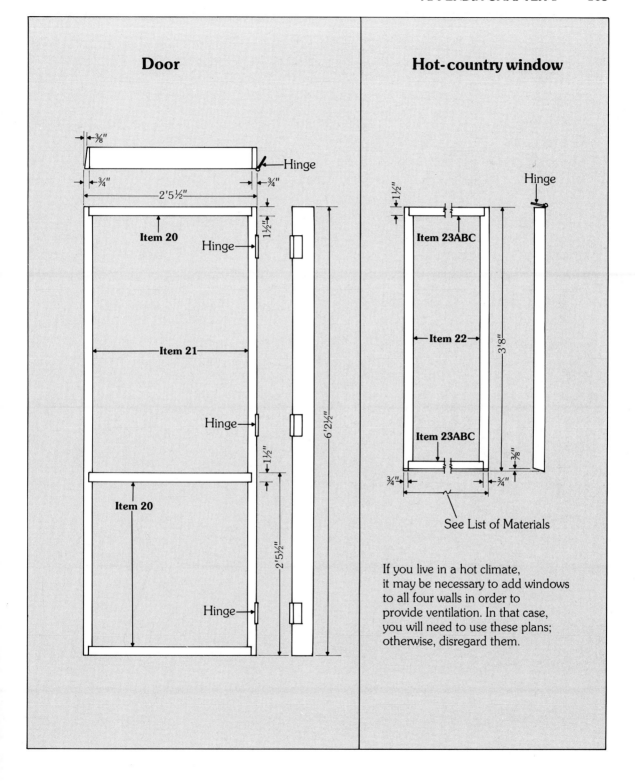

Door

Hot-country window

If you live in a hot climate,
it may be necessary to add windows
to all four walls in order to
provide ventilation. In that case,
you will need to use these plans;
otherwise, disregard them.

See List of Materials

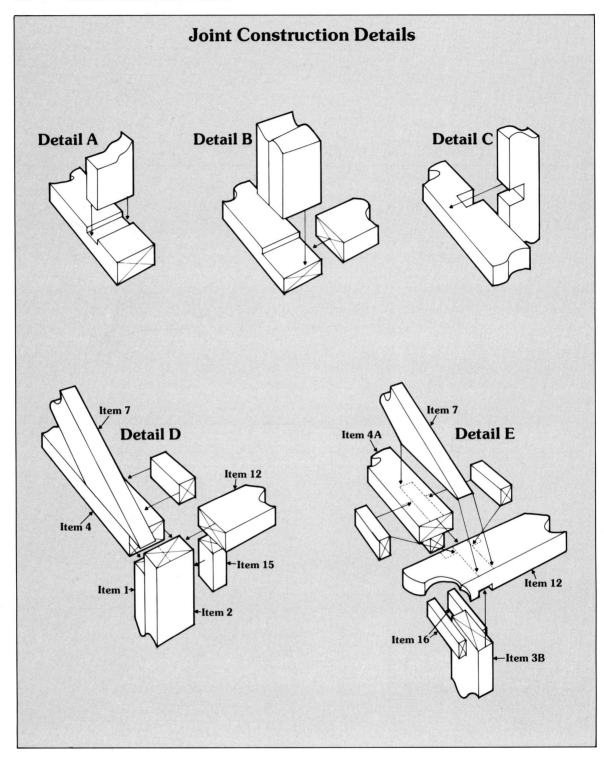

Joint Construction Details

Detail A

Detail B

Detail C

Detail D

Item 7

Item 12

Item 4

Item 1

Item 15

Item 2

Detail E

Item 7

Item 4A

Item 12

Item 16

Item 3B

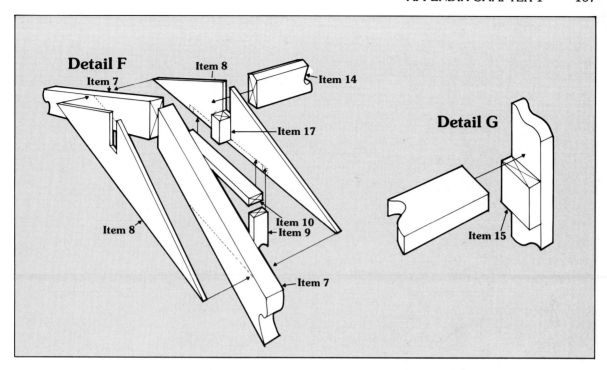

Detail F

Item 7

Item 8

Item 14

Item 17

Detail G

Item 8

Item 10
Item 9

Item 15

Item 7

List of Materials

Item	Number Required	Length	Material	Item	Number Required	Length	Material
1	4	6′5″	2″x4″ lumber	**13**	2	8′	2″x4″ lumber
2	4	6′3½″	2″x4″ lumber	**14**	1	8′	2″x4″ lumber
3	4	6′4″	2″x4″ lumber	**15**	12	4″	2″x4″ lumber
4	3	7′9″	2″x4″ lumber	**16**	4	6″	1″x2″ lumber
5	2	8′	2″x4″ lumber	**17**	3	1½″	2″x2″ lumber
6A	2	2′5¼″	2″x4″ lumber	**18**	4	8½″	1″x2″ lumber
6B	1	7′7″	2″x4″ lumber	**19**	4	9¼″	1″x2″ lumber
7	6	4′1¾″	2″x4″ lumber	**20**	3	2′4″	2″x4″ lumber
8	6	See plan	¼″ exterior plywood	**21**	2	6′2½″	2″x4″ lumber
9	4	11″	1″x4″ lumber	**22**	18	3′6″	2″x2″ lumber
10	2	10½″	1″x2″ lumber	**23A**	8	3′5½″	2″x2″ lumber
11	2	7′5″	2″x4″ lumber	**23B**	2	2′5½″	2″x2″ lumber
12	4	7′5″	2″x4″ lumber	**23C**	8	2′1½″	2″x2″ lumber

LEAN-TO GREENHOUSE

The lean-to greenhouse is an excellent structure if you have a south-facing wall of your home or garage that you can spare. It also allows direct access to the greenhouse from your home if you position it by a door.

The structure requires about 215 feet of 2"x 4" lumber, 17 feet of 1"x 2", and 2 feet of 2"x 2", plus fiberglass and siding. You will need about 95 more feet of lumber if you are in a warm climate and choose to make hinged windows to enable maximum air flow.

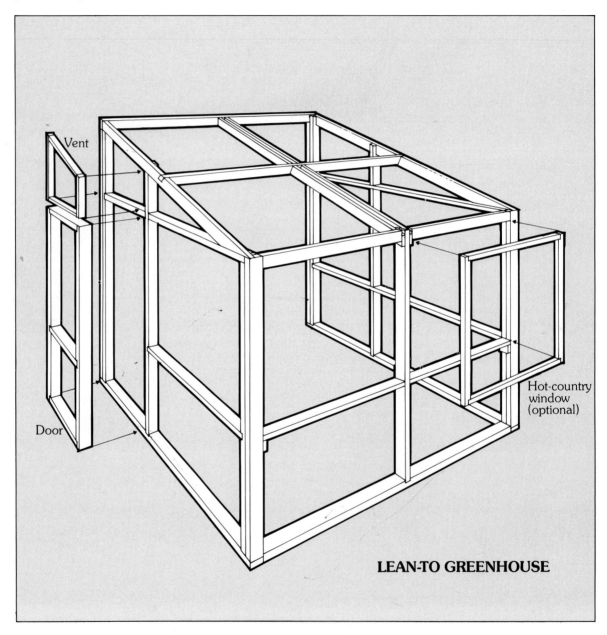

Vent

Door

Hot-country window (optional)

LEAN-TO GREENHOUSE

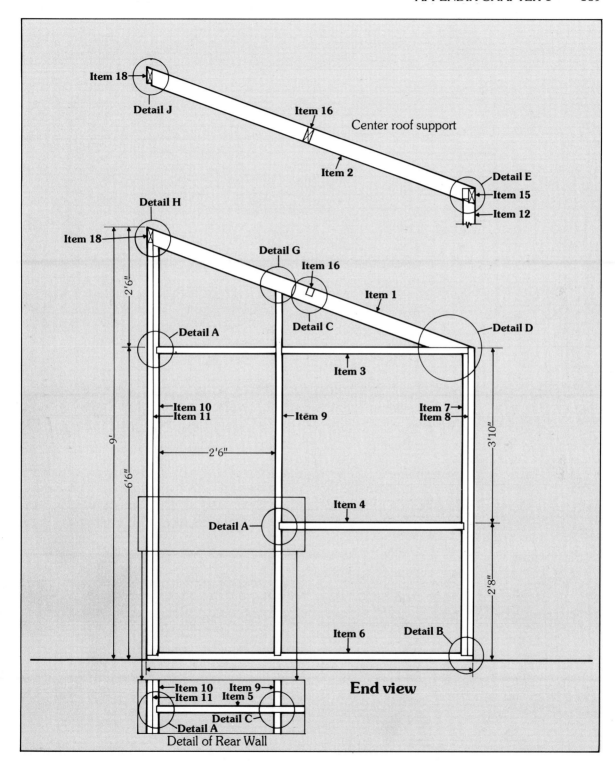

Center roof support

End view

Detail of Rear Wall

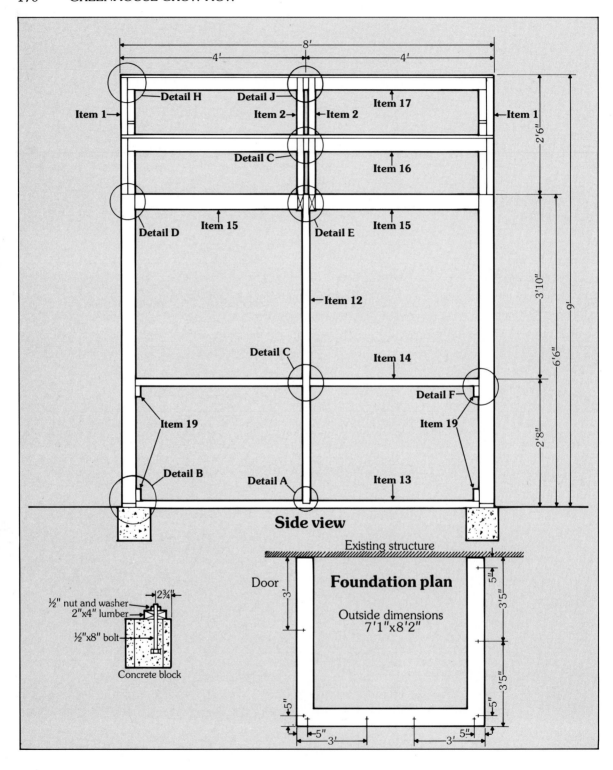

Side view

½" nut and washer
2"x4" lumber
½"x8" bolt
2¾"
Concrete block

Foundation plan

Existing structure
Door
Outside dimensions
7'1"x8'2"
3'
5"
3'5"
3'5"
5"
5"
5"
3'
3'

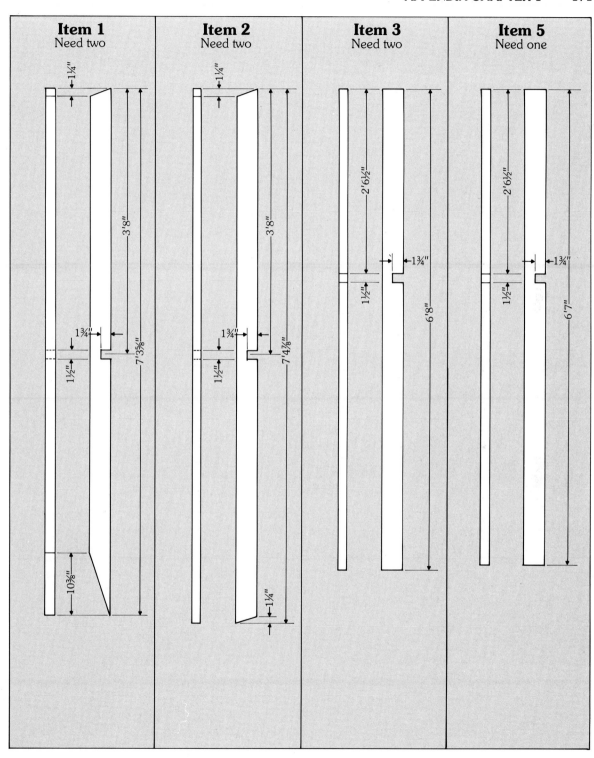

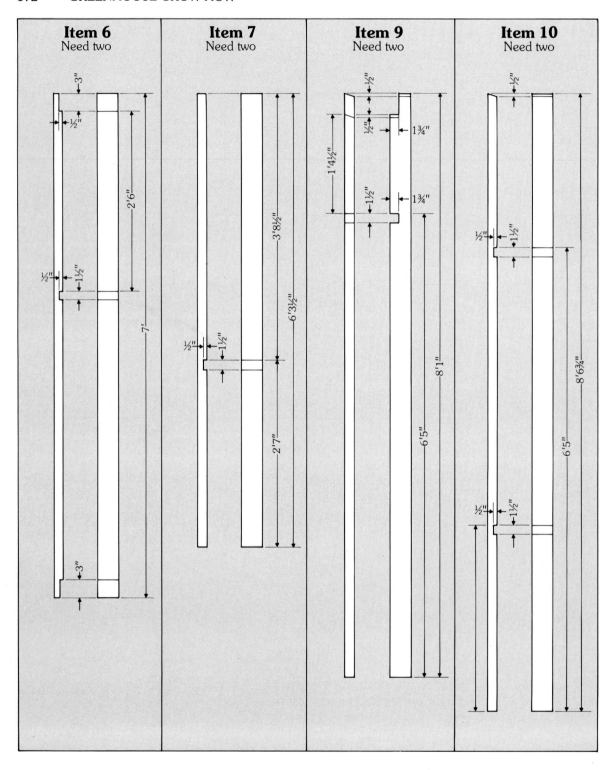

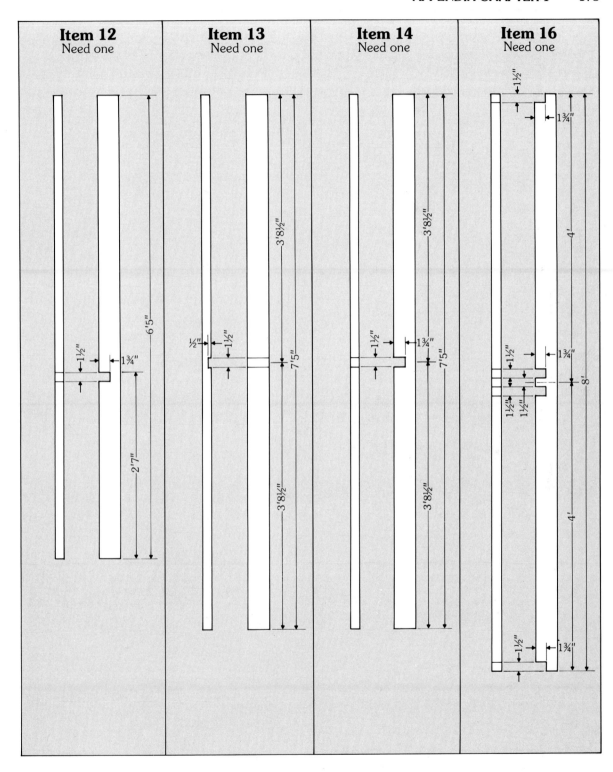

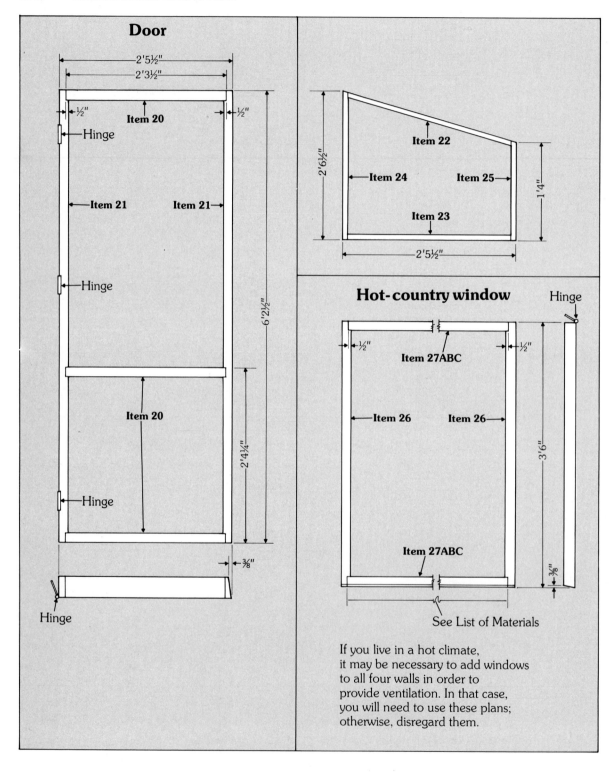

Door

2'5½"
2'3½"

½"

Item 20

½"

Hinge

Item 21   Item 21

Hinge

6'2½"

Item 20

2'4¼"

Hinge

Hinge

⅜"

Hot-country window

Hinge

½"

Item 27ABC

½"

Item 26   Item 26

3'6"

Item 27ABC

⅜"

Item 22

Item 24   Item 25

Item 23

2'6½"

1'4"

2'5½"

See List of Materials

If you live in a hot climate,
it may be necessary to add windows
to all four walls in order to
provide ventilation. In that case,
you will need to use these plans;
otherwise, disregard them.

Joint Construction Details

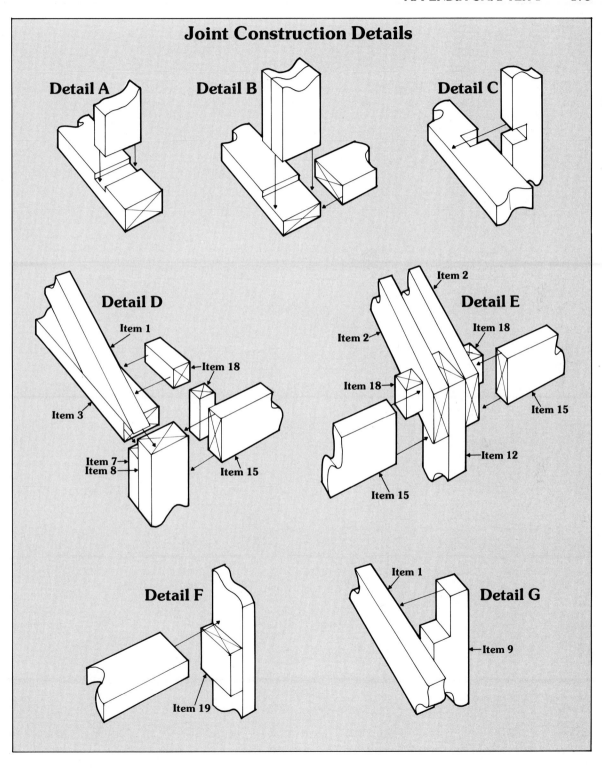

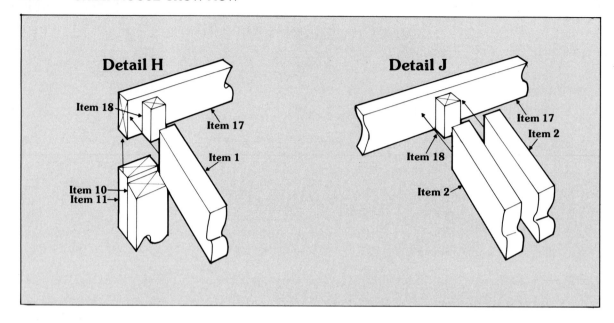

List of Materials

Item	Number Required	Length	Material	Item	Number Required	Length	Material
1	2	7'3⅜"	2"x4" lumber	16	1	8'	2"x4" lumber
2	2	7'4⅞"	2"x4" lumber	17	1	8'	2"x4" lumber
3	2	6'8"	2"x4" lumber	18	7	3"	2"x2" lumber
4	1	3'11"	2"x4" lumber	19	4	4"	2"x4" lumber
5	1	6'7"	2"x4" lumber	20	3	2'3½"	2"x4" lumber
6	2	7'	2"x4" lumber	21	2	6'2½"	2"x4" lumber
7	2	6'3½"	2"x4" lumber	22	1	2'5"	1"x2" lumber
8	2	6'5"	2"x4" lumber	23	1	2'4"	1"x2" lumber
9	2	8'1"	2"x4" lumber	24	1	2'6½"	1"x2" lumber
10	2	8'6¾"	2"x4" lumber	25	1	1'4"	1"x2" lumber
11	2	8'7½"	2"x4" lumber	26	10	3'8"	2"x2" lumber
12	1	6'5"	2"x4" lumber	27A	4	3'7"	2"x2" lumber
13	1	7'5"	2"x4" lumber	27B	4	3'10"	2"x2" lumber
14	1	7'5"	2"x4" lumber	27C	2	2' 3½"	2"x2" lumber
15	2	3'4¾"	2"x4" lumber				

PLANT ROOM

Plants normally grow out of doors or in a greenhouse where dirt and moisture do not cause problems. When you convert a room in the residence for growing plants, the following guidelines will help. If you are reticent to tackle the problems of a plant room, enlist the services of a good architect.

1. To avoid water damage to the residence structure, use waterproof materials for walls, floors, and benches; self-adhering vinyl is one of the best, and it cleans easily

2. If necessary, install a floor drain to the out-of-doors or the plumbing system

3. Install a kitchen exhaust fan near the ceiling to carry off excess water vapor

4. To maintain humidity, use a humidifier that breaks up the water into very fine droplets—you need a minimum of 50% relative humidity

5. To get more light, install plexiglass skylights

6. To ensure adequate air movement, install a small fan that is rated at about 100 cfm

FOUNDATIONS

PROCEDURE

1. Prepare the site by clearing the sod from an area slightly larger than the outside dimensions of the structure, removing about 3" or so. If you plan to run electrical or plumbing lines, or both, into the greenhouse, dig a trench deep enough to go below the frost line (check with local agricultural authorities for exact depths). Lay in the lines before you begin leveling the foundation

   Tamp the soil firmly and lay out your concrete blocks (use blocks measuring 8"x 8"x 16," and keep in mind, you will need space between them for mortar), making sure they will be level all around

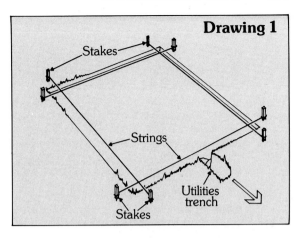

Drawing 1

Stakes

Strings

Stakes

Utilities trench

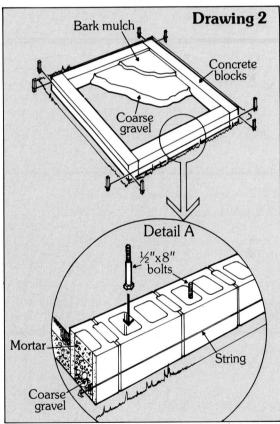

Drawing 2

Bark mulch

Concrete blocks

Coarse gravel

Detail A

½"x8" bolts

Mortar

String

Coarse gravel

This is very important! If the foundation is not level, the rest of the structure will not go together properly

2. Lay out stakes to mark off the dimensions of your greenhouse (drawing 1), and attach strings

3. Mix your mortar, and lay the blocks out end-to-end around the entire area

4. Determine the space intervals at which you will place the bolts to attach the base of the greenhouse (drawing 2); each design in the appendix includes these measurements

5. Fill all the hollow cores in the blocks ¾ full of coarse gravel (*except* the bolt holes), and finish filling with mortar to the top of the block. On the bolt holes, fill the hole with thick mortar, and insert the bolt upside down, until only 2" to 2¼" is still out; the bolt should be as vertical as you can make it (detail A)

6. When you finish with the bolts, you are ready to proceed with the construction of your greenhouse: begin by putting a 6"-8" layer of coarse gravel inside on the "floor," and top with bark mulch to make the walking easier

PREFABRICATED FIBERGLASS GREENHOUSE

You will follow the manufacturer's instructions to assemble the greenhouse, but one problem that occurs frequently with a prefabricated structure is that it is too low, so you bang your head all the time. Decide if more height is needed in your greenhouse. Figure how much, thinking in terms of 8-inch increments. You should lay the first layer solid all around, then add layers to increase height (because you will be filling in the inside with gravel and bark mulch). You will want to leave a gap where the door will be. For detailed instructions on constructing a foundation, see the preceding section.

Once you've finished the masonry, finish off the top, filling in the core, and setting bolts in positions that will be compatible with the prefabricated unit. Take a piece of exterior plywood and attach it to the bottom of the door to fill the gap. Now follow the instructions for assembly that come with the greenhouse and proceed.

PROCEDURE

1. Foundation:
Lay out and level the foundation, which can be poured concrete, concrete blocks, or 4"x 4" timbers on concrete blocks (fig. A)

2. Frame:
When you are certain everything is level, lay out the bottom sill on top of the foundation (fig. B)

Raise the uprights (fig. C), making sure to brace them temporarily—check them with a level to make certain they are plumb

Install the side strip, making sure that the nuts on the joining bolts are tight enough to give you rigidity (fig. D)

Lay out the eave plate and roof trusses (figs. E and F), install the ridge piece (fig. G)

Install the roof assembly (figs. G and H), using a C-clamp to hold pieces together prior to bolting; once the ridge is fastened and the mullions are in place, check all the nut and bolt fastenings to make sure they are tight

3. Fiberglass:
Install the fiberglass (figs. I, J, K, and L) (see appendix, chapter 2, for fiberglass construction details)

Install the gable and fiberglass (fig. M)

4. Ventilation:
Assemble the ventilator sections on the ground (fig. N)

POROUS CONCRETE WALKS

Brick laid on sand gets coated with algae and becomes slippery. Wood not only gets slippery, it rots out in a short time. Porous concrete provides a stable, non-skid, quick-draining surface for the greenhouse walks.

Be precise with the gravel size and the amount of water used. Do not use any sand or the concrete will not be porous! Mix well so the cement coats the particles of rock. Use a rake to level the poured mix; do not use a trowel—trowelling removes the

PREFABRICATED GREENHOUSE
(See procedure opposite)

cement coating and leaves the surface loose. Pour the mix 3 inches to 4 inches thick.

```
¼ CUBIC YARD MIX

700 lb. of ⅜" crushed rock
1½ sacks of Portland cement
¾ gal. of water

1 CUBIC YARD MIX

2,800 lb. of ⅜" crushed rock
5½ sacks of Portland cement
3 gal. of water for each sack of cement
```

APPENDIX
Chapter 2
Coverings

HOW TO APPLY FIBERGLASS

Suggestions

1. If possible, work with fiberglass in *warm* weather; in cold weather it is brittle and cracks easily

2. Fiberglass cuts easily with a cross-cut hand saw

3. Drill holes for all nails and screws

4. Wear gloves to protect your hands from the sharp edges

Flashing

Flashing is usually aluminum sheeting shaped to fit either the ridge or the side wall.

PROCEDURE

When fastening fiberglass to wood, use aluminum nails, 1¾" long, with a neoprene washer to seal the hole and to protect against vibration. Always pre-drill a hole in the fiberglass before putting the nail in.

If it is necessary to "patch" two pieces of ripple fiberglass together, overlap them by one ripple (2" if perpendicular to the rippling, and be sure the lower piece fits *under* the upper). Run a bead of mastic

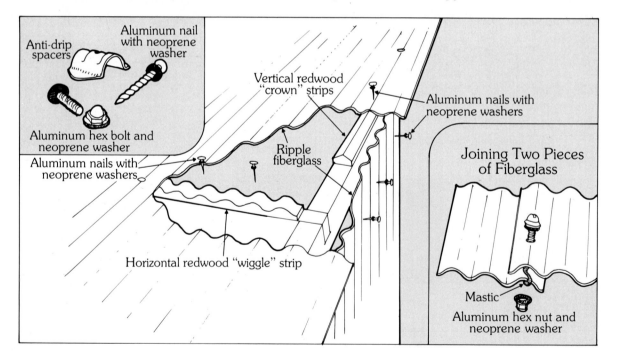

Anti-drip spacers

Aluminum nail with neoprene washer

Aluminum hex bolt and neoprene washer

Aluminum nails with neoprene washers

Vertical redwood "crown" strips

Aluminum nails with neoprene washers

Ripple fiberglass

Horizontal redwood "wiggle" strip

Joining Two Pieces of Fiberglass

Mastic

Aluminum hex nut and neoprene washer

the length of the joint to seal it, and fasten the pieces together by nailing it to a convenient truss or beam or by bolting it, using a short aluminum hex nut and

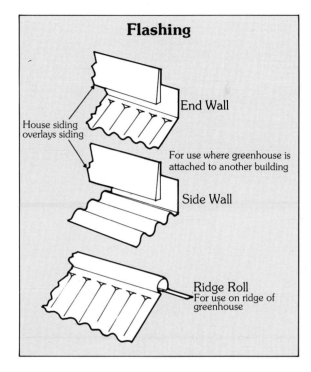

Flashing

House siding overlays siding

End Wall

For use where greenhouse is attached to another building

Side Wall

Ridge Roll
For use on ridge of greenhouse

bolt with neoprene washers on both inside and out.

When attaching ripple fiberglass (it is stronger and lighter than flat), you will use two aids: horizontal redwood "wiggle" strips and vertical redwood "crown" strips (see drawing). The "wiggle" strips are used at the ends and/or mid-points where the fiberglass is to be attached to cross-pieces, running perpendicular to the cross-pieces; the "crown" strips are for the vertical timbers, running *with* the ripple. You may also wish to use anti-drip spacers at beams mid-way down the roof or a wall. These have a hole for a nail to pass through, and hold the fiber-

glass just a bit above the wood, allowing water to flow to the corner.

When fastening the fiberglass to the top of a wall with a sloping edge, simply lay the nails through the low part of every third ripple. Make sure there is an overhang a few inches wide in the roof-piece above it.

HOW TO GLAZE WITH GLASS

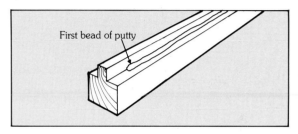

First bead of putty

1. Run a bead of putty down the bar

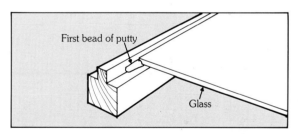

First bead of putty

Glass

2. Set the glass on top of the putty and press down lightly; allow ⅛-inch expansion room between glass and bar along each side

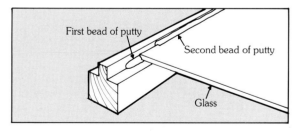

First bead of putty

Second bead of putty

Glass

3. Run a bead of top glaze along the joint of glass and wood bar to fill the space so that water cannot run in under the glass

HOW TO FASTEN POLYETHYLENE

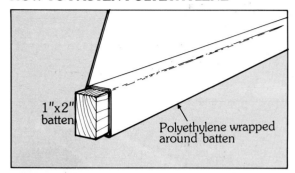

1"x2" batten

Polyethylene wrapped around batten

1. Roll a piece of 1"x2" lumber in the edge of the polyethylene for 2 or 3 wraps

2. Stretch the poly until it is taut and nail through the 1"x2" into the frame

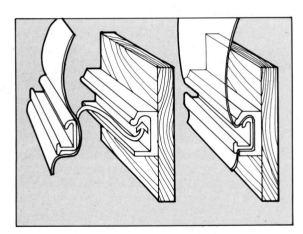

1. Fasten poly to metal by bolting or strapping a wood strip to the metal; use a 2-piece extruded aluminum device called Polylock, which can be bolted to a metal frame (costs about $.50 to $.75 per foot)

2. Permanently attach base extrusion to side board with No. 6 flathead screws through pre-punched holes provided—use 6 screws per 10-foot section

3. Proceed as described for wood frames

4. Stretch poly evenly over the locking channel and press in with the Polylock to "lock" both layers (useful in double-layer, air-inflated houses)

APPENDIX
Chapter 3
Light and Lighting

FLUORESCENT LIGHTING

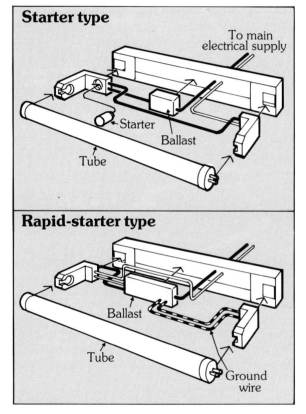

Starter type

To main electrical supply

Starter

Ballast

Tube

Rapid-starter type

Ballast

Tube

Ground wire

FIXTURE
Industrial fluorescent lights usually have a built in reflector; the channel type does not. For growing plants under artificial light, the reflector type gives better light intensity.

TUBE
There are tubes with one-pin, two-pin, and four-pin end fittings, as well as a recessed type. Those used for plant growth are usually two pin.

BALLAST
The ballast is a small transformer that regulates electrical current; it usually lasts from 10 to 12 years. Home growers can replace a ballast without difficulty.

STARTER
A starter usually lasts up to 10 years and is easy to replace.

Guidelines

1. Avoid turning fluorescents on and off more than once a day—they last twice as long if left on all the time

2. Replace when 60% of the listed service life has elapsed

3. If the tube doesn't light:
   a. Check for blown fuses
   b. Replace the tube
   c. Replace the starter
   d. Replace the ballast

4. If the ends of the tube turn black:
   a. If just one end turns black, turn the tube end for end
   b. Replace the starter
   c. Replace the tube

APPENDIX
Chapter 4
Heating

HEATED BENCH

PROCEDURE

Constructing

1. Install insulation board (styrofoam or other material) on the underside of the bottom of the bench

2. Put 2 inches of sand or vermiculite in the bench

3. Install the heat cable fastened to spacing strips of wood (see section on hotbed in appendix, chapter 1)

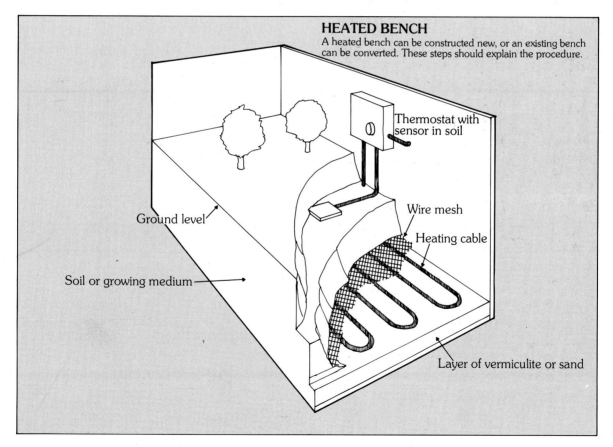

HEATED BENCH
A heated bench can be constructed new, or an existing bench can be converted. These steps should explain the procedure.

Thermostat with sensor in soil

Ground level

Soil or growing medium

Wire mesh

Heating cable

Layer of vermiculite or sand

4. Place a wire mesh over the heat cable to protect it from puncture or damage; the mesh and the cable will touch

5. Add a soil mix or growing medium to suit the crop you have in mind (up to 6 inches can be used for growing winter salad greens); pots may also be placed on top of the growing medium

6. Add a small space heater in one end of the case if you cannot maintain desired heat with the soil cable; for about $20.00 you can get an air circulating electric 1,320 watt heater that puts out about 4,500 BTUs

7. To ventilate the heated bench, raise the cover as needed, or install a small exhaust fan

TAKING TEMPERATURE READINGS

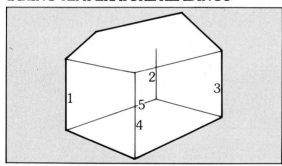

To test the heat distribution in your greenhouse, take a temperature reading in all four corners and in the center. Do this with the thermometer at bench level.

THERMOMETERS

There is enough variation in new thermometers to make it worthwhile to check for accuracy as follows: put the thermometer in a bowl of cracked ice for 30 minutes. It should then read 0°C or 32°F. If the thermometer is off by 3 degrees or more, then discard it and replace it with an accurate instrument.

ELECTRICAL HEAT DATA

1 Kilowatt	= 3,413 BTUs per hour
1 BTU per hour	= 0.293 watts
BTU's	= watts x 3.413
Wattage	= amps x voltage
Amps	= $\dfrac{\text{wattage}}{\text{voltage}}$
Voltage	= $\dfrac{\text{wattage}}{\text{amps}}$

APPENDIX
Chapter 5
Solar Heat

SOLAR HEATING TERMS

Ambient	The temperature of the atmosphere
Automatic damper	A device that regulates the flow of hot or cold air by means of a thermostat
Black body	Usually a black metal that absorbs all radiation and reflects none
Degree day	(DD) a unit of measure based on time and temperature difference; from a base of 65°F, there are as many DD units as degrees Fahrenheit between the mean temperature and the base, 65°F
Drawdown	Removing all usable heat from a storage chamber
Forced air	Air driven by a fan or blower
Heat capacity	The amount of heat needed to raise the temperature of a given mass of material one degree Fahrenheit
Incident radiation	The quantity of energy that strikes a given area of surface in a given time
Insolation	The solar radiation that reaches the earth's surface
Langley	One gram calorie per square centimeter of solar radiation
Pyranometer	A device for measuring solar radiation incident upon a surface
Radiant energy	Energy emitted from surfaces as electro-magnetic waves
Reflectance	Ratio of radiant energy reflected from a surface to the radiant energy incident upon it
Selective black paint	Absorbs more infrared than non-selective black paint
Solar altitude	The angle of the sun above the horizon
Solar furnace	A complete unit solar heating system
Vapor barrier	A layer of material impervious to moisture

SOLAR HEATING SYSTEMS

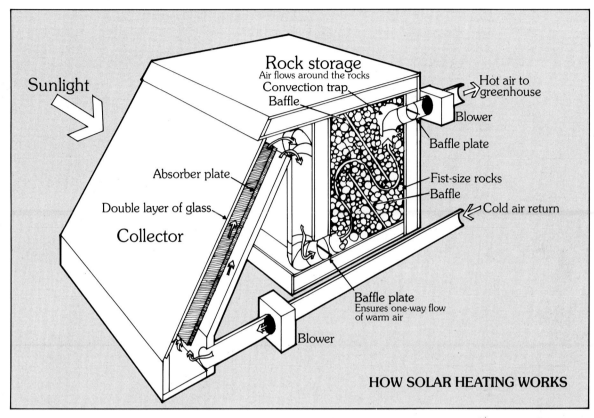

Sunlight

Rock storage
Air flows around the rocks
Convection trap
Baffle

Hot air to greenhouse

Blower

Baffle plate

Absorber plate

Fist-size rocks
Baffle

Double layer of glass

Cold air return

Collector

Baffle plate
Ensures one-way flow
of warm air

Blower

HOW SOLAR HEATING WORKS

1. The collector cover, usually double layered, admits solar heat waves and traps them in the collector

2. The absorber plate, usually black-metal plate or tubes, absorbs solar radiation

3. The heat absorbed usually is stored in water or in rocks (as shown); for the hobby greenhouse, both systems are feasible as supplementary heat (storage usually is less expensive above ground than underground because of the cost of excavation)

4. From the rock storage, a blower circulates the heated air into the greenhouse

5. Cool air from the floor of the greenhouse is recirculated through the solar collector to be reheated

CONTAINERIZED PASSIVE SOLAR HEATING SYSTEM

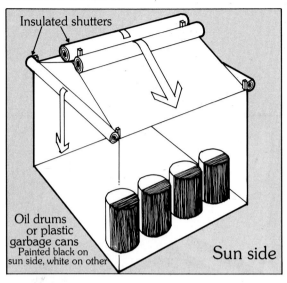

1. 1½ inch rocks in oil drums or plastic garbage cans are placed under the bench to absorb solar heat

2. The drums are painted black on the sun side and white on the heat release side; they absorb heat during the day and release it at night

3. To conserve heat at night, the entire greenhouse, including the gable ends, is covered with insulated roll-down shutters

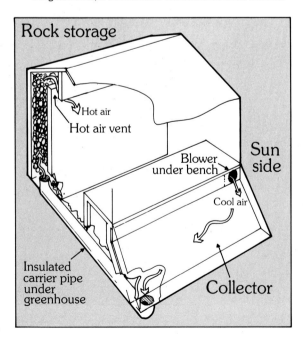

ROCK-WALL PASSIVE SOLAR HEATING SYSTEM

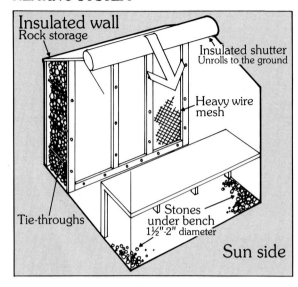

1. A rock wall on the north side of the greenhouse is used to absorb daytime heat

2. This heat is released at night into a greenhouse covered with insulating roll-down shutters

3. An insulated storage box constructed of wood and wire mesh with tie-throughs, such as those used for concrete forms, is located on the north side of the greenhouse

4. For additional heat, the ground under the benches is surfaced with rock

Passive solar heating systems require no electricity for circulation of heat

ROCK-WALL ACTIVE SOLAR HEATING SYSTEM

1. Sun shines on the collector and is absorbed by the absorber plate

2. A blower moves the heated air into the rock storage device, which is built as the insulated north wall of the greenhouse

3. The air moves through the rock storage and back into the greenhouse, where it is recirculated through the solar collector

4. As with any solar heating system, heat should be conserved at night by covering the greenhouse with insulated material

Active solar heating systems require blowers or pumps to move heat through the collector storage device and distribution systems

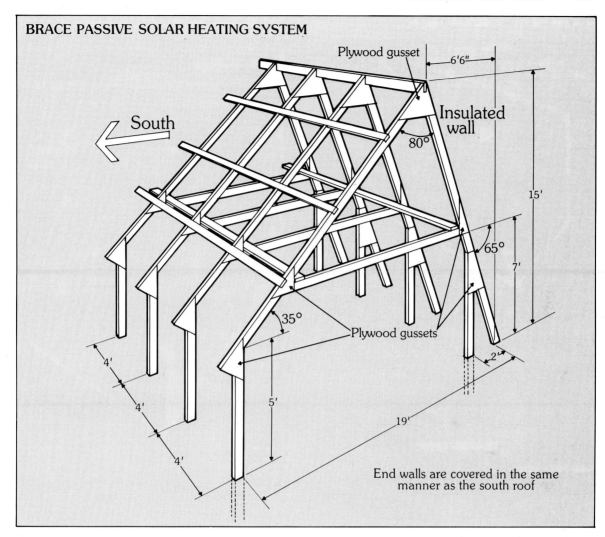

BRACE PASSIVE SOLAR HEATING SYSTEM

Plywood gusset

Insulated wall

South

80°

6'6"

15'

65°

7'

35°

Plywood gussets

2'

4'

4'

5'

4'

19'

End walls are covered in the same manner as the south roof

1. The greenhouse should be oriented on an east-west axis

2. The south-facing roof should be transparent

3. The south roof and wall sections can be translucent clear fiberglass corrugated paneling (4 or 5 ounces/square foot) 52⅝ inches wide (48-inch coverage), with an interior second layer of flat fiberglass or 4-mil polyethylene. Rafter-to-rafter cross purlins (14-foot 2"x4"s) should be every 4 feet

4. The inclined north-facing wall should be insulated with a reflective cover on the interior face

5. The north wall should be weatherable plywood or masonite insulated with polystyrene board

6. Its interior reflective surface can be single-faced aluminum building paper

7. The angles of the transparent roof and the rear inclined wall are each designed to permit optimum transmittance of solar radiation and maximum reflection of this radiation onto the plant canopy

8. The exterior should be finished in a light, reflective color

"The Development and Testing of an Environmentally Designed Greenhouse for Colder Regions," Report No. R.95; Brace Research Institute, Macdonal College of McGill University, St. Anne de Bellevue, Quebec, Canada H9X 3M1. (An experimental unit has been tested at Laval University, where a reduction of 30 to 40% has been found in the heating requirements, compared to a standard, double-layered, plastic-covered greenhouse. Preliminary results regarding productivity of tomatoes and lettuce indicate higher yields, possibly due to the increased luminosity in winter)

Passive solar heating systems require no electricity for circulation of heat

SOLAR-HEAT COMPOST BOX

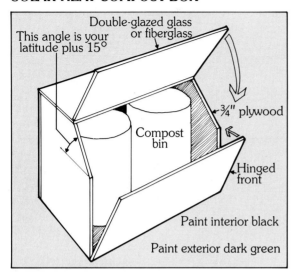

By keeping the compost bins in a solar-oriented black box, which adds heat, you can speed up the decomposition process —painted dark green, it is inconspicuous.

HEATING DATA

Solar Heat Data

K-cal — Kilocalorie: heat required to raise 1,000 grams of water 1°C (1.8°F)

BTU — British thermal unit: heat required to raise 1 lb. (454 grams) of water 1°F (5°C)

1 Food Calorie — 1K-cal

4 BTU — 1 K-cal

Insulation Data

There are many synthetic materials, manufactured both loose and pressed onto boards, for insulating. Check R-values to select which best fits your needs.

Conductance — heat moving through solid materials

Convection — heat moved by air currents

Radiation — heat moving as waves through space

R-value — the resistance of any material to heat moving through it

UNDERGROUND ACTIVE SOLAR HEATING SYSTEM

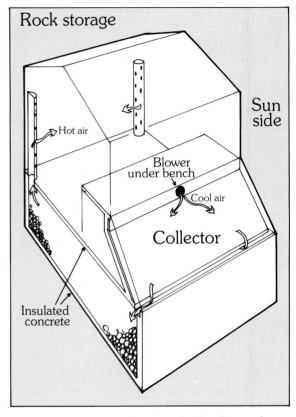

1. Rock storage area is a shallow, insulated underground basement (operates same as previous Brace system)

2. Cover at night with insulated material to conserve energy

Active solar heating systems require blowers or pumps to move heat through the collector storage device and distribution systems

R-Values for Some Common Insulating Materials

Material	Thickness	R-value
Wood	1 in.	1.25
Rockwool	3½ in.	11.00
	6½ in.	20.00
Styrofoam board	¾ in.	4.06
	1½ in.	8.12
Vermiculite	5 in.	11.00
Brown fiberglass	5 in.	11.00
Thermtron	3 in.	11.00

MANUFACTURED* ACTIVE SOLAR HEATING SYSTEM

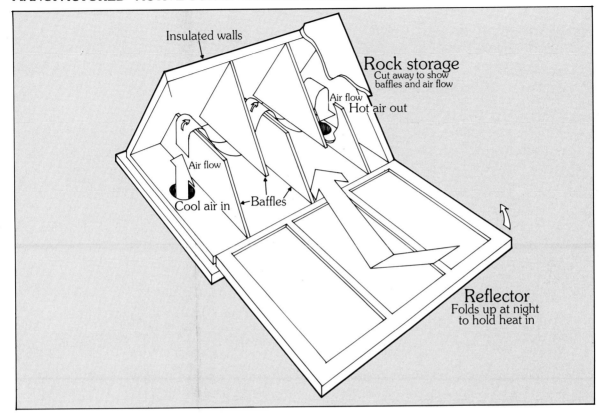

Insulated walls

Rock storage
Cut away to show
baffles and air flow

Air flow
Hot air out

Air flow
Cool air in
Baffles

Reflector
Folds up at night
to hold heat in

1. The sun shines on the reflector and bounces into the self-contained collector, where it is absorbed by a black plate

2. Two blowers move the heated air through a baffled-rock storage chamber and into the greenhouse to provide heat; the temperature of the rock storage area ranges from 75°F-180°F (23.9°C-82.2°C) — the rock will supply usable heat for up to 30 days with sunshine and from 3 to 5 days without sunshine

3. The reflector closes up over the collector at night to conserve heat in the storage chamber

4. The solar furnace can be wired to a thermostat that will cut in the residence heat or other heat supply automatically when the storage chamber heat is depleted

Active solar heating systems require blowers or pumps to move heat through the collector storage device and distribution systems

* Premanufactured, send for data: Hollick Solar Systems, 59 Greenbrook Dr., Toronto, Ontario (reprinted by permission)

HOT-WATER SOLAR HEATING SYSTEM

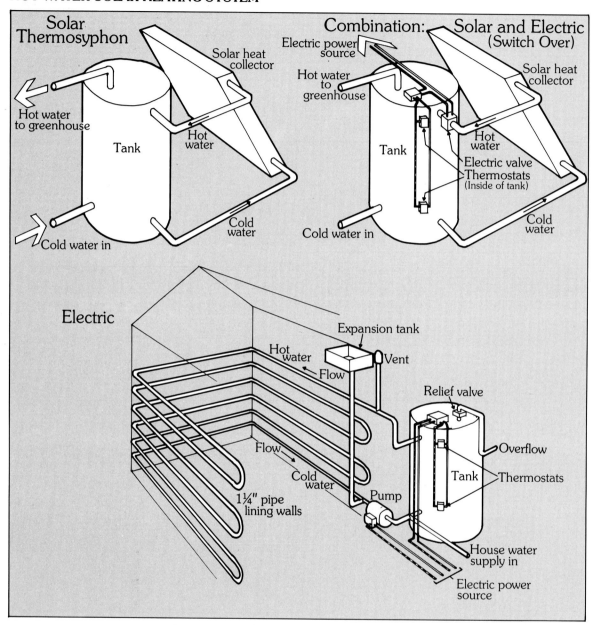

A conventional hot water system used in a residence can be adapted for use in a greenhouse. The system should be engineered properly to pipe size for BTU output, tank size, and pump capacity. Heating engineers are available for such projects.

A combination system, incorporating a simple thermosyphon, can heat the greenhouse with solar energy, using no electricity when the sun is out. When there is no solar heat available, the temperature of the water drops, and a thermostat in the hot water tank completes a circuit to close the electric valve and switch on the electric heat element in the tank. This system will supply a constant source of heated water either from solar energy or electrical current.

SUN-HEATED PIT

A sun-heated pit is basically the roof section of a greenhouse set over a pit that is lined with concrete blocks. It requires about 76 feet of 2"x 4" lumber, 31 feet of 2"x 6," 28 feet of 2"x 2," 19 feet of 2"x 8," and assorted pieces of plywood. You also will need about 150 8"x 8"x 16" cement blocks, mortar, and some drainage tiles.

Begin by referring to the section on foundations in appendix, chapter 1. You will need to dig a pit 4 feet deep and about 10 feet square. Try to select a site on higher ground to facilitate good drainage. Dig a trench downhill from your site, or to a point a small distance away, where you can dig a dry well (a hole filled with rocks).

After leveling the bottom of the pit, lay in the first row of blocks. Before you go any higher, lay in the drain tile on the outside of the foundation. Go all the way around the foundation and down the trench. Now, complete the foundation, and insert the bolts in the top rank.

From here on, the construction is mostly carpentry. Remember to have the fiberglass side face south. You can also put fiberglass on the door side, but it would be just as well to cover it with ¼" exterior plywood, perhaps additionally tacking insulation on the inside to prevent heat loss in the winter.

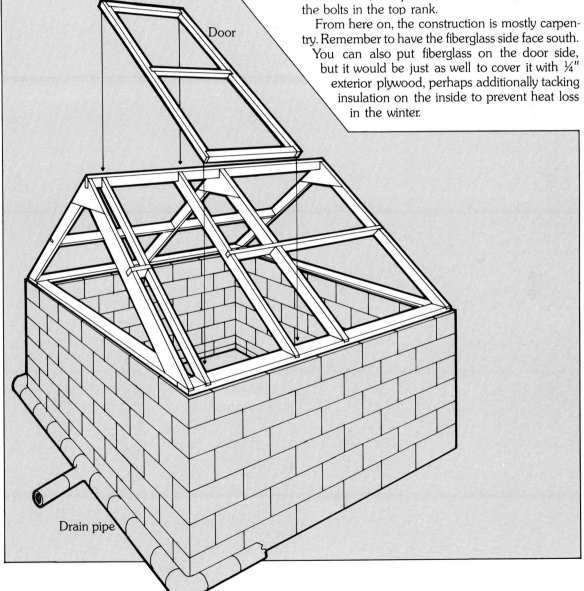

Door

Drain pipe

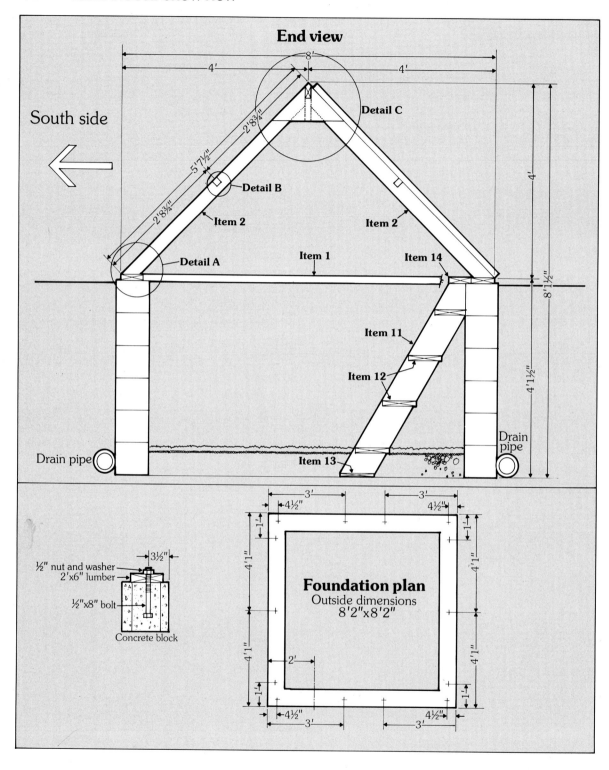

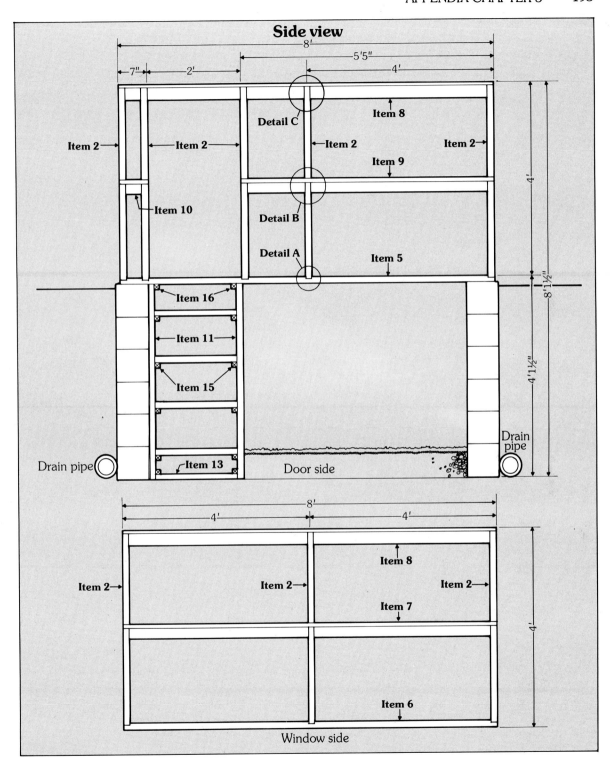

Side view

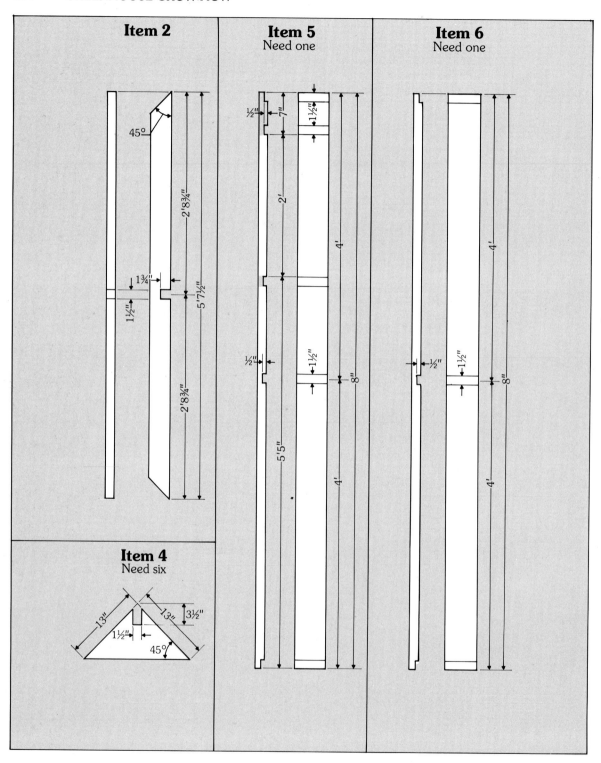

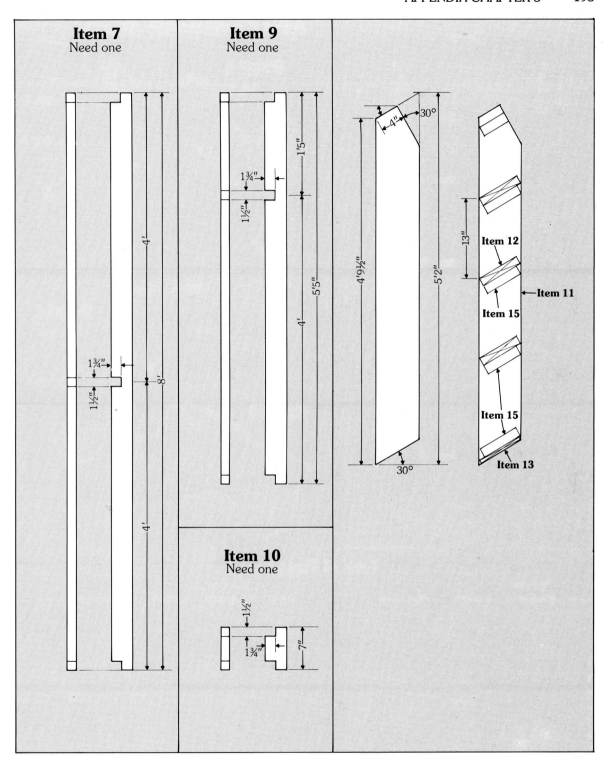

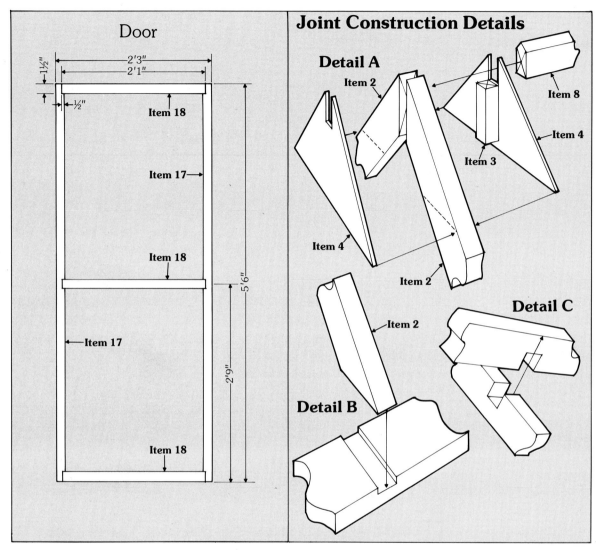

Door

Joint Construction Details

Detail A
Detail B
Detail C

List of Materials

Item	Number Required	Length	Material	Item	Number Required	Length	Material
1	2	7'1"	2"x6" lumber	10	1	7"	2"x4" lumber
2	8	5'7½"	2"x4" lumber	11	2	5'2"	2"x8" lumber
3	3	5½"	2"x2" lumber	12	4	1'9"	2"x8" lumber
4	1	13"x3'4"	¼" exterior plywood	13	1	1'9"	1"x8" lumber
5	1	8'	2"x6" lumber	14	1	1'9"	1"x6" lumber
6	1	8'	2"x6" lumber	15	10	7'	2"x2" lumber
7	1	8'	2"x4" lumber	16	2	4"	2"x2" lumber
8	1	8'	2"x4" lumber	17	2	5'6"	2"x2" lumber
9	1	5'5"	2"x4" lumber	18	3	2'2"	2"x2" lumber

APPENDIX
Chapter 6
Cooling and Shading

COOLING SYSTEMS

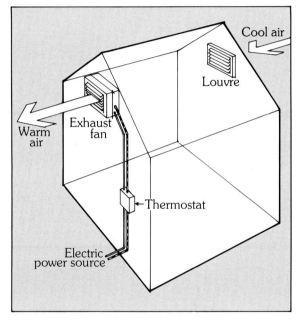

COOLING WITH EXHAUST FANS

1. Have the wiring done by a licensed electrician to meet local electrical codes

2. Mount the exhaust fan in one gable end with the louvres facing out

3. Mount the louvre *only* in the other gable end with the louvre blades facing *in*—when the thermostat turns on the exhaust fan, the louvres in the other end will open to admit cool air

COOLING WITH EXHAUST FAN AND FAN-JET

1. Mount the exhaust fan in the lower portion of one end of the greenhouse, perhaps under a bench, louvres facing in

2. Mount the fan-jet in the gable of the other end—when the thermostat turns on the exhaust fan, it also will open the motorized shutter on the fan-jet, which allows cool air to come in and circulate through the fan-jet

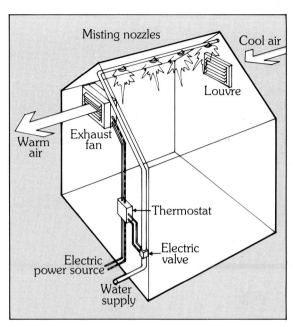

COOLING BY MISTING

When the thermostat turns on the exhaust fan, it also turns on the mist system, and the air moving through the cool water drops in temperature.

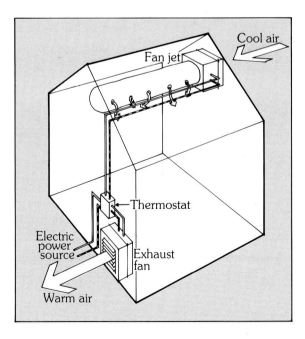

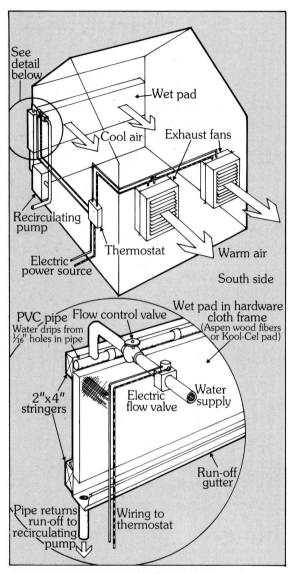

See detail below

Wet pad

Cool air

Exhaust fans

Recirculating pump

Thermostat

Electric power source

Warm air

South side

PVC pipe
Water drips from 1/16" holes in pipe

Flow control valve

Wet pad in hardware cloth frame
(Aspen wood fibers or Kool-Cel pad)

2"x4" stringers

Electric flow valve

Water supply

Run-off gutter

Pipe returns run-off to recirculating pump

Wiring to thermostat

COOLING WITH PAD AND FAN

When thermostatically controlled, the exhaust fans turn on at the same time that the water flows over the pad. Air moving through the wet pad is then cooled before entering the greenhouse.

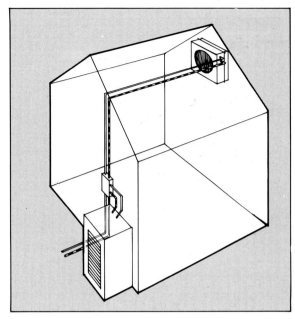

PAD AND FAN COOLER UNIT

A complete pad and fan evaporative-cooling unit is available for about $300.00 This unit is mounted outside the greenhouse and comes complete with a recirculating-pump kit and all the fittings necessary to hook up to the existing water supply and electric power source.

APPENDIX
Chapter 7
Water and Watering

AUTOMATIC WATER DISTRIBUTION SYSTEMS: SUMMARY DIAGRAM

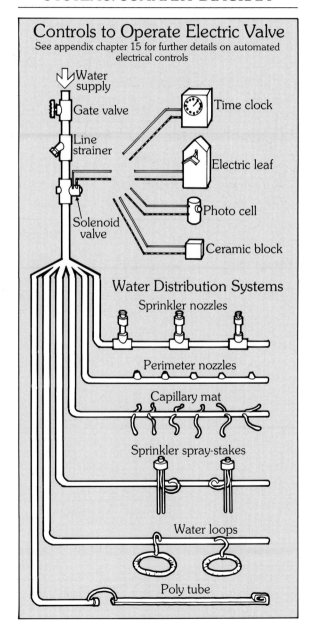

Controls to Operate Electric Valve
See appendix chapter 15 for further details on automated electrical controls

Water supply
Gate valve
Line strainer
Solenoid valve

Time clock
Electric leaf
Photo cell
Ceramic block

Water Distribution Systems
Sprinkler nozzles
Perimeter nozzles
Capillary mat
Sprinkler spray-stakes
Water loops
Poly tube

CAPILLARY WATER DISTRIBUTION SYSTEM

There are several brands of capillary mats currently in use in Europe and in the United States. The most widely used is Vattex, which was developed originally in Denmark; it is available in the United States through Vattex Corporation, 95 Main Street, Moriches, NY 11934. The procedure for converting your benches to a capillary water system follows:

1. Place a covering of 1½ mil black or clear polyethylene on top of an emptied bench

2. Check the bench to see if it is level; if it is an inch or two off, it will not make any difference, but if it is more, you should correct the problem

3. Place the capillary mat on top of the polyethylene—the mats are made either of fiberglass or of various matted fibers that you simply unroll onto the polyethylene and cut to size

FLOW TABLE
GPM Flow at 5 Feet Per Second Velocity

Pipe Size	PVC Class 160	Polyethylene Class 80	Galvanized Standard	Copper Class M	Transite 325 Ft. Hd.
½"	6.3	4.7	4.7	4.0	
¾"	10.5	8.3	8.3	8.0	
1"	17.4	13.4	13.4	12.0	
1¼"	28.7	23.3	23.3	20.3	
1½"	37.5	31.7	31.7	28.5	
2"	58.7	52.1	52.1	48.9	
2½"	86.0	74.4	74.4	76.0	
3"	127.2		114.8	108.5	110.0
4"					190.5
5"					305.0
6"					404.0

This table shows approximate flow in gallons per minute at a safe velocity (5 ft./sec.) that avoids excessive water hammer and friction loss.

MOISTURE METERS

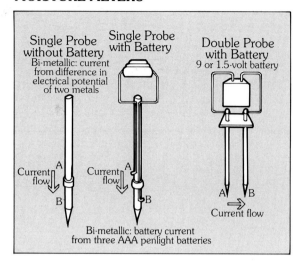

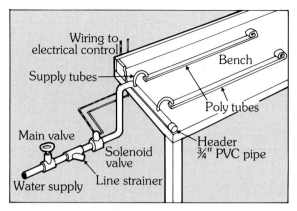

POLY-TUBE WATER DISTRIBUTION SYSTEM

There are many devices that measure the moisture content of soil, all of which operate by sending a very weak electric current through the soil water. The meter reads the salt content of the water (distilled water, which has had the impurities removed, would not register on the meter, thus it would appear that the plant was dry) and the amount of salt in the soil (old soil may well have an accumulation of salt, which, conversely, would give a wet reading when the soil really was quite dry—you can correct this condition by leaching if your water supply is not excessively high in salt). The readings, therefore, have to be interpreted in relation to both the natural salt content of the water and the age of the soil.

Although moisture meters are a good guide to water needs when you understand their operation, the judgment of the grower in regard to the appearance of the plant and the feel of the soil is still essential to good watering practices.

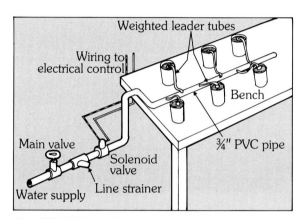

SPAGHETTI WATER DISTRIBUTION SYSTEM

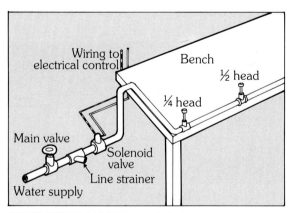

SPRINKLER-NOZZLE WATER DISTRIBUTION SYSTEM

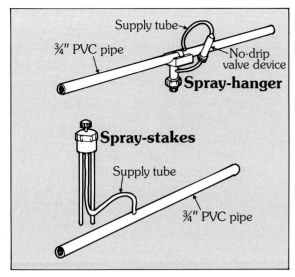

SPRAY-STAKES AND SPRAY HANGER

PLUMBED-IN SPRINKLER SYSTEM

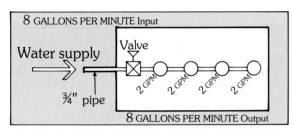

VALVE WATER DISTRIBUTION SYSTEMS

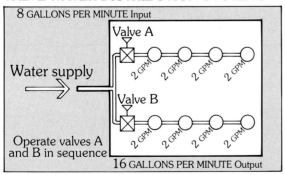

PREHEATING WATER FOR THE GREENHOUSE

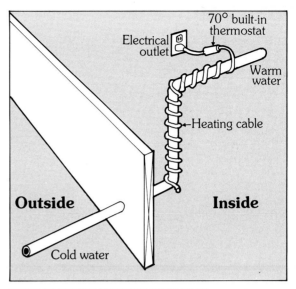

A simple means of having warm water to use on greenhouse plants is to wrap heating cable (the same type used to prevent exposed water pipes from freezing in winter) around the water pipe where it enters the greenhouse. Heating cable should cover about 10 lineal feet of pipe — then the slowly-flowing water will have the chill taken off.

APPENDIX
Chapter 8
Air

HUMIDITY CONTROL

Actual humidity, or specific humidity, refers to the number of grains of water-vapor moisture in a cubic foot of air, usually abbreviated as gr/cu/ft. Relative humidity (RH) is a measure of the amount of water vapor in the air expressed as a percentage of the amount it *could* hold at a given temperature. When an hygrometer reads 50% RH, for example, the air is holding 50% as many gr/cu/ft of water as it could at the existing temperature. Relative humidity is the measurement used to maintain the proper humidity when growing plants.

Temperature and relative humidity

Relative humidity varies from night to day due to temperature fluctuations—for every 20-degree rise in temperature, the capacity of the air to hold moisture is doubled and the RH is halved. If a night temperature is 50° with 50% RH, for instance, when the sun warms the air in the morning to 70°, the relative humidity drops to 35%.

Guidelines for control of relative humidity

1. To raise RH:
   Decrease the temperature (for example, shade the roof)

   Turn on the mist system or humidifier

   Admit outside air if the RH is higher out-of-doors

2. To lower RH:
   Increase the temperature

   Keep good air circulation

   Admit outside air if the RH is lower out-of-doors

Greenhouse humidity at night

If the greenhouse cools from 70° with 100% RH (110 gr/cu/ft) to 50° at night, then the capacity of the air to hold moisture is halved and 55 gr/cu/ft is condensed as liquid drops of water on plants and other surfaces, which creates the ideal conditions for disease organisms. Do the following to avoid this situation:

1. Do not water late in the day or at night

2. Keep the night temperatures high

3. Keep air circulating continually

APPENDIX
Chapter 9
Soils and Media

AEROBIC COMPOSTING

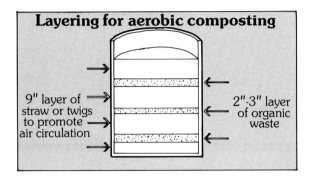

Layering for aerobic composting

9" layer of straw or twigs to promote air circulation

2"-3" layer of organic waste

ANAEROBIC COMPOSTING

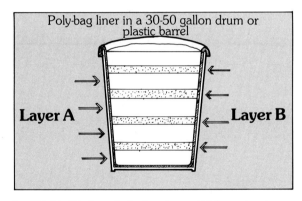

Poly-bag liner in a 30-50 gallon drum or plastic barrel

Layer A   **Layer B**

1. Put 6 to 8 inches of mixed garden and kitchen refuse in the bottom of the bag, layer A

2. Add 3 cups of dried steer manure, 1 cup of lime, and 1 cup of blood meal, layer B

3. Alternate layers until bag is full

4. Add 1 quart of water and tie the bag tightly to prevent escaping odors

5. Cover barrel and store in heated area such as basement or greenhouse

6. Uncover for use in 2 to 3 months

DO-IT-YOURSELF COMPOST BIN

Materials
One sheet ¼" exterior grade plywood
One piece ½" exterior grade plywood 33" square
5' of 1"x 2" lumber
6" of 2"x 2" lumber
Four hook-and-screw-eye closures
1" round-head brass screws
¾" round-head brass screws
Cuprinol (Copper Napthanate #14, Florist's Green)
36" square heavy wire mesh

PROCEDURE
Cutting
1. Plywood (see detail A):

    Cut the sheet of ¼" plywood in half lengthwise

    Use a saber saw, or drill with hole-saw attachment, to cut 2" diameter holes, as shown in plans

    Cut the piece of ½" plywood into a circle 33" in diameter

2. 1"x 2" lumber:

    Cut four pieces 1'2" long

3. 2"x 2" lumber:

    Cut one piece 30" long

    Cut two pieces 14¼" long

Assembling
1. The upper part needs only to have the hook-and-screw eye attached in a fashion that will allow the ends to be brought together snugly—measure carefully!

2. The lower part needs to have the same treatment, but then attach the 1"x 2" lumber (as shown in detail B), using the brass screws and going *through* the plywood, *into* the lumber

3. Assemble to top (as shown in detail C), again going through the plywood into the lumber, this time using 1" screws

4. Coat all the wood with the Cuprinol and let air for a week before filling with compost

DO-IT-YOURSELF COMPOST BIN

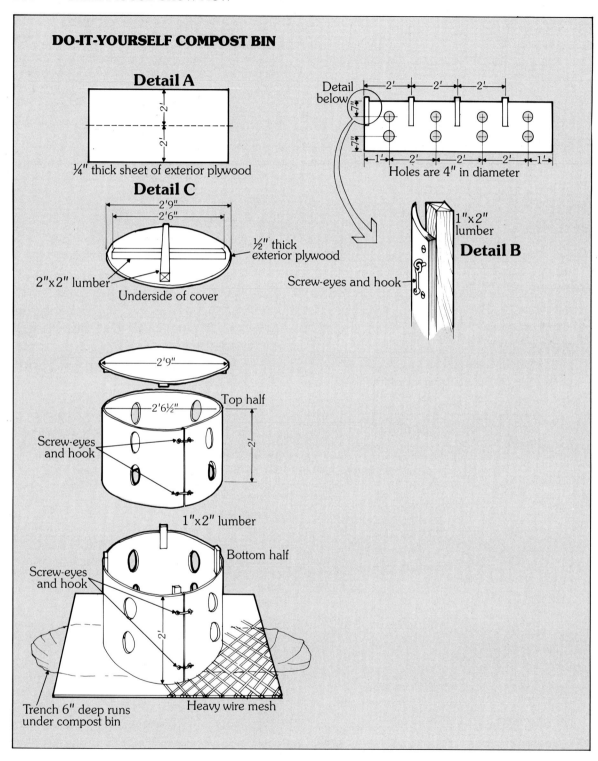

Detail A

¼" thick sheet of exterior plywood

Holes are 4" in diameter

Detail below

Detail C

2'9"
2'6"

½" thick
exterior plywood

2"x2" lumber
Underside of cover

1"x2"
lumber

Detail B

Screw-eyes and hook

2'9"

2'6½"   Top half

2'

Screw-eyes
and hook

1"x2" lumber

Bottom half

Screw-eyes
and hook

2'

Trench 6" deep runs
under compost bin

Heavy wire mesh

BENCH HYDROPONICS

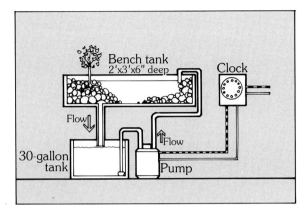

1. Time clock C starts pump P—self-priming, 5.6 gpm

2. Box fills in approximately 6 minutes

3. Nutrient solution immediately begins to drain through ¼-inch outlet hole, going back to the stock tank

4. Box empties in about 1 hour

5. Recycle as needed using time clock

SOIL PASTEURIZATION

Required temperatures

Temperatures required to kill pathogenic or undesirable organisms include:

180°F (82°C)	Most weed seed
160°F (71°C)	All plant disease-causing bacteria, most plant viruses and soil insects
140°F (60°C)	Worms, slugs, centipedes; many pathogenic fungi and bacteria

Baking soil at home

A simple way of pasteurizing soil in small batches is to bake the soil in the oven by the following procedure:

1. Place the soil mix in a pan 3 to 4 inches deep and add enough water to moisten the soil thoroughly

2. Cover the pan with aluminum foil, and insert a meat thermometer through the foil into the soil

3. Set the oven at 200°F (93°C) for ½ hour; watch the meat thermometer to make certain the temperature in the soil mix does not go higher than 180°F (82°C)—temperatures about 180°F will kill beneficial bacteria

4. Remove the soil from the oven and allow it to cool

Chemical treatment

Use 40% formaldehyde as follows:

1. Dilute 2 tablespoons in 3 pints of water

2. Sprinkle the dilution evenly over a layer of soil mix 1 inch thick and 2 feet square

3. Mix the soil thoroughly—wear rubber gloves

4. Place the soil in a pot or flat that has been scrubbed with Clorox or Javex

5. Allow to stand for 24 hours, and water thoroughly

6. Let the treated mix stand until the odor of formaldehyde is gone, which may take two weeks; fumes of formaldehyde will kill or damage most plants

APPENDIX
Chapter 11
Nutrition

HOW TO PREPARE A FERTILIZER SOLUTION FOR HYDROPONIC GROWING

The ingredients (single-element fertilizers) for a hydroponic solution are available from greenhouse suppliers and fertilizer companies. They often are called "simples" to distinguish them from mixed fertilizers.

PROCEDURE

Stock solution

1. Get four clean 1-gallon jugs and mark them A, B, C, D

2. Add water and dissolve the following nutrients in the appropriate jug:

    | Jar A | 16 oz. | Potassium nitrate | 1 gal. water |
    | Jar B | 34 oz. | Calcium nitrate | 1 gal. water |
    | Jar C | 18 oz. | Ammonium phosphate | 1 gal. water |
    | Jar D . | 39 oz. | Magnesium sulphate | 1 gal. water |

3. Store the four stock solutions in a cool place, out of the light

Final solution

1. Put 25 gallons of water in a clean drum or garbage can

2. Add the stock solutions to the 25 gallons as follows:

    | From Jar A | 24 oz. |
    | From Jar B | 16 oz. |
    | From Jar C | 8 oz. |
    | From Jar D | 4 oz. |

3. You now have a final solution ready to be used on plants grown hydroponically

4. Minor elements usually are sufficient in the water supply—if minor elements are needed, however, purchase a soluble trace elements mix; for example, Peters Soluble Trace Elements Mix, S.T.E.M., which contains sulfur, boron, copper, iron, manganese, molybdenum, and zinc—add: 2 ounces of S.T.E.M. to the 25 gallons of water (follow the manufacturer's directions for other brands)

5. You now have a final solution with both major and minor elements to be used in a hydroponic growing facility (see chapter 11)

APPENDIX
Chapter 11
Nutrition Deficiency Symptoms
See plate 24, facing page 85

APPENDIX
Chapter 12
Growth Regulation and Control

PLANTS FOR BONSAI

A great many small trees and some shrubs can be used for bonsai whether they are tropical for indoor use or temperate for outdoor use. Outdoor bonsai should be protected from cold winds and severe frosts. Usually slow-growing plants with small leaves and flowers make the best bonsai subjects. Following are some suggestions for both indoor and outdoor bonsai plants:

Indoors
Araucaria excelsa
Araucaria bidwillii
Ardisia crenulata
Carissa grandiflora
Citrus mitis
Citrus taitensis
Coffea arabica
Euphorbia splendens
Euphorbia lactea
Ficus diversifolia
Ficus rubiginosa variegata
Ficus retusa nitida
Ficus stricta
Gardenia radicans florepleno
Gardenia jasminoides
Malpighia coccigera
Osmanthus heterophyllus
Parthenocissus tricuspidata
Serissa foetida

Outdoors
Acer palmatum
Acer buergerianum
Acer trifidum
Chamaecyparis obtusa
Cryptomeria japonica
Cotoneaster adpressa
Cotoneaster microphylla
Daphne odora
Enkianthus perulatus
Fagus crenata
Ginkgo biloba
Juniperus chinensis sargenti

Malus prunifolia
Malus sieboldii
Picea jezoensis
Picea glauca conica
Pinus parviflora
Pinus pentaphylla
Pinus thunbergii
Pinus Mugho
Prunus mume
Prunus subhirtella pendula
Punica granatum
Pyracantha koidzumi
Rhododendron obtusum amoenum
Rhododendron kiusianum
Rhododendron indicum
Taxus cuspidata nana
Zelkova serrata

LEAF STRUCTURE IN LIGHT AND IN SHADE

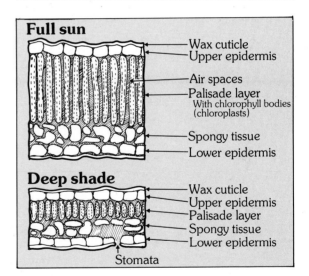

We usually think of plants growing in sunlight or under shade without realizing the leaf structure in each situation is different. The full-sun leaf is thick, with long palisade cells to absorb higher light intensities. The deep-shade leaf is thin, with short palisade cells to receive low light.

If you purchase a plant that has been grown in full sun and move it into a shady location, growth slows down, and the plant may die. Conversely, if you purchase a plant grown in shade, it may be injured or killed by moving it into full sun. Give the new plant a chance to adapt slowly to different light conditions. Some plants, for example, have the capacity to adapt by putting out new leaves with the deep shade structure. Most plants will do well in partial shade if you do not know the actual light requirements

**APPENDIX
Chapter 13
Insects and Pests**
See plates 25-28
between pages 116-117

**APPENDIX
Chapter 14
Plant Diseases**
See plates 29-32
between pages 116-117

RATING TOXICITY OF CHEMICALS

All substances we use to control pests and diseases have a toxicity rating. The standard method of rating toxicity is to test the chemical on animals, often mice, and determine the dosage necessary to kill 50% of the test animals (usually written as LD50); the dose is expressed as milligrams of the chemical per kilogram of body weight of the animal. So if 1 mg/kg of the chemical kills 50% of the test animals, the LD50 rating is 1. Chemicals with an LD50 rating of 1 perhaps would be fatal to man in amounts from a trace to a grain. Law requires that chemicals be labeled to indicate LD50 rating.

APPENDIX
Chapter 15
Automation

AUTOMATED GREENHOUSE

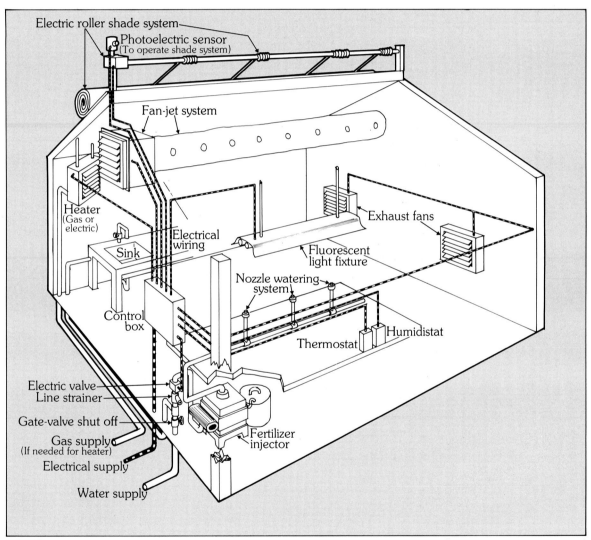

Electric roller shade system
Photoelectric sensor
(To operate shade system)
Fan-jet system
Heater
(Gas or electric)
Electrical wiring
Sink
Exhaust fans
Fluorescent light fixture
Nozzle watering system
Control box
Humidistat
Thermostat
Electric valve
Line strainer
Gate-valve shut off
Gas supply
(If needed for heater)
Fertilizer injector
Electrical supply
Water supply

For an illustration of the different systems available for automatic electrical control, see chapter 7 appendix

AUTOMATIC CONTROLS

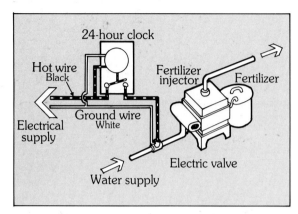

AUTOMATIC CONTROL OF NUTRIENTS
Fertilizing with soluble fertilizer through the watering system

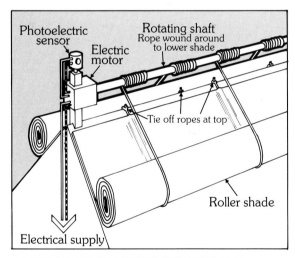

AUTOMATIC CONTROL OF SHADING

1. Wiring should be done to meet local codes

2. When the light reaches a specified high intensity, the photo cell activates a small electric motor that lets the shade roll down

3. When the light intensity drops, as on a rainy day or evening, the shade rolls back up

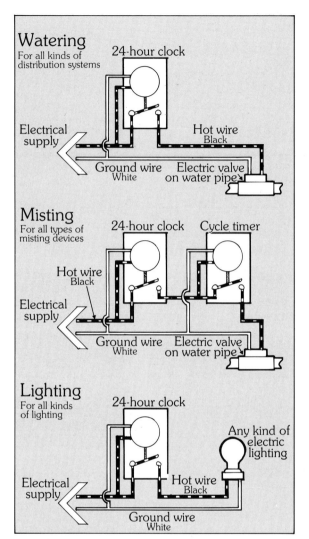

Watering
For all kinds of distribution systems

Misting
For all types of misting devices

Lighting
For all kinds of lighting

AUTOMATIC CONTROL WITH ELECTRIC CLOCKS

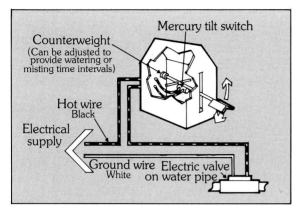

AUTOMATIC CONTROL WITH ELECTRIC LEAF

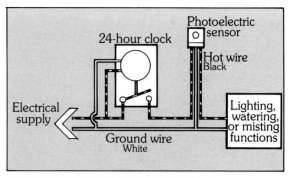

AUTOMATIC CONTROL WITH PHOTOELECTRIC CELL

Lighting

1. Use 24-hour clock

2. Will turn lights on at evening or on cloudy days and keep them on as long as the clock commands

Watering

1. Use 24-hour clock

2. Will turn water on when bright and sunny, applying water when the clock commands

3. Will not water on rainy days

Misting

1. Use cycle timer

2. Will mist when bright and sunny at intervals and duration as programmed on cycle timer

3. Will not mist on cloudy, rainy days

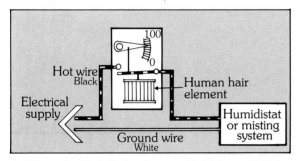

AUTOMATIC CONTROL WITH HUMIDISTAT

1. Dial is pre-set at desired humidity

2. When the air dries, the human hair element stretches to close the circuit and turn on the humidifier or mist system

3. When the mist goes on, it wets the hair element, which contracts to shut off the system

AUTOMATIC TEMPERATURE – ALARM SYSTEM

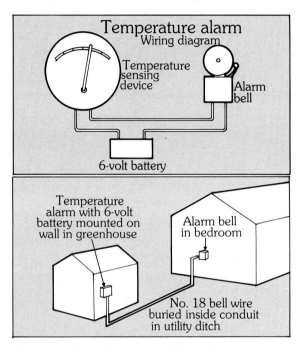

Temperature alarms that operate on battery power are available to set off an alarm system automatically at a pre-set temperature level.

Operation: when temperature gets too low or too high, as set on the temperature alarm, the bell rings

AUTOMATIC CONTROL WITH THERMOSTATS

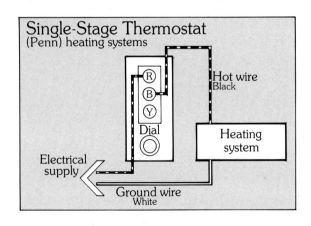

1. When temperature rises to dial setting, heater goes off

2. When temperature drops approximately 3°F (1.7°C), heater goes on

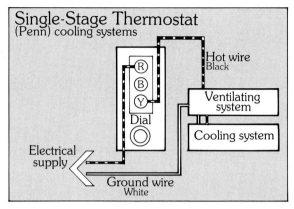

1. When the temperature rises, the ventilating and/or cooling systems go on

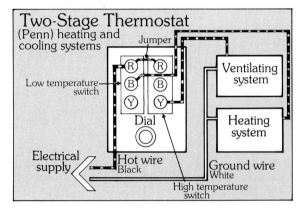

1. When temperature increases to dial setting, the heating system turns off

2. A further temperature increase of 3°F (1.7°C) will turn on the fan or the ventilating system

APPENDIX
Chapter 17
Propagation

HARDWOOD AND SOFTWOOD CUTTINGS

Hardwood

Deciduous

These procedures will apply to most stiff-stemmed woody plants outdoors or in the greenhouse, such as dogwood, ficus, jasmine, lilac, spirea, forsythia,

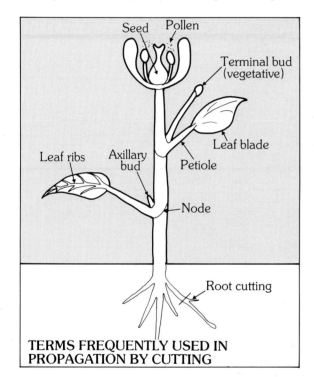

Seed Pollen
Terminal bud (vegetative)
Leaf blade
Leaf ribs Axillary bud Petiole
Node
Root cutting

TERMS FREQUENTLY USED IN PROPAGATION BY CUTTING

wisteria, honeysuckle, rose, olive, quince, grape, plum, willow, and poplar.

1. Take cutting 4 to 30 inches (with at least 2 buds) in early morning in the fall

2. Treat with Hormodin #3; Hormex #3, 4, 5, 6; Rootone #10; Seradix B #3; or equivalent

3. Stick in ½ peat, ½ coarse sand and gravel, or growth cube, such as Jiffy 7

4. Supply bottom heat 70°F (21.1°C) for 4 weeks, while keeping top cool at 40°F-50°F (4.4°C-10°C)

5. Remove bottom heat and store at above-freezing temperatures in basement, attic, shed, or garage, under low light conditions

6. Keep at 35°F-40°F (2°C-4.5°C) until spring

7. Plant outside in soil spaced 2 inches apart when frost is out of the ground

8. Feed when growth starts with 1 teaspoon per gallon of 20-20-20 or equivalent (*do not feed in summer*)

9. Plant in permanent location in the fall or early the next spring

Needle evergreen

Most junipers, yews, arbor-vitae, and cypress root fairly well. The spruces, hemlocks, pines, and firs, however, do not root readily and are perhaps better grown from seed.

1. Take cuttings 4 to 6 inches in early morning during late fall from young stock plants; wound the base of the cutting by cutting or crushing

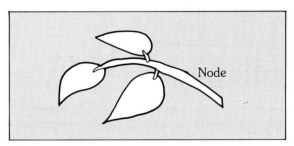

Node

HERBACEOUS CUTTING

1. Take tip cutting 3 to 5 inches long with 2 or 3 leaves of soft-stemmed plants such as Geranium, Fuchsia, Coleus, Begonia

2. Treat with Hormodin #1, Hormex #1, Seradix B #1, Rootone, or equivalent

3. Stick in sand; Jiffy 7 pellet; or ½ sand, ½ vermiculite or perlite

4. Bottom heat of 75°F-80°F (23°C-27°C), air temperature 70°F (21°C)

For more information on specialized propagation procedures, see the sources at the end of text chapter 17.

2. Treat with hormones as for hardwood deciduous cuttings

3. Stick in sand or ½ peat, ½ sand, or Jiffy 7 type block, with bottom heat of 75°F-80°F (24°C-26.5°C)

4. Supply mist on a cycle of 12 seconds every 6 minutes, or 5 seconds every 10 minutes during daylight hours

5. Time to produce root varies from 1 month to 1 year, depending on the type of plant

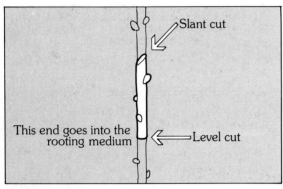

HARDWOOD AND SOFTWOOD CUTTINGS

Softwood

Deciduous and evergreen

Cuttings can be taken from plants such as forsythia, magnolia, weigela, azalea, gardenia, ivy, and pyracantha.

1. Take freshly matured cuttings 4 inches long, usually in the spring or early summer, from new growth; strip leaves except for 1 or 2 tip leaves, or trim large leaves, and pinch out tip buds

2. Treat with Hormodin #1, Hormex #1, Seradix B #1, Rootone, or equivalent

3. Stick in ⅓ peat, ⅓ sand, ⅓ vermiculite or perlite; Jiffy 7 pellet; or equivalent

4. Bottom heat of 75°F-80°F (23°C-27°C) in the soil and air temperature of 70°F (21°C)

5. Rooting time is 2 to 5 weeks; as soon as substantial roots show, transplant to pot

6. With succulent plants that exude juices, let them air dry until a crust forms on the lower end; this will avoid contamination by pathogenic microorganisms

7. Mist 5 seconds every 10 minutes or use closed-propagation case

Needle evergreen

Use same procedure as listed under hardwoods.

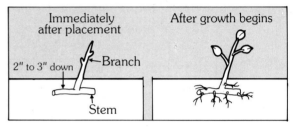

TRUNCHEON CUTTING

A truncheon is a piece of hardwood stem, including a bud, which when buried 2 to 3 inches in the medium, will produce a shoot from the bud and roots from the old stem or the new shoot. This method may be used on many hardwood deciduous species.

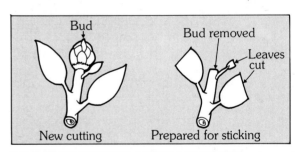

BROADLEAF EVERGREEN CUTTING

1. Take cutting 4 to 6 inches long in early summer, as soon as new growth matures; reduce leaf surface by cutting leaves in half on large-leafed plants, and pinch out any flower buds (for example, of rhododendron, camelia, azalea (evergreen), holly, citrus)

2. Wound base and treat with hormone as for needle evergreens and hardwood deciduous

3. Stick in ½ peat, ½ sand, or Jiffy 7 type block, with bottom heat of 75°F (24°C)

4. Supply mist on 5-seconds-every-10-minutes cycle during the day, or place in closed propagation case

5. Transplant as soon as roots show

LEAF CUTTING

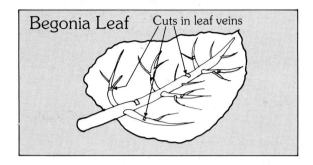

Begonia Leaf — Cuts in leaf veins

1. Cut the large veins on the under surface of the leaf (for example, of begonia, african violet, gloxinia, peperomia)

2. Dust the cuts with hormone as for herbaceous cuttings

3. Pin the leaf flat on the rooting medium, with the cut veins down

4. Mist 5 seconds every 10 minutes, or use a closed-propagation case

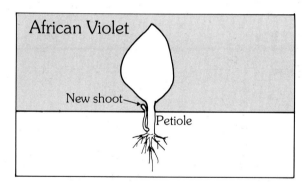

African Violet — New shoot — Petiole

PETIOLE LEAF CUTTING

1. Roots grow at the base of the petiole (for example, of Begonia Rex, sansevieria, euphorbia, hoya)

2. Dust with hormone; pin to rooting medium; mist as for whole leaves

Pieces of Sansevieria stem also will root readily; cut 3 to 4 inches, and treat with hormone; plant in herbaceous medium

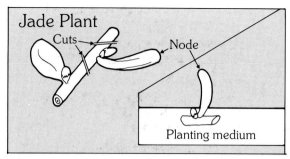

Jade Plant — Cuts — Node — Planting medium

LEAF BUD CUTTING

1. A leaf bud is the unit that occurs at each node on the stem, consisting of leaf blade, petiole, and axillary bud—take the entire node for the cutting (for example, of rhododendron, jade, lemon, camelia, black raspberry)

2. Apply hormone (moisten and dip in Hormoden #1 or equivalent)

3. Insert ½ inch into a ½-sand, ½-vermiculite medium

4. Maintain bottom heat of 75°F-80°F (23°C-27°C) air temperature of 70°F (21°C)

ROOT CUTTING

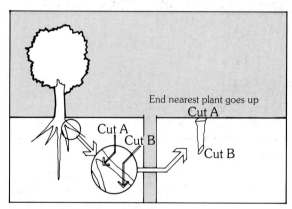

End nearest plant goes up — Cut A — Cut B

Root cuttings are best taken from young plants in the dormant season; for example, if the plant flowers in the fall, take root cuttings in the spring, or if the plant is spring flowering, take cuttings in the summer after bloom. You want to get root sections that are full of stored food. Note also that roots have polarity, and must be oriented when planted.

LAYERING

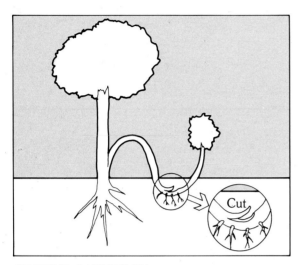

GROUND LAYERING

1. Wound or slice cutting and treat with #3 or strongest rooting compound

2. Bury the one-year old stem 6 to 12 inches in the ground (some propagators wound the portion of the stem that is buried by notching or slicing)

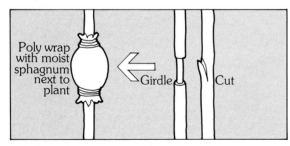

AIR LAYERING

You are trying to provide an underground environment for root production—one that is dark, warm, moist, and nutritious.

1. Select last year's growth on an actively growing branch

2. Cut or girdle the bark of the stem from 6 to 18 inches back of the tip

3. Treat with the strongest rooting compound (for example, #3 Hormodin or stronger, as in Hormex 4.5% indole butyric acid)

4. Place some moist sphagnum moss (not baled peat) around cut area—the sphagnum should be *moist only, not wringing wet*

5. Wrap the sphagnum in polyethylene, and secure both ends

around the branch with twistems, string, or tape so that water will not run down the branch into the air layer packet —the polyfilm allows gas exchange but not water vapor

6. Support the air-layer branch so it is not blown around in the wind

FERNS

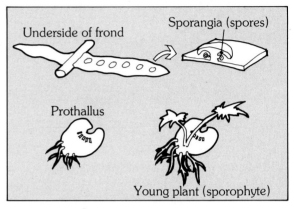

FERN REPRODUCTION

Ferns have a different life cycle than higher plants and are propagated best by spore germination.

1. Locate spores and make cutting

    a. Locate the spores formed in the sporangia on the underside of the frond

    b. Cut off whole pieces of frond and let them dry for about a week

    c. Keep the temperature at about 70°F (21°C)

2. Moisten the medium and sow spores

    a. Tap the spores out on a sheet of white paper, and sow them evenly over a pasteurized mix of ⅔ peat and ⅓ perlite or vermiculite

    b. Cover the flat with glass

    c. Keep bottom heat at 70°F (21°C) and air temperature at 65°F-75°F (18°C-24°C)

3. Spores germinate to produce prothallia; transplant and space out the prothallia

4. When the prothallus produce sporophytes, transplant again; in 3 to 6 months young mature plants will appear

CACTUS

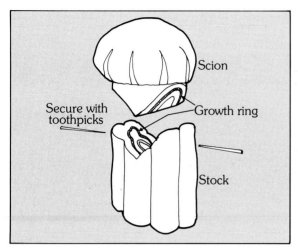

Scion

Secure with toothpicks

Growth ring

Stock

GRAFTING CACTUS

One of the best grafts for many cacti is the cleft graft. Proceed as follows:

1. Cut the stock plant off horizontally—check the exposed end for the growth layers, usually a growth ring of actively dividing tissue, which must be matched for a successful grafting

2. Cut a wedge-shaped notch in the stock plant

3. Shape the end of the scion to fit the wedge in the stock

4. Place the scion firmly on the stock and secure with toothpicks

5. Keep the graft area dry and the plant well watered

SEED DORMANCY

SEED DORMANCY TABLE

Dormancy Condition	Treatment Procedures	Seeds
Seed coat impermeable	Scarification (mechanical, acid, hot water)	Legumes, geraniums
Chemical inhibitors in the seed coat	Soaking, leaching, chemicals	Fleshy fruits; iris, citrus, cucurbits, roses
Internal rudimentary embryo and other internal factors	Moist chilling (stratification) chemical	Selected species of herbaceous and woody plants

PROPAGATION OF ORCHIDS

As mentioned in the text, seeds of orchids are so small that a single Cattleya pod may produce 25,000 to 35,000 seeds! There is much written about the difficulties of growing orchids from seed, and of course you do have to wait several years for flowering, but the time and care invested can be well rewarded. Following are some guidelines:

1. Extract seed from pod and place in a test tube

2. Soak in calcium hypochlorite for 5 to 10 minutes until seeds sink to bottom of tube

3. Rinse the seed in distilled water and pour into a test tube or flask containing a nutrient medium, or buy a ready-mixed culture medium from one of the scientific supply houses

4. It takes several weeks for germination, up to 6 months before the small plants can be transplanted into larger flasks, and about a year before the seedling can be put into a pot

The most common procedures are:

Scarification

1. Mechanical (use a 10x hand lens so you can see to avoid injuring the embryo:

    a. If the seed is large enough, rub it on a piece of fine sandpaper until the outer coat is perforated

  b. For fine seed, line a jar with sandpaper and shake the seed until the seed coat is perforated

2. Chemical:

  a. Place dry seeds in a dish and cover with sulphuric acid, which eats the seed coat (the soaking time varies with the type of seed—fairly soft seed coats may require only 10 minutes, for example, while tough resinous coats may require several hours)

  b. Check the thickness of the seed coat with the hand lens; when you can see the white tissue under the seed coat, remove the seed and rinse with water at once

  c. Leave under running water 10 minutes (caution: sulphuric acid is highly corrosive and reacts with water to cause splattering; wear neoprene gloves and protect your eyes)

3. Hot water:

  a. Immerse the seed in water heated to 170°F-212°F (77°-100°C)

  b. Remove the water from the heat source at once

  c. Leave the seed in the water and let cool for 24 hours

Leaching

1. Place the seed in a dish under running water that is warm to the touch for 3 to 4 hours

2. Run a gentle stream so that the seed sits in water

3. Remove and plant

4. With some seeds, chemical treatment may take the place of leaching—try soaking the seed in a 300 ppm solution of kinetin for 3 minutes; remove and plant (see General Appendix, tables and measures, for ppm data)

Moist chilling (stratification)

1. Soak the seed for 24 hours and drain

2. Place the seed in a mix of 1 part sand to 1 part chopped sphagnum peat moss (the mix should be 3 times the volume of the seed)

3. Moisten the mix and keep moist during the chilling period

4. Place in a poly bag or container that permits aeration

5. Store in a refrigerator at 35°F (1.7°C) for 1 to 4 months, depending upon the species of seed

6. Remove and plant the seed in shade, at cool air temperatures of about 65°F (18.3°C)

Chemical treatments

If you are inclined to experiment, you can try chemical treatments instead of the chilling procedure (see General Appendix, tables and measures, for ppm data):

1. Gibberellins:

  a. Soak the seed for 24 hours in a 5 ppm solution of .5% potassium gibberellate (1 teaspoon per gallon of water)

  b. If this does not break dormancy, increase the strength of the solution

  c. Remove and plant

2. Ethaphon (Florel):

  a. Soak the seed for 5 minutes in a 300 ppm (1 ounce per gallon of water) solution

  b. Remove and plant

3. Potassium nitrate:

  a. Moisten some blotter paper with .2% solution of potassium nitrate

  b. Place the seed on blotter paper in a small dish

  c. If the blotter dries before germination, remoisten with plain water

GENERAL APPENDIX
General Sources of Information and Supply

SOURCES OF INFORMATION

For most problems involving insects, soils, disease, and cultural methods, the handiest source of help is your local nursery, garden center, or seed store where you usually will find a knowledgeable person who is familiar with these problems, or can tell you where to get the help you need. For the professional expertise of plant physiologists, pathologists, and entomologists, go to the nearest source on the following lists.

CANADA:

Alberta

Alberta Dept. of Agriculture, Edmonton, Alberta T6G 2E1

Alberta Horticultural Assoc., c/o Mrs. Frank Adamson, Corresponding Secretary, Lacombe, Alberta T0C 1S0

Botanic Garden, Director, Dept. of Botany, University of Alberta, Edmonton, Alberta T6G 2E1

Calgary Parks and Recreation Dept., Horticultural Extension Officer, P.O. Box 2100, Calgary, Alberta T2P 2M5

British Columbia

Botanical Gardens, Director or Coordinator, University of British Columbia, Vancouver, British Columbia V6T 1W5

British Columbia Council of Garden Clubs, c/o Mrs. Joyce Goodman, Corresponding Secretary, 862 Shasta Crescent, Coquitlam, British Columbia V3J 6G3

Dept. of Agriculture, Victoria, British Columbia

Van Dusen Botanical Gardens, Curator, 37th and Oak St., Vancouver, British Columbia

Manitoba

Canada Dept. of Agriculture, Research Station, Morden, Manitoba

Manitoba Horticultural Assoc., Secretary, c/o Manitoba Dept. of Agriculture, 908 Norquay Bldg., Winnipeg, Manitoba R3C 0P8

New Brunswick

Fredericton Garden Club, c/o Dr. Dorothy Farmer, 165 Liverpool St., Fredericton, New Brunswick E3B 4V6

New Brunswick Dept. of Agriculture and Rural Development, Plant Industry Branch, P.O. Box 6000, Fredericton, New Brunswick

Newfoundland

Agricultural Div., Dept. of Mines, Agriculture and Resources, Confederation Bldg., St. John's, Newfoundland

Newfoundland Horticultural Society, P.O. Box 1033, St. John's, Newfoundland A1C 5M3

Nova Scotia

Nova Scotia Assoc. of Garden Clubs, c/o Mrs. J.J. Holmes, Secretary, 17 Cameron St., Dartmouth, Nova Scotia B2Y 2G7

Soils and Crops Branch, Nova Scotia Dept. of Agriculture and Marketing, Truro, Nova Scotia

Ontario

Arboretum and Horticultural Science Dept., Ontario Agricultural College, University of Guelph, Guelph, Ontario N1G 2W1

Civic Garden Centre, Edwards Gardens, 777 Lawrence Ave. E., Don Mills, Ontario M3C 1P2

Highrise Gardeners of Toronto, c/o Civic Garden Centre, Edwards Gardens, 777 Lawrence Ave. E., Don Mills, Ontario M3C 1P2

Horticultural Research Institute, Director, Ontario Ministry of Agriculture and Food, Vineland Station, Ontario L0R 2E0

The Niagara Parks Commission, School of Horticulture, Superintendent, P.O. Box 150, Niagara Falls, Ontario L2E 6T2

Ontario Horticultural Assoc., Secretary, c/o Ontario Ministry of Agriculture and Food, Parliament Buildings, Queen's Park, Toronto, Ontario M7A 1A3

Royal Botanical Gardens, Director, P.O. Box 399, Hamilton, Ontario L8N 3H8

Prince Edward Island

Canada Dept. of Agriculture, Research Branch, Charlottetown, Prince Edward Island

Prince Edward Island Rural Beautification Society, c/o Mr. Keith L. Brehaut, Bunbury Nursery, P.O. Box 70, Charlottetown, Prince Edward Island C1A 7K2

Provincial Horticulturist, P.O. Box 1600, Charlottetown, Prince Edward Island C1A 7K2

Quebec

Montreal Botanical Gardens, Director, 4101 Sherbrooke St. E., Montreal, Quebec H1X 2B2

Morgan Arboretum, MacDonald College, McGill University, P.O. Box 500, St. Anne de Bellevue, Quebec H9X 3L6

Provincial Council of Horticultural Societies of Quebec, c/o Mr. E. B. Jubien, Secretary, 150 Vivian Ave., Town of Mount Royal, Quebec H3P 1N7

Technical Institute of Agriculture, Agronomist, P.O. Box 40, St. Hyacinthe, Quebec J2S 7B2

Saskatchewan

Dept. of Agriculture, Government of Saskatchewan, Regina, Saskatchewan

Saskatchewan Horticultural Assoc., Secretary, c/o Extension Div., University of Saskatchewan, Saskatoon, Saskatchewan S7N 0W0

Yukon and Northwest Territories

Inquiries should be addressed to: Canada Dept. of Agriculture Research Station, P.O. Box 29, Beaverlodge, Alberta

UNITED STATES:
Alabama

Alabama Polytechnic Institute, Auburn, AL 36830

Alaska

University of Alaska, College (or Experiment Station), Palmer, AK 99645

Arizona

University of Arizona, Tucson, AZ 85721

Arkansas

University of Arkansas, Fayetteville, AR 72701 (or

Cooperative Extension Service, 1201 McAlmont Ave., Little Rock, AR 72203)

California

University of California, Berkeley, CA 94720 (or Agricultural Extension Bldg., Riverside, CA 92502; or Davis, CA 95616)

Connecticut

University of Connecticut, Storrs, CT 06268 (or Connecticut Agricultural Experiment Station, New Haven, CT 06501)

Delaware

University of Delaware, Newark, DE 19711

Florida

University of Florida, Gainesville, FL 32611

Georgia

University of Georgia, Athens, GA 30602 (or Agricultural Experiment Station, State of Georgia, Coastal Plain Station, Tifton, GA 31794)

Hawaii

University of Hawaii, Honolulu, HI 96844

Idaho

University of Idaho, Extension Service, Boise, ID 83707 (or Agricultural Experiment Station, Moscow, ID 83843)

Illinois

University of Illinois, Urbana, IL 61801

Indiana

Purdue University, Lafayette, IN 47907

Iowa

Iowa State University, Ames, IA 50010

Kansas

Kansas State University, Manhattan, KS 66502

Kentucky

University of Kentucky, Lexington, KY 40506

Louisiana

Louisiana State University, University Station, Baton Rouge, LA 70813

Maine

University of Maine, Orono, ME 04473

Maryland

University of Maryland, College Park, MD 20740

Massachusetts

University of Massachusetts, Amherst, MA 01002

Michigan

Michigan State University, East Lansing, MI 48823

Minnesota

Institute of Agriculture, University of Minnesota, St. Paul, MN 55165

Missouri

University of Missouri, Columbia, MO 65201

Montana

Montana State College, Bozeman, MT 59715

Nebraska

College of Agriculture, University of Nebraska, Lincoln, NE 68503 (or Scott's Bluff Experiment Station, Mitchell, NE 69357)

Nevada

University of Nevada, Reno, NV 89504

New Hampshire

University of New Hampshire, Durham, NH 03824

New Jersey

State College of Agriculture, Rutgers University, New Brunswick, NJ 08903

New Mexico

New Mexico State University, University Park, NM 88003

New York

New York State College of Agriculture, Cornell University, Ithaca, NY 14850 (or Agricultural Experiment Station, Geneva, NY 14456 or Ornamentals Research Laboratory, Farmingdale, NY 11735)

North Carolina

North Carolina State College, State College Station, Raleigh, NC 27607

A&T College, P.O. Box 1014, Greensboro, NC 27420

North Dakota

North Dakota State University, State College Station, Fargo, ND 58102

Ohio

Ohio State University, Columbus, OH 43210 (or Agricultural Experiment Station, Wooster, OH 44691)

Oklahoma

Oklahoma State University, Stillwater, OK 74074

Oregon

Oregon State University, Corvallis, OR 97330

Pennsylvania

Pennsylvania State University, University Park, PA 16802

Puerto Rico

University of Puerto Rico, Rio Piedras, PR 00923

Rhode Island

University of Rhode Island, Kingston, RI 02881

South Carolina

Clemson Agricultural College, Clemson, SC 29631

South Dakota

South Dakota State College, Brookings, SD 57006

Tennessee

University of Tennessee, Knoxville, TN 37916

Texas

Texas A&M College, College Station, TX 77840 (or Box 476, Weslaco, TX 78596; Tyler Experiment Station No. 2, R.6, Tyler, TX 75701)

Texas Tech., Agricultural Bldg., Lubbock, TX 79406

Utah

Utah State University, Logan, UT 84321

Vermont

University of Vermont, Burlington, VT 05401

Virginia

Virginia Polytechnic Institute, Blacksburg, VA 24060

(or Virginia Truck Experiment Station (truck crops), Norfolk, VA 23501; Piedmont Fruit Research Laboratory, Charlottesville, VA 22906; or Winchester Fruit Research Laboratory, Winchester, VA 22601)

Virgin Islands

Officer in Charge, Virgin Islands Agriculture Project, Kingshill, St. Croix, VI 00850

Washington

Washington State University, Pullman, WA 99163 (or Western Washington Experiment Station, Puyallup, WA 98371)

West Virginia

West Virginia University, Morgantown, WV 26505

Wisconsin

University of Wisconsin, Madison, WI 53706 (or Peninsular Branch Experiment Station, Sturgeon Bay, WI 54235)

Wyoming

University of Wyoming, Laramie, WY 82070

All states have at least one extension horticulturist to answer questions on cultural management of garden plants. Some have an extension entomologist (insects, mites, rodents) and also may have an extension plant pathologist (diseases). Write to the specialist in care of the department of agriculture at your state college or university. The department also probably has free bulletins, circulars, pamphlets, spray schedules, and so forth, which you may obtain on request.

STANDARD REFERENCE WORKS

CANADA:
Chatelaine's Gardening Book. Lois Wilson. McLean-Hunter, 481 University Ave., Toronto, Ontario M5W 1A7

UNITED STATES:
Encyclopedia of Gardening. Norman Taylor. Houghton Mifflin, 2 Park St., Boston, MA 02107

Encyclopedia of Organic Gardening. J.I. Rodale. Rodale Press, Emmaus, PA 18049

Exotica 3. Alfred B. Graf. Roehrs, East Rutherford, NJ 07073

Hortus Third. The L.H. Bailey Hortorium, Cornell University. Macmillan, 666 3rd Ave., New York, NY 10022

The Standard Cyclopedia of Horticulture. L.H. Bailey. Macmillan, 666 3rd Ave., New York, NY 10022

WORLD:
The Royal Horticultural Society Dictionary of Gardening. Royal Horticultural Society. Clarendon Press, Oxford, England

SOURCES OF SUPPLY

The following companies are suppliers for greenhouse operation and plant culture. Since some of the companies are wholesale only, some retail only, and some both, contact the supplier before attempting to purchase supplies.

Many hobby-greenhouse growers gradually turn their greenhouses into income-producing businesses, which entitles purchasing from any wholesaler. All of the firms listed will assist you in locating items that you need if they cannot provide them.

CANADA:

Eastern Region

Source	Structures Coverings and Prefabs	Climate Control Equipment	Growing Supplies and Equipment	Seed
Ball Superior, Ltd. 1155 Birchview Dr. Mississauga, Ontario L5H 3E1	yes	yes	yes	yes
Equipment Sales & Consultants (Humex Products) 2241 Dunwin Dr. Mississauga, Ontario L5L 1A3	yes	yes	yes	no
Ickes-Braun of Canada 90 Bartlett Rd. Beamsville, Ontario	yes	yes	yes	no
Lord & Burnham 325 Welland Ave. St. Catharines, Ontario L2R 6V9	yes	yes	no	no

Source	Structures Coverings and Prefabs	Climate Control Equipment	Growing Supplies and Equipment	Seed
W. H. Perron Co., Ltd. 515 Labelle Blvd. Chomedey, Quebec	yes	yes	yes	no
Plant Products Co. 314 Orenda Rd. Bramalea, Ontario L6T 1G1	no	yes	yes	no
The Plant Room 6373 Trafalgar Rd. Horby, Ontario L0P 1EO	yes	yes	yes	no
Stokes Seeds, Ltd. 39 James St. St. Catharines, Ontario L2R 6R6	no	yes	yes	yes
Vanhof & Blokker 1773 Mattawa Ave. Mississauga, Ontario L4X 1K5	yes	yes	yes	no
Vaughn-Jacklin Corp. 49 Pioneer Tower Rd. Kitchener, Ontario	yes	yes	yes	yes

Central Region

Source	Structures Coverings and Prefabs	Climate Control Equipment	Growing Supplies and Equipment	Seed
Buckerfields, Ltd. 120 Lombard St. Winnipeg, Manitoba	no	yes	yes	yes
Gales Wholesale 3004 13th Ave. Regina, Saskatchewan	yes	yes	yes	no
Gardeners Sales, Ltd. 984 Powell St. Winnipeg, Manitoba	yes	yes	yes	yes
Green Thumb Nursery 960 Assiniboine Ave. E. Regina, Saskatchewan	yes	yes	yes	yes
Pioneer Greenhouse Supply Co. 175 Essar N. Winnipeg, Manitoba	yes	yes	yes	yes

Western Region

Source	Structures Coverings and Prefabs	Climate Control Equipment	Growing Supplies and Equipment	Seed
Apache Seeds, Ltd. 10136 149th St. Edmonton, Alberta	yes	yes	yes	yes
Golden West Seeds 1108 6th St. S.E. Calgary, Alberta	yes	yes	yes	yes
Greenleaf Garden Supply 4612 Dawson St. Burnaby, British Columbia	yes	yes	yes	yes
David Hunter Nursery 3030 Kingsway Vancouver, British Columbia	yes	yes	yes	yes
Paridon Bulb Co. P.O. Box 1006 Coquitlam, British Columbia	yes	yes	yes	no
Harry Sharp & Sons 620 Malkin St. Vancouver, British Columbia	yes	yes	yes	no
Smith & Gordon Horticulturists 8115 76th Ave. Edmonton, Alberta	yes	yes	yes	yes
Chris Walters Sales (MacPenny Systems) RR 4 Salmon Arms, British Columbia	no	yes	yes	no
Westcan Horticultural Specialists 1902 11th St. S.E. Calgary, Alberta T2G 3G2	yes	yes	yes	no
Woodward the Florist 635 Fort St. Victoria, British Columbia	yes	yes	yes	yes

Source	Structures Coverings and Prefabs	Climate Control Equipment	Growing Supplies and Equipment	Seed
UNITED STATES:				
Eastern Region				
Apopka Growers Supply P. O. Box 1147 Apopka, FL 32703	yes	yes	yes	no
Al-Tex Nursery Supply P. O. Box 86 Semmes, AL 36575	yes	yes	yes	yes
Brawley Seed Co. P. O. Box 597 Mooresville, NC 28115	yes	yes	yes	yes
Brighton By Products P. O. Box 23 New Brighton, PA 15066	no	yes	yes	no
Cassco P. O. Box 550 Montgomery, AL 36101	yes	yes	yes	no
W. J. Connell Co. 210 Needham St. Boston, MA 02164	yes	yes	yes	yes
Fischer Greenhouse Dept. 4 Linwood, NJ 08221	no	yes	yes	no
Florida Agri-Supply P. O. Box 658 Jacksonville, FL 32201	yes	yes	yes	no
E. C. Geiger & Co. P. O. Box 2852 Harleysville, PA 19438	yes	yes	yes	no
Fred C. Gloeckner 15 E. 26th St. New York, NY 10008	yes	yes	yes	yes
W. W. Grainger, Inc. (132 stores, in all states)	no	yes	yes	no
Griffin Greenhouse Supply 349 Main St. Reading, MA 01867	yes	yes	yes	no

Source	Structures Coverings and Prefabs	Climate Control Equipment	Growing Supplies and Equipment	Seed
Lord & Burnham Irvington, NY 10533	yes	no	no	no
Merrimack Farmers Exchange Concord, NH 03301	yes	no	yes	yes
Geo. W. Parks Seed Co. 540 Cokesbury Rd. Greenwood, SC 29647	no	yes	yes	yes
Piedmont Garden Supply P. O. Box 36 Salesbury, NC 28144	yes	yes	yes	yes
Px Primex 435 W. Glenside Ave. Glenside, PA 19038	yes	yes	yes	yes
Al Saffer & Co. 130 W. 28th St. New York, NY 10001	yes	yes	yes	no
X. S. Smith Co. Drawer X Red Bank, NJ 07701	yes	yes	no	no
Spurgeon Supply Co. Rt. 3, Mwy. 411 Maryville, TE 37801	yes	yes	yes	no
Vaughn-Jacklin Corp. Chimney Brook Rd. Boundbrook, NJ 08805	yes	yes	yes	yes
Central Region				
Geo. J. Ball, Inc. P. O. Box 335 W. Chicago, IL 60185	yes	yes	yes	yes
Campbell Distributing 333 N. Main St. Springfield, MO 65806	yes	yes	yes	no
Capital Equipment Co. 1007 Center St. Little Rock, AR 72203	no	yes	yes	no

Source	Structures Coverings and Prefabs	Climate Control Equipment	Growing Supplies and Equipment	Seed
Z. W. Credle Co. 4608 Dodge St. Omaha, NE 68132	yes	yes	yes	no
Florist's Products, Inc. 1843 Oakton St. Des Plaines, IL 60018	yes	yes	yes	no
Forestry Suppliers P. O. Box 8397 Jackson, MI 39204	no	yes	yes	no
Fosters, Inc. P. O. Box 1114 Waterloo, IA 50704	yes	yes	yes	no
Johnson Floral Supply 3333 Edwards St. N.E. Minneapolis, MN 55418	no	yes	yes	no
F. A. Martiny & Sons 2822 Magazine St. New Orleans, LA 70119	yes	yes	yes	yes
National Greenhouse Co. 400 E. Main St. Pana, IL 62557	yes	yes	no	no
Stuppy Supply Co. 120 E. 12th Ave. N. Kansas City, MO 64116	yes	yes	yes	no
Vaughn-Jacklin Corp. 5300 Katrina Ave. Downer's Grove, IL 60515	yes	yes	yes	yes

Western Region

Source	Structures Coverings and Prefabs	Climate Control Equipment	Growing Supplies and Equipment	Seed
Geo. J. Ball-Pacific P. O. Box 9055 Sunnyvale, CA 94088	yes	yes	yes	yes
Joe Berger Co. 900 Lind Ave. S.W. Renton, WA 98055	yes	yes	yes	yes

Source	Structures Coverings and Prefabs	Climate Control Equipment	Growing Supplies and Equipment	Seed
Environmental Dynamics 3010 CEA Vine Riverside, CA 92507	yes	yes	yes	no
Germain's, Inc. 4820 E. 50th St. Los Angeles, CA 90085	no	yes	yes	yes
Jacobs Bros. Supply 8928 Sepulveda Blvd. Sepulveda, CA 91343	yes	yes	yes	no
Lawn & Garden Supply P. O. Box 11220 Phoenix, AZ 85017	yes	yes	yes	yes
J.M. McConkey & Co. P. O. Box 309 Sumner, WA 98390	yes	yes	yes	no
Mid Coast Distributors P. O. Box 1528 Medford, OR 97501	yes	yes	yes	no
Pacific Agro Co. 503 Houser Way Renton, WA 98055	no	yes	yes	no
Pacific Coast Supply 430 Hurlingame Ave. Redwood City, CA 94036	yes	yes	yes	no
Alfred Teufel Nursery 12345 N.W. Barnes Rd. Portland, OR 97229	yes	yes	yes	no

Alaska

Source	Structures Coverings and Prefabs	Climate Control Equipment	Growing Supplies and Equipment	Seed
Tongass Trading Co. P. O. Box 468 Ketchikan, AK 99401	yes	yes	yes	yes

Hawaii

Source	Structures Coverings and Prefabs	Climate Control Equipment	Growing Supplies and Equipment	Seed
Island Supply 130 Halekauila St. Honolulu, HI 96810	yes	yes	yes	yes

HORTICULTURAL SOCIETIES

CANADA:
Canadian horticultural organizations are well organized and numerous. Ontario, for example, has 50,000 members who belong to 242 societies, under the Ministry of Agriculture and Food, Agriculture and Horticultural Societies Branch, 1200 Bay St., Toronto, Ontario. Write or call your provincial department of agriculture for names and addresses of societies.

Professional or Commercial

Canadian Society for Horticultural Science, E.J. Hogue, Secretary, Research Station, P.O. Box 457, St. Jean, Quebec J3B 6Z8
UNITED STATES:
Indoor Light Gardening Society of America, Inc., 4 Wildwood Dr., Greenville, SC 29607 ($5.00)

Contact the state departments of agriculture for further information and addresses of horticultural associations.

Professional or Commercial

American Horticultural Society*, 7931 E. Boulevard Dr., Alexandria, VA 22308

American Society for Horticultural Science, P.O. Box 109, St. Joseph, MI 49085

Horticultural Research Institute, 230 Southern Bldg., Washington, DC 20005

International Plant Propagator's Society, Rutgers State University, New Brunswick, NJ 08903

WORLD:
International Society for Horticultural Science, Dr. G. de Bakker, Secretary General, P.O. Box 9595, The Hague, Netherlands

PLANT SOCIETIES

The fee listed includes annual membership dues and subscription to the society's publication.

CANADA:
The Canadian Rose Society, 12 Castelgrove Blvd., No. 18, Don Mills, Ontario M3A 1K8 ($12.50)

---

* Publishes the *Directory of American Horticulture*

The Civic Garden Centre, 777 Lawrence Ave. E., Don Mills, Ontario M3C 1P2 ($5.00)

The Rhododendron Society of Canada, 4271 Lakeshore Rd., Burlington, Ontario ($5.00)

For addresses of other Canadian plant societies, write to the Civic Garden Centre; it is the hub of plant society activity in Ontario.

UNITED STATES:
African Violet Society of America, Inc., P.O. Box 1326, Knoxville, TN 37901 ($6.00)

American Amarylis Society (see American Plant Life Society)

American Begonia Society, Inc., 1431 Coronado Terrace, Los Angeles, CA 90026 ($4.00)

American Bonsai Society, 229 North Shore Dr., Lake Waukomis, Parsville, MO 64151 ($10.00)

American Camellia Society, P.O. Box 212, Fort Valley, GA 31030 ($7.50)

American Fern Society, University of Rhode Island, Dept. of Botany, Kingston, RI 02881 ($5.00)

American Fuchsia Society, 1600 Prospect St., Belmont, CA 94002 ($4.00)

American Gloxinia and Gesneriad Society, P.O. Box 174, New Milford, CT 06776 ($5.00)

American Ivy Society, 128 W. 58th St., New York, NY 10019 ($5.00)

American Orchid Society, Botanical Museum of Harvard University, Cambridge, MA 02138 ($12.50)

American Plant Life Society (American Amarylis Society), P.O. Box 150, La Jolla, CA 92037 ($5.00)

American Primrose Society, 14015 84th Ave. NE, Bothell, WA 98011 ($5.00)

American Rhododendron Society, 2232 NE 78th Ave., Portland, OR 97213 ($10.00)

American Rock Garden Society, 99 Pierpont Rd., Waterbury, CT 06705 ($5.00)

American Rose Society, 4048 Poselea Pl., Columbus, OH 43214 ($10.50)

Bonsai Clubs International, 445 Blake St., Menlo Park, CA 94025 ($5.00)

Bromeliad Society, P.O. Box 3279, Santa Monica, CA 90403 ($7.50)

Cactus and Succulent Society of America, Inc., P.O. Box 167, Reseda, CA 91335 ($10.00)

Epiphyllum Society of America, 218 E. Graystone Ave., Monrovia, GA 91016 ($10.00)

Herb Society of America, 300 Massachusetts Ave., Boston, MA 02115 ($12.50)

Hobby Greenhouse Assoc. of America, 45 Shady Dr., Wallingford, CT 06492 ($5.00)

International Aril Society, Mrs. Richard A. Wilson, Secretary, 11500 Versailles Ave. NE, Albuquerque, NM 87111 ($4.00)

International Geranium Society, 2547 Blvd. Del Campo, San Luis Obispo, CA 93401 ($4.00)

New England Wildflower Society, Hemenway Rd., Framingham, MA 10701 ($5.00)

North American Lily Society, Rt. 1 Box 395, Colby, WI 54431 ($7.50)

The Palm Society, 7229 SW 54th Ave., Miami, FL 33143 ($10.00)

Saintpaulia International, P.O. Box 10604, Knoxville, TN 37914 ($4.00)

Professional or Commercial

Bedding Plants, Inc., 4479 Seneca Dr., Okemos, MI 48864

RESEARCH BULLETINS
AND TRADE MAGAZINES

The fee listed includes annual membership dues and subscription to the society's publication.

CANADA:
The Canadian Florist, P. O. Box 697, Streetsville, Ontario ($6.00)

UNITED STATES:
Colorado Flower Growers Assoc. 2785 N. Speer Blvd., Denver, CO 80211 ($50.00)

Florida Foliage Grower and *Florida Flower Grower*, Dept. of Ornamental Horticulture, University of Florida, 115 Rolfs Hall, Gainesville, FL 32611

Illinois State Florists Assoc., 1426 Morris Ave., Berkeley, IL 60163 ($10.00)

The Maryland Florist, Allied Florists of Greater Washington, Inc., 8630 Fenton St., Suite 520, Silver Springs, MD 20910 ($5.00)

The Michigan Florist, Michigan State Florists Assoc., 1152 Haslett Rd., Haslett, MI 48840 ($10.00)

Minnesota State Florists Bulletin, Minnesota Commercial Flower Growers, 1021 Larpeneur Ave. W., St. Paul, MN 55113 ($5.00)

Missouri State Florists News, 3008 N. Ten Mile Dr., Jefferson City, MO 65101 ($10.00 for out-of-state subscribers)

New York State Flower Industries, Inc., 900 Jefferson Rd., Rochester, NY 14623 ($7.50)

Ohio Florists Assoc. 2001 Fyffe Court, Columbus, OH 43210 ($10.00 for out-of-state subscribers)

Pennsylvania Flower Growers, P.O. Box 247, Chalfont, PA 18914 ($12.00)

Connecticut Florists Assoc., P.O. Box 352, West Haven, CT 06516 ($35.00)

The Florist's Review, 310 S. Michigan Ave., Chicago, IL 60604 ($15.00)

Tables and Measures

CONCENTRATION DATA

1 part per million (p.p.m.):

1 mg. per liter

1 mg. per kilogram

1 mg. per 9/10 qt. (approximate)

.0001%

1% solution:

10,000 p.p.m.

10 g. per liter

1.28 oz. per gallon

.1%	= 1,000 p.p.m.	= 1,000 mg. per liter
.01%	= 100 p.p.m.	= 100 mg. per liter
.001%	= 10 p.p.m.	= 10 mg. per liter
.0001%	= 1 p.p.m.	= 1 mg. per liter

Percentage of Emulsifiable Concentrate (EC) Converted to Pounds Used per Gallon

Percentage	equals	Pounds per Gallon
10-12		1
15-20		1.5
25		2
40-50		4
60-65		6
70-75		8
80-100		10

DILUTION DATA

Measurement Conversion Table

Percentage	Dilution or Rates	Parts per Million (p.p.m.)	Grams per Liter	Ounces per Gallon
1	1:100	10,000	10	.35 (⅓)
.1	1:1,000	1,000	1.0	.03
.01	1:10,000	100	.1	.003
.001	1:100,000	10	.01	—
.0001	1:1,000,000	1	.001	—

Volume and Weight Measurement Equivalents

Common to Metric

Common Measure: Volume	Common Measure: Weight	equals	Metric Measure: Volume	Metric Measure: Weight
1 tsp.	.17 oz.	=	5c.c.	4.85.g.
1 Tbs. or 3 tsp.	.50 g.	=	15c.c. or ml.	14.2 g.
2 Tbs. or 6 tsp.	1 oz.	=	29.57c.c. or ml.	28.35 g.
1 pt.	16 oz. or 1 lb.	=	473c.c. or ml. or .473 l.	453.6 g.
1 qt. or 2 pt.	32 oz.	=	946c.c. or ml.	907.2 g. or .907 kg.
1 gal. or 4 qt. or 8 pt.	128 oz.	=	3.785 l.	3.628 kg.

Conversions to Smaller Quantity from 100 Gallons for Liquid Concentrations

100 Gallons	50 Gallons	10 Gallons	5 Gallons	3.5 Gallons	1 Gallon*
2 gal.	1 gal.	1.6 pt.	12.8 oz.	½ pt. or 8 oz.	2.56 oz. or 5⅒ Tbs.
1 gal.	2 qt.	12.8 oz.	6.4 oz.	4 oz.	1.28 oz. or 2⅗ Tbs.
2 qt.	1 qt.	6.4 oz.	3.2 oz.	2 oz.	3⅘ tsp.
1 qt.	1 pt.	3.2oz.	1.6 oz.	1 oz.	2 tsp.
1 pt.	1 c.	1.6 oz.	.8 oz.	½ oz.	1 tsp.
4 oz.	2 oz.	.4 oz.	.2 oz.	⅛ oz.	¼ tsp.

Conversion to Smaller Quantity from 100 Gallons for Wettable Powder (WP) Concentrations

100 Gallons	50 Gallons	10 Gallons	5 Gallons	3.5 Gallons	1 Gallon*
5 lb.	2.5 lb.	8 oz.	4 oz.	2.5 oz.	4⅘ tsp.
4 lb.	2 lb.	6.4 oz.	3.2 oz.	2 oz.	3⅘ tsp.
3 lb.	1.5 lb.	4.8 oz.	2.4 oz.	1.5 oz.	2⅘ tsp.
2 lb.	1 lb.	3.2 oz.	1.6 oz.	1 oz.	2 tsp.
1 lb.	½ lb.	1.6 oz.	.8 oz.	.5 oz.	1 tsp.
½ lb.	4 oz.	.8 oz.	.4 oz.	¼ oz.	½ tsp.
4 oz.	2 oz.	.4 oz.	.2 oz.	⅛ oz.	¼ tsp.

FERTILIZER WEIGHTS*

24 Tbs. per pound	Ground limestone Sulphate of potash 0-0-50 Nitrate of soda 15-0-0
32 Tbs. per pound	Calcium nitrate 15-0-0
36 Tbs. per pound	Superphosphate 0-20-0 Complete 4-12-8 Complete 5-10-5 Muriate of potash 0-0-50 Nitrate of potash 13-0-44
40 Tbs. per pound	Ammonium nitrate 33-0-0 Epsom salts
44 Tbs. per pound	Ammonium sulphate 20-0-0 Ammonium phosphate 11-48-0

*Approximate

Aluminum sulphate
(acidifying)

64 Tbs. per pound Hydrated lime
Sulphur

LIQUID VOLUME EQUIVALENTS

Gallons	Quarts	Pints	Fluid Ounces	Cups	Table-spoons	Tea-spoons	Milliliters or Cubic Centimeters
1	4	8	128	16			
	1	2	32	4			
		1	16	2	32		473
			1	⅛	2	6	30
				1	16	48	240
					1	3	15
						1	5

METRIC AND COMMON MEASUREMENT CONVERSION TABLES
Distance Measurement Equivalents

Metric to Common		Common to Metric	
Metric equals Common		Common equals Metric	
1 cm.	.394 in.	1 in.	2.54 cm.
1 m.	3.281 ft. or 1.094 yd.	1 ft.	30.5 cm. or .305 m.
1 km.	.621 mi.	1 yd.	.914 m.
		1 mi.	1.609 km.

Volume Measurement Equivalents

Metric to Common		Common to Metric	
Metric equals Common		Common equals Metric	
1 l. or 1000 ml. or c.c.	1.06 qt. or 2.1 pt.	1 gal. or 4 qt.	3.785 l.
1 ml. or c.c.	0.34 fluid oz.	1 qt. or 2 pt.	.946 l.
		1 pt.	.473 l.
		1 fluid oz.	29.6 ml. or c.c.

Weight Measurement Equivalents

Metric to Common		Common to Metric	
Metric equals Common		Common equals Metric	
1 kg. or 1,000 g.	2.2 lbs.	1 lb.	453.6 g.
1 g. or 1,000 mg.	.035 oz. (or ¼ tsp.*)	1 oz.	28.35 g.

Water Measurement Equivalents

Metric Volume and Weight		Common Volume & Weight	
Volume equals Weight		Volume equals Weight	
1 ml. or c.c. of water	1 g.	1 pt. of water	1 lb.
1 l. of water	1 kg.	1 gal. of water	8.34 lbs.

One Cup Measurement Equivalents

Metric	Common
236.5 ml. or c.c.	8 fluid oz., or .5 pt., .25 qt., 16 Tbs., 48 tsp.

METRIC MEASUREMENT

Prefixes

The metric system, like money, is arranged in tens:

Mega	= one million	1,000,000
Kilo	= one thousand	1,000
Hecto	= one hundred	100
Deca	= ten	10
Deci	= one tenth	$1/10$
Centi	= one hundredth	$1/100$
Milli	= one thousandth	$1/1,000$
Micro	= one millionth	$1/1,000,000$

Measurements

These prefixes combine with the basic units of the meter for linear measure, the gram for weight or volume, and the liter for liquid measure:

Linear measure:	Millimeter	$1/1,000$	mm.
	Centimeter	$1/100$	cm.
	Meter	1	m.
	Kilometer	1,000	km.

*approximate

Weight measure:	Milligram	$\frac{1}{1,000}$	mg.
	Centigram	$\frac{1}{100}$	cg.
	Gram	1	g.
	Kilogram	1,000	kg.
Liquid measure:	Milliliter	$^1/_{1,000}$	ml.
	Centiliter	$^1/_{100}$	cl.
	Liter	1	l.
	Kiloliter	1,000	kl.
Volume measure:	Cubic centimeters		c.c.

SOIL VOLUME EQUIVALENTS
Size of Pot

Common	equals	Metric
2¼ in.		75 c.c.
3 in.		200 c.c.
4 in.		500 c.c.
5 in.		900 c.c.
6 in.		1,500 c.c.
7 in.		2,500 c.c.
8 in.		3,300 c.c.
1 pt.		400 c.c.
1 qt.		800 c.c.
1 gal.		2,250 c.c.
8-in. hanging basket		2,150 c.c.
10-in. hanging basket		4,000 c.c.

Volume Measurement

1,728 cubic in. = 1 cubic ft.
27 cubic ft. = 1 cubic yd.

POWER DATA

1 BTU   =   0.293 watt/hour

1 kw/hour   =   3,413 BTUs

Wattage   =   Amps x voltage

Amps   = $\dfrac{\text{Wattage}}{\text{Voltage}}$

Voltage   = $\dfrac{\text{Wattage}}{\text{Amps}}$

TEMPERATURE CONVERSION CHART*
Fahrenheit (F) and Centigrade (or Celsius, C)

F°	C°	F°	C°	F°	C°
−40	−40	40	4.4	84	28.9
−30	−34.4	41	5.0	85	29.4
−20	−28.9	42	5.6	86	30.0
−10	−23.3	43	6.1	87	30.6
0	−17.8	44	6.7	88	31.1
1	−17.2	45	7.2	89	31.7
2	−16.7	46	7.8	90	32.2
3	−16.1	47	8.3	91	32.8
4	−15.6	48	8.9	92	33.3
5	−15.0	49	9.4	93	33.9
6	−14.4	50	10.0	94	34.4
7	−13.9	51	10.6	95	35.0
8	−13.3	52	11.1	96	35.6
9	−12.8	53	11.7	97	36.1
10	−12.2	54	12.2	98	36.7
11	−11.7	55	12.8	99	37.2
12	−11.1	56	13.3	100	37.8
13	−10.6	57	13.9	101	38.3
14	−10.0	58	14.4	102	38.8
15	−9.4	59	15.0	103	39.4
16	−8.9	60	15.6	104	40.0
17	−8.3	61	16.1	105	40.5
18	−7.8	62	16.7	106	41.1
19	−7.2	63	17.2	107	41.6
20	−6.7	64	17.8	108	42.2
21	−6.1	65	18.3	109	42.7
22	−5.6	66	18.9	110	43.3
23	−5.0	67	19.4	111	43.8
24	−4.4	68	20.0	112	44.4
25	−3.9	69	20.6	113	45.0
26	−3.3	70	21.1	114	45.5
27	−2.8	71	21.7	115	46.1
28	−2.2	72	22.2	116	46.6
29	−1.7	73	22.8	117	47.2
30	−1.1	74	23.3	118	47.7
31	−0.6	75	23.9	119	48.3
32	0.0	76	24.4	120	48.9
33	0.6	77	25.0	121	49.4
34	1.1	78	25.6	122	50.0
35	1.7	79	26.1	123	50.5
36	2.2	80	26.7	124	51.1
37	2.8	81	27.2	125	51.6
38	3.3	82	27.8	140	60.0
39	3.9	83	28.3	160	71.1
				200	93.3
				212	100.0

*Conversion formula:

$$°C \times {}^9/_5 + 32 = °F$$

$$[°F - 32] \times {}^5/_9 = °C$$

GLOSSARY

Acidic   Soil having a pH of 1.0 to 7.0 (see pH)

Adsorption   Adhesion of molecules of water to individual soil particles

Aerate   Prepare soil so that it is loose enough to permit air to reach all of the root system

Aerobic   Living or active only in the presence of oxygen; usually refers to bacteria

Aggregate   The large component of a concrete mix, usually gravel; used to designate the growing medium for hydroponics

Aircap   A double-layer polyethylene, quilted into one-half inch bubbles containing air

Air drainage   Movement of cold air, which runs down-hill like water

Alkaline   Soil having a pH of 7.0 to 14.0 (see pH)

Alkaloid   Organic compounds manufactured by plants; often poisons or medicines (for example, Caffeine, morphine, cocaine, nicotine)

Allelopathy   The study of inhibitors or toxic chemicals that are given off by plants into the air or soil

Ambient   The temperature of the atmosphere

Anaerobic   Living or active in the absence of free oxygen; usually refers to bacteria

Antibiotic   A chemical substance produced by an organism that inhibits the activity of a microorganism

Atrium   A central court surrounded by four walls and open to the sky

Automatic damper   A device that regulated the flow of hot or cold air by means of a thermostat

Bacterium   A microscopic unicellular plant without chlorophyll; may be a disease-causing organism. Survives winters because of resistant resting spores

Biodegradable   Any material that is broken down by decomposition bacteria

Black body   Usually a black metal that absorbs all radiation and reflects none

Bolting   Rapid growth of the plant to produce seed; fostered by high temperatures and long days

BTU   (British Thermal Unit) the amount of heat required to raise the temperature of one pound of water one degree Fahrenheit

Cambium   The rapidly dividing tissue between the bark and the wood in woody plants

Capillary attraction   A force resulting from the interaction of adhesion, cohesion, and surface tension, which causes water to rise in a tube or a fine textured material such as a mat or a soil mix

Carpel   The seed-bearing organ of a plant

Catalyst   A substance that effects a chemical reaction, but undergoes no chemical change itself

Cellulose   One of the substances composing the cell wall of woody plants ($C_6H_{10}O_5$)

Chelates   Chemicals that prevent binding or tie up of compounds in the soil; used with minor nutrient elements to make them readily available to the plant

Chlorophyll   The green pigment in plants that "traps" the energy of light

Clone   A group of organisms propagated from an individual organism (for example, cuttings from one stock plant, tissue culture from one leaf)

Companion planting   The practice of planting insect-repellent plants with ornamentals or vegetables

Controller   An electronic device for controlling the environment in the greenhouse

Controlled release   Fertilizers that are formulated to release the nutrients at a pre-established rate over a long period

Copolymer   A type of plastic material whose molecular arrangement makes a strong polyethylene sheeting

Cultivar   A cultivated variety of plant

Cycler   A timing device that operates over and over at a preset interval and does not shut off unless controlled by a timer

Damping off   A name for any of several fatal diseases

that turn the stems of seedlings black at the soil level; also called black leg

Degree day   (DD) a unit of measure based on time and temperature difference; from a base of 65°F, there are as many DD units as degrees Fahrenheit between the mean temperature and the base, 65° F

Diffusion   The process in which molecules of one substance mix with those of another, usually through soil or cell walls

Dormancy   The resting state of a plant or seed in which growth ceases and life processes slow down

Drawdown   Removing all usable heat from a storage chamber

Dry weight   The weight of plant tissue after drying to remove all liquids

Ecosystem   A specifically defined environment, including all the organisms that live in it

Enzyme   Organic compounds that act as catalysts

Etiolation   Tall, spindly growth in low light

Exotic   A plant introduced into an area where it is not native

Flat   A shallow tray used to start seed or cuttings

Foliar feeding   Applying soluble fertilizers to the leaves of plants

Footcandle   A measure of light intensity: the amount of light received on a white surface one foot away from an international candle

Forced air   Air driven by a fan or blower

Frond   The leaf of a fern

Fungus   A primitive plant that has no chlorophyll; it may cause disease or decompose organic matter

Fungicide   A compound that kills fungi

Genus   The name of a group of plant species (for example, family: Rosaceae; genus: Rosa; species: odorata rugosa carolina)

Growth chamber   A specialized box or room in which complete control of the environment is achieved

Growth regulators   Chemicals that modify or change the growth process

Habitat   The locality that is the natural abode of a plant; sometimes a large area

Harden off   Slowing plant growth to produce tougher tissues by gradually withholding water and fertilizer and lowering the temperature

Hardy   Plants that can withstand frost and cold

Heat capacity   The amount of heat needed to raise the temperature of a given mass of material one degree Fahrenheit

Heel cutting   Any cutting that has a piece of older stem wood at the base

Hormone   A chemical that regulates, triggers, or controls a growth process

Host   A plant that provides nourishment for parasitic bacteria, fungus, or virus

Humidity (relative)   A percentage designation of the amount of water vapor in the air compared to the maximum the air could hold at that temperature

Hydroponics   The growing of plants in water or a water bath containing fertilizers

Hyphae   Microscopic thread-like pieces of fungus that are dispersed like spores

Incident radiation   The quantity of energy that strikes a given area of surface in a given time

Injector   A device that automatically meters a predetermined amount of soluble fertilizer into the flow of water

Inorganic   Usually, a compound not containing carbon, which is derived from mineral sources

Insolation   The solar radiation that reaches the earth's surface

Ion   An electrically charged atom or group of atoms—positively charged is a cation; negatively charged is an anion

Lanai   Term in Hawaii for a covered porch that contains plants

Langley   One gram calorie per square centimeter of solar radiation

Larva	An insect stage of development before adulthood; usually a grub, a maggot, or a caterpillar
Leaching	To filter water down through a material such as soil until soluble substances are removed
Lime	Used to adjust the pH of the soil; occurs as limestone, hydrated lime, sugar beet lime, and dolomite (dolomite contains magnesium as well as calcium carbonate)
Limiting factors	The factors that limit plant growth, such as water, temperature, light, nutrition, soil, and air
Lorotex	A woven polyethylene material with high tear strength
Major elements	Nitrogen, phosphorus, potassium
Medium	A name designating the material in which the root system grows
Metabolism	The chemical and physical processes that sustain life
Minor elements	Calcium, magnesium, sulfur, boron, manganese, copper, zinc, iron, molybdenum, chlorine
Oedema	Water blisters on the leaf caused by an excess of soil moisture and low transpiration
Parasite	An organism that lives in or on, and obtains its nutrients from, a host plant
Pasteurization	The process of heating soil to about 140°F (60°C) to kill pathogenic bacteria without killing decomposition bacteria
Pathogen	An organism capable of causing disease in a host plant
pH	The symbol for relative acidity; on a scale of 1.0 to 14.0 the acidic values are 1-7 and the alkaline values 7-14; a value of 7 is neutral
Pheremones	Female insect secretions used as bait in insect traps to attract males
Phloem	The stem tissue in which fluids are transported
Photoperiod	The length of day or night in which a plant grows
Photoperiodism	The response of plants to dark periods
Photosynthesis	The process by which plants manufacture sugars from soil, water and carbon dioxide using the energy of sunlight
Phytotoxicity	The sensitivity of plants to toxic chemicals in the soil or air
Polarity	Roots grow down with gravity; stems grow up against gravity—if cuttings of stem or root are reversed, growth diminishes or stops
Pupa	The insect resting form during which the larva changes to the adult form
Pyranometer	A device for measuring solar radiation incident upon a surface
Radiant energy	Energy emitted from surfaces as electromagnetic waves
Reflectance	Ratio of radiant energy reflected from a surface to the radiant energy incident upon it
Respiration	The process by which plants burn sugars to provide growth energy, during which they give off water and carbon dioxide as waste products
Respirator	A nose and mouth mask worn to protect against some harmful dusts and chemicals; provides less protection than a gas mask
Resting stages	Forms of fungi and bacteria that can survive winter, usually because of an impervious outer coating
Salts	Compounds, such as chlorides and sulfates, which may be necessary for plant growth in small quantities, but produce damage when used in excessive amounts; most fertilizers contain soluble salts
Scarify	To file, cut, or otherwise abrade the coating of a seed to assist germination
Scion	A small shoot or twig taken from a plant, which is to be grafted on a rooted growing understock
Scorch	Dry plant tissue that has turned brown
Selective black paint	Absorbs more infared than non-selective black paint

Simples	Fertilizers containing only one element, such as Urea (45% nitrogen), or unformulated materials, such as calcium nitrate (16% nitrogen)	Synergist	A compound that, when combined with other compounds, yields unpredictable results in addition to the predictable effects of the individual compounds
Siphon	A device that operates on the vacuum principle to put chemicals into a flow of water	Tensiometer	A device for measuring soil moisture content, often activating an electrical circuit to turn water on or off
Solar altitude	The angle of the sun above the horizon	Timer	A device that regulates time functions on a twenty-four hour basis
Solar furnace	A complete unit solar heating system	Tissue culture	A propagation technique for reproducing entire plants from one or just a few cells
Sorus	The fruiting structure of the fern		
Spaghetti system	Watering through small plastic tubes, one tube per pot	Toxic	Poisonous
Sphagnum (milled)	Sphagnum moss from the top of the bog that has been dried and finely ground	Trace elements	See minor elements
Spore	The reproductive body of fungi and bacteria; usually smaller than a seed	Transpiration	The process by which water evaporates from the leaves of the plant into the air
Sterilization	Heating soil to 212°F (100°C) to kill off nearly all living entities	Turgor pressure	The pressure inside plant cells, created by the diffusion of water through cell walls, which keeps the plant rigid
Stick	A term used to describe the act of putting a cutting into a rooting medium	Vapor barrier	A layer of material impervious to moisture
Stomata	Openings in the leaf that permit gaseous exchange with the air	Virus	A submicroscopic infecting agent that causes disease
Stress	The condition of a plant that has made adjustments to a shortage of water	Wetting agent	A chemical that lowers surface tension of liquids to make wetting easier
Sun pit	A greenhouse structure with the eave at ground level, oriented to trap winter sun	Wilt	A condition in which the plant loses turgor pressure in the tissues; usually from lack of water

INDEX

About the Author

John Pierce holds degrees in botany from Clark University and the University of Michigan, and brings to his readers over forty years of experience in all aspects of horticulture.

Self-employed for ten years in nursery production and landscape design, and for twenty years a community college instructor in botany and horticulture, Pierce has served as a staff member of the New York Botanical Garden; Director of the Trailside Botanical Museum, Bear Mt., New York; Director, Japanese School of Horticulture of Everett Community College, Everett, Washington; and was an environmental botanist with Environmental Professionals Northwest.

As a member of the International Plant Propagators Society and International Society for Horticultural Science, he has traveled widely in the interests of horticultural communication—his latest venture being a seed exchange with Tadjikistan, U.S.S.R.

John Pierce resides with his wife Marian at Niagara-on-the-Lake, Ontario, Canada.

Acknowledgments

A reference book is the crystallized expression of the effort and expertise of many people. The author gratefully acknowledges the assistance of Dean Charles Skinner, Everett Community College, for providing a twenty-year teaching opportunity in horticulture; of Robert and Jun Brandenburg for sharing years of experimental research on hobby greenhouses; and of Dave Kalamar for the years of researching the problems of a commercial grower.

In addition, my thanks to Ted Marston, publisher, whose professionalism turned a lifetime of experience into a book; to Melinda Jones for perceptive editorial skill; and to Marian Pierce for countless hours as secretary-critic.

I am grateful, too, for constructive encouragement from Glen Hunt, Lois Wilson, Carl Swanson, Frank and Leni Forsdike, Herschel Swanson, Art and Ethel Hansen, and Frank Brooks.

I would also like to thank Emily Johnson, Angela Hollis, Roselyn Pape, Jon. Hersh, and Valerie Muller for significant contributions in editing, design, and production of this book.

Finally, invaluable information was contributed by the following institutions: Agriculture Canada Research Station, Vineland, Ontario; Brooklyn Botanic Garden; Civic Garden Center, Toronto, Ontario; Cornell University; Institute of Botany, Tadjik, USSR; International Botanical Congress; International Society for Horticultural Science; New York Botanical Garden; Niagara Parks Commission School of Horticulture; Ohio State University; Potash Institute of Canada, Toronto, Ontario; Royal Botanical Garden, Hamilton, Ontario; U.S. Department of Agriculture, Agricultural Research Center, Beltsville, Maryland; University of Alaska; University of California, Davis; University of Florida; University of Guelph, Guelph, Ontario; and Washington State University.

Photo Credits

Color plates:
John Pierce: 1, 2, 3, 6, 7, 9, 10, 13, 14, 15, 16
Goldsmith Seeds: 4, 5
Steve Marts: 8, 10, 12
Kim Steele: 10, 11

Illustrations and figures:
John Pierce: 29, 30, 33, 34, 36, 39, 45, 47, 48, 50, 51, 55, 56, 62, 63, 64, 68, 72, 81, 87, 91, 111, 120, 121, 123, 125, 126, 133, 137, 148, 149
Steve Marts: opposite 1, 12, 14, 18, 22, 29, 30, 31, 38, 46, 54, 66, 78, 82, 101, 128, 134, 137, 141, 145, 147
Ted Marston: 92
Kim Steele: 143
Norman Comp: 118
Growhouse Corporation: 14
Jim Kight: 26
Derald Mauerman: 52, 56, 124
Jack Jarvie: 99
David Scharf: 100
U.S.D.A.: 112
Dr. W. G. Kemp: 113, 114
Mouth-to-mouth resuscitation drawing (p. 150) by Hilber Nelson